Equity in and through Education

The Comparative Education Society in Europe

VOLUME 5

Series Editor

Stephen Carney, *Roskilde University, Denmark (CESE President)*

Editorial Board: The CESE Executive Committee

Carlo Cappa, *University of Rome, Italy*
Eleftherios Klerides, *University of Cyprus, Cyprus*
Hans-Georg Kotthoff, *Freiburg University of Education, Germany*
Paul Morris, *UCL Institute of Education, England*
Eleni Prokou, *Panteion University of Social and Political Sciences, Greece*
Michele Schweisfurth, *University of Glasgow, Scotland*

The Comparative Education Society in Europe (CESE) is an international non-profit making association of scientific and educational character. CESE was founded in 1961 in London and is a founding society of the World Council of Comparative Education Societies (WCCES).

CESE has traditionally promoted a space for dialogue amongst scholars, specialists and young researchers from the field of education and other disciplines. More specifically, its purpose is to encourage and promote comparative and international studies in education by:

- promoting and improving the teaching of comparative education in institutions of higher learning;
- stimulating research;
- facilitating the publication and distribution of comparative studies in education;
- interesting professors and teachers of other disciplines in the comparative and international dimension of their work;
- co-operating with those who in other disciplines attempt to interpret educational developments in a broad context;
- organising conferences and meetings;
- collaborating with other Comparative Education Societies across the world in order to further international action in this field.

Every two years CESE organises an international conference of high scholarly standards which attracts academics, scholars, practitioners and students from all parts of Europe and around the world. Throughout its history, CESE has organised twenty-four such conferences, a special conference for the 25th anniversary of the Society, a symposium, and two 'CESE In-Betweens'. In-Betweens are international symposia organised between the biennial conferences. A web site of CESE is maintained at http://www.cese-europe.org/

The titles published in this series are listed at *brill.com/ciec*

Equity in and through Education

Changing Contexts, Consequences and Contestations

Edited by

Stephen Carney and Michele Schweisfurth

BRILL
SENSE

LEIDEN | BOSTON

Cover illustration: May Carney

All chapters in this book have undergone peer review.

Library of Congress Cataloging-in-Publication Data

Names: Carney, Stephen, editor.
Title: Equity in and through education : changing contexts, consequences, and contestations / edited by Stephen Carney and Michele Schweisfurth.
Description: Leiden ; Boston : Brill, [2018] | Series: The comparative education society in Europe, ISSN ; Volume 5 | Includes bibliographical references and index.
Identifiers: LCCN 2018003585 (print) | LCCN 2018008078 (ebook) | ISBN 9789004366749 (E-book) | ISBN 9789004366725 (pbk. : alk. paper) | ISBN 9789004366732 (hardback : alk. paper)
Subjects: LCSH: Educational equalization--Cross-cultural studies. | Multicultural education--Cross-cultural studies.
Classification: LCC LC213 (ebook) | LCC LC213 .E678 2018 (print) | DDC 379.2/6--dc23
LC record available at https://lccn.loc.gov/2018003585

ISBN: 978-90-04-36672-5 (paperback)
ISBN: 978-90-04-36673-2 (hardback)
ISBN: 978-90-04-36674-9 (e-book)

Copyright 2018 by Koninklijke Brill NV, Leiden, The Netherlands.
Koninklijke Brill NV incorporates the imprints Brill, Brill Hes & De Graaf, Brill Nijhoff, Brill Rodopi, Brill Sense and Hotei Publishing.
All rights reserved. No part of this publication may be reproduced, translated, stored in a retrieval system, or transmitted in any form or by any means, electronic, mechanical, photocopying, recording or otherwise, without prior written permission from the publisher.
Authorization to photocopy items for internal or personal use is granted by Koninklijke Brill NV provided that the appropriate fees are paid directly to The Copyright Clearance Center, 222 Rosewood Drive, Suite 910, Danvers, MA 01923, USA. Fees are subject to change.

This book is printed on acid-free paper and produced in a sustainable manner.

CONTENTS

Introduction   1
Stephen Carney and Michele Schweisfurth

1. Equity against the Odds: Three Stories of Island Prisons, Education and Hope   13
   Elaine Unterhalter

2. Holocaust Education in Transition: A Transnational Perspective   29
   Masako Shibata

3. Implementing Multicultural Curriculum for Equity: Islam in Hong Kong Education   43
   Liz Jackson

4. Educational-Work Projects and Post-Graduate Pathways of Secondary Students in Chile: Individual Strategies in an Unequal Education System   59
   Leandro Sepúlveda and María José Valdebenito

5. The European Qualifications Framework as an EU Policy Instrument for the Marketisation of Adult and Lifelong Education   81
   Eleni Prokou

6. Necessity or Right? Europeanisation and Discourses on Permeability between Vocational Education and Training and Higher Education in Germany and France   97
   Nadine Bernhard

7. Mentoring in Widening Access to Higher Education   119
   Jan McGhie

8. Discourse and Desire: Wellbeing as Escape from Nepali Village Life   139
   Joanna Nair

9. Doing Equality through Greater Transparency? Troubling Surveillance Expansion in the Russian School System   157
   Nelli Piattoeva

10. Contesting the Cities: A Comparative Perspective on the Geographically Specific Tendencies in Urban Education Policies   175
    Sezen Bayhan

CONTENTS

11. Parental Involvement in Disadvantaged Districts of Santiago: Intergenerational Consequences for Equity of a Market-Driven Educational System   191
    Marcela Ramos

12. Interrogating Equity Discourses: Conceptual Considerations and Overlooked Complexities   209
    Marianna Papastephanou

Index   223

STEPHEN CARNEY AND MICHELE SCHWEISFURTH

INTRODUCTION[1]

In one widely used illustration of the difference between the concepts of equality and equity, three people of different heights are depicted looking over a fence to watch a sports match.[2] Each has a crate on which to stand in order to achieve the goal. From an *equality* perspective, the available resources are distributed equally. However, in this configuration, only the tallest can see comfortably over the fence with the shortest of the three still facing the wall of exclusion. A contrasting illustration adopts an *equity* perspective. Here, a focus on redistribution means that there are no crates for the tallest of the three spectators but, rather, a distribution of resources according to need. Equity is thus understood to involve a 'levelling of the playing field' in order to make the situation fairer for the disadvantaged. Now, at least, everyone can watch the match.

This simple illustration is powerful in demonstrating a basic difference between the two concepts but it reinforces some unfortunate messages that make it an imperfect metaphor for the social world. The height of the three people is something inherent to them that social policy cannot easily fix. Nevertheless, thoughtful intervention can help each actor by compensating for deficits that are beyond the control of the individual. However, much of the disadvantage encountered in the world is located not in the traits of people themselves but, rather, in social structures and value systems which constrain opportunity. Being a girl, for example, is not in itself a disadvantage, but becomes so if teachers assume female learners are less able or if gender-based discrimination is tolerated. Much faith has been placed in education as a means to increase the life chance of people from lower social strata and thus to create greater social equity. However, and contrary to many of our best efforts, intergenerational cycles of poverty are persistent, if not reinforced through a wide range of mechanisms that connect dynamics related to families, society and education.

Inequalities in Glasgow, the city that hosted the 27th Conference of the Comparative Education Society in Europe (CESE) on which this volume is based, are no exception. For example, research in 2008 demonstrated that a boy living in Calton, an area of high deprivation, had an average life expectancy of 54 years, while a boy of the same age from the affluent suburb of Lenzie could expect to live to 82 (WHO, 2011). Relative income poverty accounts for some but not all of this discrepancy. Considerable faith has been invested in education to address these social inequalities, and targeted policy and school-level interventions by the

Scottish Government concerned with the 'Attainment Gap' focus on narrowing the gulf between the educational outcomes of those from different social strata. Schools, therefore, do matter. We all know what they can do to transform lives and worlds for the better. However, the research literature—especially from Anglo-American contexts, but increasingly mirrored by findings from continental Europe, East Asia and Latin America—makes clear that new forms of exclusion are emerging to consolidate those that have always troubled us. With a focus on social class, Reay (2014) writes about the English system:

> The working classes have always been excluded from formal education, and in particular any form of elite education, but now we are seeing invidious processes of excluding within the state educational system. Predominately working-class schools across the sector are more surveillant, are more obsessed with the audit culture, deliver a narrower curriculum, and have higher degrees of regulation than their more middle-class counterparts. (p. 317)

Here, the problem is identified as an imposed policy framework fixated on issues of basic literary and numeracy. This framework is enforced by individualised regimes of testing that celebrate "competitive learning dispositions" and which create a "sense of shame and failure in those positioned at the bottom of assessment hierarchies" (p. 318). Unsurprisingly, learners in such contexts internalise many negative lessons from school, primary of which is that education is about extrinsic matters and, as we have known since the great British educational ethnographies of the 1960s and 70s, largely not meant for them. Evoking the work of Ashurst and Venn (2014) and Ball (2010), Reay (2014) reminds us that we must now think in terms of a "political economy of exclusion that is fuelled by the current neoliberal reconstitution of all areas of society not just education" (p. 318). Expedient and short-sighted policy makers, strategic parents, objectified university managers and applied academic research are all part of a toxic cocktail that makes progressive attempts to deal with inequalities in schooling all the more difficult.

Thirty years of neo-liberal reform have thus brought into sharp relief the difference between those who benefit from education and those who do not, helping to make equity a prominent policy discourse. European countries have traditionally been divided into those which reflect both the inclination and the resources to invest in measures to promote equity, with Scandinavian countries at one extreme cast as 'universalistic' (inclusive, employment-focused and with strong welfare rights) and South European countries classed as 'sub-protective' due to pressing structural deficits (Gallie & Paugam, 2000). In the so-called Global South, international agreements such as the United Nations Millennium Development Goals (2000–2015) and the Sustainable Development Goals (2015–2013) have emphasised the potential of education to redress poverty and its associated inequalities. This includes, for example, promoting girls' education as an investment in improving child health. The Sustainable Development Goals are explicit in the demand that by 2030, nations "ensure that all girls and boys complete free, equitable and quality primary and secondary education leading to relevant and effective learning outcomes" ("UN Sustainable Development", 2017). What chance that this lofty vision will come to pass? Widening the access to *quality* higher education presents further challenges. As a non-compulsory sector requiring considerable financial investments and increasingly subject to the fickle winds of academic migration/flight, international league tables and policy demands for immediate relevance, the possibility that all able students might progress to this level remains a fantasy.

Middle-income countries such as South Africa and Chile, held up as examples to the rest of the developing world, have some of the greatest income inequalities on the planet, mirrored and reinforced through educational inequalities. In South Africa these are largely the legacy of racial apartheid, while in Chile, market forces and parental expectations to pay for schooling create a highly stratified system. Even in Sweden, a context usually presented as a 'gold standard' of equity and social justice, we have seen the development of one of the most market-based systems of education in the world with the establishment of 'independent schools', school vouchers and free school choice (Björklund et al., 2006). Here, the quasi-market also includes the possibility for profitmaking by private firms that 'invest' in the system (Lundahl et al., 2014). Such cases are far from unusual, as the contributions to this book illustrate. There is a long way still to travel.

Work on equity in education is vast and ongoing and this volume cannot hope to capture all of the multiple intellectual pathways currently being forged by a new generation of scholars. In order to provide a fuller frame for reading the contributions brought together here, it is useful to consider the broad value positions that guide thinking about equity and inequality in education. Drawing on Labaree (2003), Rizvi and Lingard (2010) outline three positions: democratic equality, social mobility and social efficiency. They point out that these three are not mutually exclusive or located in some relative hierarchy of desirability.

The 'democratic equality' position aims to connect education to civic purpose, political awareness and active participation in society. From this perspective, education is a public good, implying that "maximum benefit to society can only be realized if every member of a community is educated to realize their full potential" (Rizvi & Lingard, 2010, p. 78). Whilst economic relevance is important, it is very much subsidiary to social and cultural goals. In contrast, the 'social mobility' position suggests that education should be envisaged as a resource to enable individuals to achieve their goals. It views education as "both inherently rivalrous and desirably competitive, serving the functions of allocating economic benefits and social status to individuals". Put crudely, "social rewards should be based on both effort and intelligence" with the spoils going to those who "work harder and have inherently superior skills and talent" (p. 78). Cruel and uncaring? From this perspective, it is the market and its apparently neutral mechanisms that facilitate social formation with the state working in the background to ensure access and opportunity. Finally, Labaree (2003) offers the value position of 'social efficiency'. Here, the focus is on shaping educational outcomes less to the needs of democratic society (however defined) or individual advancement and fulfilment but, rather, to "the system's capacity to make an adequate return on investment, assessed in terms of its contribution to producing workers with knowledge, skills and attitudes relevant to increasing productivity within the knowledge economy". Once conceptualised within a competitive market logic, the 'social efficiency' position views education as able to realise public goals for economic growth and social cohesion as well as private ones oriented towards individual actualisation through the market (p. 78).

There is a rather nasty underbelly to visions that draw part of their programme from the ideology of the 'enterprise society' and what Foucault (2008) called homo æconomicus: the "entrepreneur of himself" (p. 226). Drawing on insights from Foucault's lectures on the Birth of Biopolitics, Venn notes:

> that inequality is not only a by-product of a system based on competition, but is required as a condition; inequality is seen to be an inherent and necessary feature of free market economy, and is justified on the basis of its necessary and regulating role as a mechanism, which means that the state must not intervene to 'compensate the effects of economic processes…social policy cannot take equality as its objective', and this is because 'the economic game, precisely with the inequality effects proper to it, is a kind of general regulatory mechanism of society….' (Venn, 2009, p. 213, citing Foucault, 2004, 2008)

Here, we are talking about a 'moral economy' (p. 219) where inequality is both naturalised and made visible as a core aspect of public policy. In Venn's analysis of contemporary biopolitics, such inequality must be made transparent in 'networks and circulations' (p. 222) that tie the modern, de-territorialised subject of education to a common—increasingly global—project of reform:

> it is not just inequality as a necessary regulating mechanism which is in question, but the return, after the interregnum of the welfare state, to a zero-sum game of systematic dispossession not offset by active redistribution at the national or the global scale. This zero-sum economic game, because of the conflicts it generates, requires new mechanisms that attempt to ensure relatively docile, if not compliant, populations in the form of massively intrusive surveillance, new forms of subjugation using new tools for the government of conduct. (Venn, 2009, pp. 225–226)

This is a fundamental rethinking of the role of inequality in society, not as something to be identified and corrected but, rather, a form of governance central to the workings of contemporary neoliberal systems of control. Here, technologies such as PISA, school inspection, instrumentalised teacher training, educational vouchers and so forth are inserted into a system of relations aimed at *remaking* education, schooling and learning not only in particular contexts but across time and space.

Whilst many scholars are cautious about reading the world through the language of globalisation theory, there is sense in which it is now becoming necessary to talk about a common space of/for education policy (Carney, 2009). The language here is vast—ideology, discourse, network, scape, scale, convergence and isomorphism are just some of our contemporary signposts—but does not obscure the 'fact' that more people are using fewer value positions when they manage and manipulate policy variables. Rizvi and Lingard (2010) note the 'global shift towards a neoliberal value orientation' that takes clearest form in privatisation efforts that 'assume the validity of market mechanisms' to solve the problems of government:

> In educational policy discourses, this has involved a reorientation of values from a focus on democracy and equality to the values of efficiency and accountability, with a greater emphasis on human capital formation allegedly demanded by the new knowledge industries, and required by nation-states to participate and compete successfully in the global economy. (p. 72)

This reorientation does not mean that issues of equality, democracy, social justice and, even, dignity and decency are being abandoned. Rather, they become 're-articulated' in the *service* of the economy (p. 72). Part of that re-articulation takes form as what Cowen (2018, p. 31) calls 'new vocabularies of persuasion' where notions of 'choice', 'diversity' and for example 'transparency' come to the fore. Such transformation presents a challenge for scholars who must develop new language, concepts and an awareness of the nature of policy metamorphous. It also exposes the limits and dangers of an emerging 'comparative education of solutions' that dovetails into the language of economy and which can only respond to it by using that self-same language. If this is the 'current situation', how did it come to pass?

In Popkewitz's terms, education reflects a system of 'reason', one that is "historically produced and governing" (2008, p. 144). When thinking of schooling and school pedagogy in the nineteenth century, we find the cosmopolitanism of the enlightenment embodying "cultural theses about how individuals are and should live through the applications of 'reason' and rationality to affect personal and collective life". The 'citizen', 'worker', parent' and 'child' can thus all be understood as being *made* with/ through a certain mode of thought and an attachment to a certain understanding of science that might "tame the uncertainty of change so that the future can be contemplated and people act in 'the pursuit of happiness', liberty and freedom" (p. 143). In our time, that project has been not only about "secular life, reason, and rationality" but a type of planning that would "change the child who would embody (the) civic virtues and modes of living". There is a salvation narrative here where the new person becomes "*responsible* for the future" (p. 143, our emphasis).

In similar fashion, comparative education can be thought of as embodying a certain historically-contingent 'reason'. Like the broader field of education in general, the post-second world war 'mobiliser' (or 'Holy Grail' to linger in Cowen's language) was 'equality of educational opportunity' (p. 30) and comparativists followed the equality 'quest' across the vast lands of context, theory and method. By the time of the cold-war, comparative education, "swung to 'read' and to intervene" in a "new world", creating a mode of scholarship that was "structural-functionalist, useful, applicable, and blinkered historically—overall, a policy-oriented science embedded in political assumptions about both the domestic and the international world". Salvation par excellence!

Cowen (2018) takes this brief historical sweep and poses the awkward question: was this a sorry form of preparation (if not naïve collaboration) for the current age of economic globalisation where only 'robust' 'science' will do? (p. 34). This is an important challenge, as a new generation of comparative researchers are at the forefront of change, charged with delivering a "specific notion of 'progress', to construct applied social 'sciences' that will be useful, and to contribute to public policy in education" (Cowen, 2018, p. 30). All in the name of the global knowledge economy. Of course, there are many comparative educations and whilst the academic policy entrepreneur of solutions appears to set the course for what counts as meaningful within many university and policy making systems, this is by no means the only future.

As our objects of analysis change before our eyes in new and subtle configurations, an *academic* comparative education is needed more than ever. In this sense, the current volume has much to offer. Not only do we bring together established voices who have lived through the policy transformations of the past 30 years, we introduce a number of younger scholars and less familiar contexts where our general argument about rising inequality as a new structural condition in education can be both extended and challenged. This conversation brings into dialogue scholars from the high technology societies of which we are most familiar, peripheral contexts struggling to be heard in the new discourse of 'excellence' as well as 'poster' cases of reform where neo-liberal policies are claimed to have sparked educational improvement and societal change. In all cases, our authors reflect an approach to comparative education that is contextually-rich, historically-aware, sensitive and provisional. We suggest that it is only from such scholarship that new insights into our current predicament might emerge and that we might illustrate the power of comparative research to push the boundaries of what might be thought and written.

If one acknowledges the salvation narrative embedded in the western enlightenment thought (Popkewitz, 2000), then it is fitting that our volume begins with an exploration of the relation between equity and hope. *Elaine Unterhalter* grounds her chapter in the life and work of a key comparativist—Joseph Lauwerys—drawing out compelling themes that speak to our current times. Principle amongst those is the potential of education as the glue that might bind refugees (like Lauwerys) to a common national mission and as the frame for a shared understanding of humanity. The notion of 'free men living in equality' (Lauwerys, 1945) positions education centrally in projects of social transformation. However, as Unterhalter notes, this call also exposed a lack of sensitivity to the gendered nature of post-war educational visions that, whilst not fully in the minds of these early planners, are nonetheless urgent now. In a brave comparative endeavor, she brings together stories of hope from three very different people, times and contexts. Education—as enlightening, grounded in issues of justice, dignity and collective freedom—bind them together. Whilst Louise Michel, Antonio Gramsci and Nelson Mandela responded to very different circumstances, education was a promise that bound their journeys to a common, greater good and, in her own striking phrase, 'offer(ed) some niche of protection against the humiliations and denials of humanity' (Unterhalter, this volume).

The vision that education can lead to social change, indeed a deep resetting of value systems, is the theme of *Masako Shibata's* analysis of the rise of holocaust education after world war two. Here, education and injustice intersect in new commitments not only to address the crimes of the past but also, and of possibly more importance, to establish a new understanding of the rights of humans. Holocaust education becomes part of a common language for defining global norms related to how societies should address the challenges confronting minority groups and for building multi-ethnic and multi-cultural polities. Whilst the chapter is not grounded explicitly in a 'world culture' or institutionalist theoretical framework, there is a strong sense in which, internationally, governments must now be *seen* to be addressing their own earlier failures. Here, the language of rights is unfolded in part through the common or collective reconstruction of the past.

Staying in Asia, albeit in a very different context, *Liz Jackson* introduces us to the challenges of multicultural education in Hong Kong. With Islam in focus, her stark conclusion is that Hong Kong persists in projecting 'prejudicial, discriminatory, and xenophobic attitudes' toward ethnic and cultural minorities and that these attitudes present significant barriers to equity and social justice. Even though policy prescriptions regarding multiculturalism and non-discrimination reflect increasingly global norms and dispositions, are well known, and spread widely throughout the region, the actual needs of minorities and the challenges they face remain 'poorly understood'. Here, we see issues of textbooks and teacher preparation coming to the fore with pre-service teachers themselves identifying a 'lack(ing) of criticality' in the materials they have to work with. As 'performative' artefacts, textbooks in Hong Kong lead students towards viewing "cultural diversity, intercultural mixing, and ethnic minorities in society as problematic, rather than recognising how prejudice, inequity, and discrimination operate, and may be bolstered (such as by anti-multicultural worldviews) in majority practices and norms" (Jackson, this volume). Here, and in contrast to the antiracist strides documented by Shibata above, the challenge of achieving equity through education becomes layered in practices that are barely made visible.

Three chapters deal with less emotive or contested matters but are nonetheless central to the thematic orientation of the volume. In the first of these, *Leandro Sepúlveda and María José Valdebenito* explore post-secondary educational pathways in Chile. As we have mentioned earlier, Chile is often held up as a successful case of societal regeneration through education. Certainly, enrolments and completion rates in formal school suggest a major transformation is under way but this chapter also exposes some deep differences in aspirations, expectations and types of participation where socio-economic disadvantage shapes both the engagement in education and the degree of vulnerability within the system. Privatisation in education is one important factor in distorting participation in education as well as educational outcomes with students from lower socio-economic backgrounds making pragmatic decisions that reinforce existing social inequalities but which now become legitimate through the politics of choice.

Eleni Prokou's analysis of the European Qualifications Framework extends this problematique. Here, the cherished goal of social transformation through 'critical conscientisation' is being compromised by the marketisation of adult and lifelong learning. What was once viewed as an educational provision for the good of both the individual and society has now switched logics with the mantra of 'lifelong learning' signaling an invitation to individuals to create their own futures. In the process of remaking education through the templates of lifelong learning, it appears that the imperatives of skills, relevance and employability are replacing the earlier goals of social inclusion and active citizenship. In this sense, education policy is contributing to a remaking of persons as productive and economically calculating consumers. How those subjectivities will serve a Europe in search of a renewed collective purpose and identity remains to be seen.

In the third chapter of this trio, *Nadine Bernhard* explores permeability in postsecondary vocational education and training within and across national education systems as well as at the European level, noting that the dominance of a certain type of 'functionalist argumentation' suggests that equity and equality of opportunities are very much secondary to the reform demand for economic transformation. Here, it seems that stratified skill formation systems without 'bridges' between different educational sectors can affect the possibilities for favorable education and employment outcomes. Resonating with Sepúlveda and Valdebenito's study in Chile, it appears that the structural characteristics of educational systems and individual life courses intersect in ways that policy makers are barely aware of, all to the disadvantage of those groups already adversely affected by social inequalities.

Given that widening access to education is an important part of any equity programme, and that education is being transformed by the logic of capital, it should therefore be important that communities of practice are established to enable new entrants to master the language and dispositions needed to negotiate implicit educational values. In her study of mentoring in Scottish higher education, *Jan McGhie* illustrates the role to be played by student facilitators as they support young people during their first encounters of higher learning. When done thoughtfully, mentoring can support students' longer-term decisions about entering higher education, not least in breaking the hidden codes of how to study and learn; things often beyond the reach of parents and peers who themselves have little experience of these worlds. The great promise of student mentoring in higher education is long-term retention of non-traditional student cohorts, and thus the promise of deep and lasting social change.

In an innovative study of a community education in Nepal, we find a resonance with much of the above but also an important challenge to the general tenor of 'equity research'. *Joanna Nair* reports findings from a long-term engagement with marginalised groups, noting that 'well-being' and 'escape' are interconnected projects. As she notes: 'Women and dalits value symbolic resources as means to attain wellbeing through either *talk* of escape, which gives them a sense of greater equity and freedom as well as improving their self-image, or through *actual* escape from the village for better opportunities and for liberty from (the) gender or caste restrictions...' (Nair, this volume, emphasis added). This is an important message and one that must be heard by scholars in particular who would otherwise insist that education serves primarily social and political functions. What if society is structurally-unequal and conventional education unreflexively (or, for that matter, enthusiastically) reproduces that? In such cases—and they are widespread in the Global South in particular—the reasonable action is to use any new, individualising, educational provision as a means not to *transform* one's limited world but to *transcend* it. Is this a call for a return to an educational ideal based upon the values of social cohesion and mutual respect? Perhaps. The economically charged re-articulations of education outlined earlier may be problematic in their own right but we should not assume that the dreams and aspirations of a new type of educational subject—one swirling within what Appadurai (1996) famously termed an 'ideoscape' of promises of a different world—will be content within an educational system rebuilt upon the great 'equality' movements of the post-war epoch.

In many of the above contributions, there appears a fine line between the attempts by policy makers to enshrine hope and potential into reformed systems and the regressive consequences of placing those hopes in the invisible hands of the market. In the following chapters, we find policy makers acting to enhance their control of social and political processes by deploying economically-informed discourses of efficiency, choice and, even, 'quality' to redefine the meaning of 'equality'. In some cases, this appears to be strategic and tactical, in others we see the emergence of new systems of reason where policy makers in particular (but also other stakeholders) are swept along with the new language of change.

Nelli Piattoeva provides a thought-provoking critique of how a logic of 'equity' can be misused, in this case to tighten control of the system. As she explains in relation to the surveilliance of exams by the Russian Federation authorities, the 'rhetoric of equality' offers a 'powerful justification narrative' for the introduction of standardisation. She starts by offering the concept of surveillant assemblage as "a situated accumulation of different and often mutually contradictory discourses, practices, technologies etc" and shows how this assemblage has expanded greatly in the Russian school system since 2014. Here, as elsewhere, cheating is presented as a threat to equality of opportunity, with surveillance 'tools' then introduced to support social and educational equality. In this sense, equality then functions as a "kind of mythology that gives meaning and legitimacy to surveillance practices and their proliferation" (Piattoeva, this volume).

Whilst reporting upon a very different context, *Sezan Bayhan's* courageous study of school relocations and de-secularisation in Turkey shows the dramatic consequences of connecting global discussions of equity in education to the 'specific cultural character' of that country's neo-liberalisation. Here, education reform frames parental choice in terms of being able to choose a religious school where a 'single interpretation of Islam is taught'. Not unlike the charter or grant maintained school movements that 'extend publicly funded choice into the private sphere', she notes that the growth of *Imam Hatip* schools in Turkey is partly the consequence of their active promotion and endorsement by policy makers themselves. In a context of the "spatial and material neglect of secular public schools" this pushes middle class parents towards private solutions in education (Bayhan, this volume). Rather than open a new space for the disadvantaged to move in, she shows that these policies are exacerbating the deterioration of conditions in public schools and are widening disparities and inequalities in education.

Marcela Ramos takes us back to Chile with an exploration of the beliefs and aspirations of parents from the lower middle-class as they negotiate the politics and economics of school choice. Ramos shows how these parents, formed during the early market-based dictatorship of the 1980s, become "managers of their children's educational trajectories", basing their decisions on a certain neo-liberal understanding of schooling as enabling individual success. Here, they were on the lookout for opportunities and ready to act strategically to maximise the any possible advantage. Whilst individual agency comes to the fore, issues of social equity and justice drift to the background. Parents, it seems, come to embody the logic of the system and are ever ready to pass that on that legacy.

Taken together, the contributions outlined here suggest that equity in education is a contentious signifier for an enormous range of policy ideals and practices. In many cases, we see attempts to reinforce new articulations of well-known commitments to access, opportunity and social efficiency in education, seemingly in the service of the economy. In others, we see scholarship that challenges the emerging neo-liberal settlement in order to unravel regressive steps towards a less equal and less just world.

Our final contribution takes distance to these positions by asking us to interrogate the very meaning of equity through the dominant discourses that give it unnecessarily limited form. *Marianna Papastephanou* notes that equity in education is all things to all people, bridging notions such 'equality, inclusion, tolerance, social justice or diversity' as well as inserting them into 'strings of nouns that operate in justificatory, normative-prescriptive and comparative ways'. Searching for precision in what we mean by 'equity' could serve to "reveal(s) the multiplicity of meanings" it has taken over time. We might also consider the meaning(s) of equity by interrogating its opposite: inequity. In much of the literature, equity is "arbitrarily associated with mere inclusion, tolerance and respect of diversity" and thus remains vague. Additionally, much equity thinking promotes the "egocentric, monological Western world view", leaving "untouched the liberal idealised subject" and thus obscuring perspectives that prioritise "solidarity and interconnectedness" such as the African notion of *Ubuntu*. Finally, we are in danger of consolidating "univocal discourses"

INTRODUCTION

at a time when social and global equity considerations should make theoretical diversity a necessity (Papastephanou, this volume).

Undoubtedly, equity deserves attention as it emerges in policy and is consolidated and contested in ministries, classrooms and communities. It behoves scholars of education to explore its multiple forms and potentialities, both to examine the concepts with which we approach the world but, as importantly, to extend those into new, uncharted and potentially uncomfortable territory. We hope that this collection will inspire such travel.

NOTES

[1] This volume has its origins in the 27th Conference of the Comparative Education Society in Europe (CESE), hosted by the Robert Owen Centre for Educational Change at the University of Glasgow, Scotland in Summer 2016. The conference theme was 'Equity in and through education: Changing contexts, consequences, and contestations'.
[2] https://edtrust.org/the-equity-line/equity-and-equality-are-not-equal/

REFERENCES

Appadurai, A. (1996). *Modernity at large: Cultural dimensions of globalization*. Minneapolis, MN: University of Minnesota Press.
Ashurst, F., & Venn, C. (2014). *Inequality, poverty, education: A political economy of school exclusion*. Basingstoke: Palgrave Macmillan.
Ball, S. (2010). New class inequalities in education: Why education policy maybe looking in the wrong place! Education policy, civil society and social class. *International Journal of Sociology and Social Policy, 30*(3–4), 155–166.
Björklund, A., Clark, M., Edin, P., Fredriksson, P., & Krueger, A. (2005). *The market comes to education in Sweden: An evaluation of Sweden's surprising school reforms*. New York, NY: Russel Sage Foundation.
Carney, S. (2009). Negotiating policy in an age of globalization: Exploring educational "policyscapes" in Denmark, Nepal and China. *Comparative Education Review, 53*(1), 63–88.
Cowen, R. (2018). Narrating and relating educational reform and comparative education. In E. Hultqvist, S. Lindblad, & T. Popkewitz (Eds.), *Critical analysis of educational reforms in an era of transnational governance* (pp. 23–40). Cham: Springer.
Foucault, M. (2008). *The birth of biopolitics* (G. Burchell, Trans.). Houndmills: Palgrave Macmillan.
Gallie, D., & Paugam, S. (2000). The social regulation of unemployment. In D. Gallie & S. Paugam (Eds.), *Welfare regimes and the experience of unemployment in Europe*. Oxford: Oxford University Press.
Labaree, D. F. (2003, May). The peculiar problems of preparing educational researchers. *Educational Researcher, 32*(4), 13–22.
Lundahl, L., Arreman, I. E., Holm, A.-S., & Lundström, U. (2014). *Gymnasiet som marknad* [Upper secondary school as a market]. Stockholm: Boréa Bokförlag.
Popkewitz, T. (2000). Reform as the social administration of the child: Globalization of knowledge and power. In N. C. Burbules & C. A. Torres (Eds.), *Globalisation and education: Critical perspectives* (pp. 157–186). New York, NY: Routledge.
Popkewitz, T. (2018). Reform and making human kinds: The double gestures of inclusion and exclusion in the practice of schooling. In E. Hultqvist, S. Lindblad, & T. Popkewitz (Eds.), *Critical analysis of educational reforms in an era of transnational governance* (pp. 133–150). Cham: Springer.
Reay, D. (2014). Inequality, poverty, education: A political economy of school exclusion. *Subjectivity, 7*(3), 316–319.

Rizvi, F., & Bob, L. (2010). *Globalizing education policy*. London: Routledge.
United Nations. (2017). *Sustainable development goals 4*. Retrieved from https://sustainabledevelopment.un.org/sdg4
Venn, C. (2009). Neoliberal political economy, biopolitics and colonialism: A transcolonial genealogy of inequality. *Theory, Culture & Society, 26*(6), 206–233.
World Health Organisation. (2011). Behind the Glasgow effect. *WHO Bulletin, 89*(10), 706–707.

Stephen Carney
Roskilde University
Denmark

Michele Schweisfurth
University of Glasgow
Scotland

ELAINE UNTERHALTER

1. EQUITY AGAINST THE ODDS

Three Stories of Island Prisons, Education and Hope[1]

The key theme of this chapter concerns the ways in which equity in education is linked with hope. This association comes from one of the earliest appearances of the word equity in English. In Wycliff's translation of the Bible into English in 1382 he coined the word equity in a passage from the Book of Malachi. The verses describe the prophet ferociously condemning the priests of Israel for neglecting their covenant with God. But it also holds out the notion that the prophet will express 'the law of truth' and walk with God 'in peace and equity', and through this engage the priests to 'keep knowledge'. I want to step off from this early coining of the word equity to explore some of its attributes linked to knowledge and hope, and consider education as a site for examining power and difference, drawing on a number of facets of comparative study.

The first comparative move I want to make is with the biography of Joseph Lauwerys from which I want to take two themes with resonance today. The first is the theme of the equitable inclusion of refugees who come, like Lauwerys' family did, in time of war, to a country where they did not speak the language. In 1914, Lauwerys' family came as refugees to England from Brussels. Their experience was that people in different kinds of organisations supported schooling for refugee children. Lauwerys initially attended a Catholic independent day school, Ratcliff College in Leicestershire, and from 1915 he went to school in Bournemouth, where his family later joined him. Although he left school early and worked as a shop assistant, he was encouraged and supported though the Co-Operative movement to obtain the necessary qualifications for university entry, and in 1927 obtained a BSc from King's College London after years of part-time study (Halls, 2004). While we cannot simply read off from these personal experiences with his own education to Lauwerys' later work reaching across barriers and boundaries to understand different kinds of education and develop collaborations (Maclean, 1981), we also cannot discount the resonance of these relationships in Lauwerys' vision of education as a site of hope. This speaks to us across more than a hundred years, when we witness today the biggest movement of people ever recorded in history. So many among the millions fleeing oppressions are children, hoping for education. An aspect of that hope is that people will walk in equity with them. But all too often we disappoint these children and their families. No schools are provided and we are disoriented about the policies and practices we should adopt. Humanitarian aid is insufficient and only 2% of this goes on education (UNESCO, 2015; Albright, 2016). We may know education is important for refugees but, as practitioners, researchers, taxpayers, voters, fellow human beings, we do not always take the appropriate next steps. Will understanding equity better help in this engagement?

This links with my second theme from Lauwerys' biography, which concerns seeing education policy and practice as a site of hope, and the equitable provision of education as a means to realise this. At the height of World War 2, at a time when it was not at all evident who would win or lose, and when the suffering and anxiety was immense, Lauwerys led an inquiry, initiated by the Committee of Allied Ministers of Education. This met in London under R. A. Butler to plan educational reconstruction after the war. The work of this committee fed into the efforts that established UNESCO. Lauwerys' own writings at this time link equality with reaching across boundaries and hope. In a series of articles for *The New Era* written between 1944 and 1945, Lauwerys argued for education systems to work towards integration rather than deepening divisions, and to consider the ways in which individuals and institutions in education interact (Lauwerys, 1944, 1945a). He argued for the importance of developing a well-informed public, through education. He wrote that education should seek to foster "the humane ideals of social democracy and abate religious, racial, national and class conflicts". His list of the means to do this included the curriculum, the organisation of schools, the provision of early childhood education, and education exchanges to widen horizons (Lauwerys, 1945a). In 1945, summing up a symposium on future education after the war, Lauwerys emphasised a vision of education oriented to 'free men living in equality' (Lauwerys, 1945b). I take this to be a meaning, common at the time, but dissonant to us, where men meant humans. The context of Lauwerys' writings have him emphasising equality, even if he did not have a language to articulate some of the important inequalities of gender we have come to understand in the decades that followed. From that time Lauwerys expressed links of education with hope (Hall, 2004; McLean, 1981). The way that equity is positioned on this terrain is something I want to explore in some depth.

The analysis is organised around a number of intersecting questions. Firstly, what different approaches are apparent in how equity is used as a concept in education? How do aspects of comparative and international education feature in these discussions? How do these different approaches articulate the relationship between what works in education and the way that equity matters? I also want to consider the value of these comparative moves. As a community of scholars many of us, like Lauwerys, invest in education great aspiration to develop knowledge, skill, understanding, connect across social, cultural, economic, political and historical divisions, and contribute to some challenge to injustice. But a whole body of scholarship tells us how much education falls short of this ideal. How and why do we balance our critical insights and our hopes? Do we talk in the voice of the condemning prophet or in the tones of equity and hope and what is the relationship between them in education?

I want to centre my discussion on the notion of education as a complicated terrain in which equity and hope are mixed with many other dynamics. To illustrate this, I want to give three examples of political activists, given long and brutal prison sentences for standing up for justice, freedom, and equalities. All three, despite the inhumanity and degradation of their imprisonment, used the space for education, and never doubted that the process of education was a way to put into practice something of the dynamic of hope, equity and challenge to unjust structures.

My first example is Louise Michel. She was a schoolteacher, born in 1830 in the Haute-Marne region of France. She moved to Paris in 1856 and taught in a school for poor children in Montmartre, loving the work, her fellow teachers and the children (Michel, 1981, pp. 38–40). She was an active participant in political circles in Paris, critical of the Second Empire, and a leading figure in the Paris Commune, elected President of the Women's Vigilance Committee. The Commune was defeated in May 1871 with immense brutality. Michel was arrested, held in a cell from which she could hear the executions of her comrades, and tried in December 1871. Her speech to the court included a defiant taunt to the authorities that "any heart that beats for liberty has the right only to a small lump of lead" (Michel, 1981, p. 87). However, she was not sentenced to death but condemned to imprisonment on New Caledonia in the South Pacific, at that time a French colony. Michel, together with 169 other deportees, 20 of whom were women, set off in 1873. Her imprisonment lasted six years, until in 1880, with a changing politics in France, she was pardoned, and returned to a life of activism. What is striking for the theme of this chapter is that during her time of imprisonment she engaged very actively in education, opening a school, directing plays, and organising music.

The indigenous Melanesian people, the Kanaks, were being deprived of their land by French settlers in New Caledonia. Some political prisoners joined in, but Louise Michel refused to participate in this dispossession. She learned the Kanak language, collected and wrote down Kanak legends and songs, and taught Kanak children and adults. She did this in the face of fury from the prison administrators, who decried her school for filling "the heads of these Canaques with pernicious doctrines about humanity, justice, freedom and other useless things" (quoted in Maclellan, 2004, p. 15). She describes her active approach to teaching reading, writing and mathematics, the spaces she created so that the Kanaks she taught could reflect on the knowledge she imparted linked to their own understandings (Michel, 1981, pp. 117–118). This image where she describes playing a piano, with some notes silent, and her Kanak pupils supplementing their own music into the spaces, appears to distil her pedagogic approach.

> ...the piano served me as a teaching method that produced good results. With this piano, whose broken hammers or strings made some notes in a run silent, the pupils realized there were gaps and filled them in with their own notes. Sometimes they sang notes from the piece they were studying, and at other times they searched their own musical phrases to fill the gaps. Thus they

created motifs which were often strange and sometimes beautiful. ...I tried out this method on my regular schoolchildren as well as in my Sunday class for the Kanaks. (Michel, 1981, p. 118)

This pedagogy of dialogue, reaching across boundaries of what is known and unknown, appreciating what is strange and unexpected, and making new knowledge is a theme I will return to as an important feature of equity in education.

When the Kanaks rose in protest against their land dispossession Louise Michel reached across boundaries of race and economic philosophy to support their cause writing: "The Kanaks were seeking the same liberty we had sought in the commune" (Michel, 1981, p. 112). She constructed an image of a symbolic bond tying the struggles together in the story she told of two of her former pupils, Kanak rebel leaders, who came to see her the night before they went to join the insurgency. She gave them "my red scarf, the red scarf of the Commune, that I had hidden from every search" (Michel, 1981, p. 112). They were not seen again, but the image of education as a space in which people can come together and establish the ties of friendship and aspiration to challenge injustice, even in the face of the harsh repression of dispossession, imprisonment and scorn, invites us to ask what is it about this site of hope, and how does it talk to the notion of equity?

My second example of prisoners using the space of education, and, initially, an island confinement, somewhat like New Caledonia, to organise an alternative to the inhumanity of incarceration, is Antonio Gramsci, a journalist, member of the Italian Communist Party and an anti-Fascist. Gramsci and other Communist Party deputies were arrested in November 1926, in the midst of a spate of repression by the Fascist government against its opponents. Sentenced, initially to five years imprisonment, under hastily imposed Laws on Public Security, Gramsci was given a sentence of internment on the island of Ustica, with a number of other political prisoners, from different political parties. Here they set up a school. Gramsci's account in a letter of December 1926 to his friend, the economist Pietro Sraffa, describes the organisation and the connections made:

> Here in Ustica there are thirty of us political prisoners; we've already initiated a series of elementary and general cultural courses for the various groups of prisoners; we will also begin a series of lectures. Bordiga directs the scientific section, while I have the historical-literary section; this is the reason I've ordered certain particular books. Let's hope that in this way we will spend our time without becoming completely brutalized and at the same time help our friends, who represent the entire gamut of political parties and cultural backgrounds. Here with me there are Schiavello and Fiorio from Milan; among the Maximalists there is also the former deputy Conca, from Milan. Among the Unitarian Socialists there is Attorney Sbaraglini from Perugia and a magnificent Molinellese peasant type. There is a Republican from Massa and six Anarchists who have a complicated moral makeup; the rest are Communists, that is the great majority. There are three or four who are illiterate, or almost;

the education of the others varies, but the general average is very low. All of them, however, are very glad to have the school, which they attend with great assiduity and diligence. (Gramsci, 2011a, pp. 52–53)

It is clear that the educational space of the school the prisoners established provides a meeting ground across divisions of politics, regions and levels of learning. Their instruction is organised into a 'series' of lectures, and they consider distinctions between scientific and cultural-historical areas of knowledge. Books were available because Sraffa had established an open account for Gramsci with a bookseller in Milan (Buttiegieg, 2011, p. 86) and the knowledge books hold are a central underpinning. The school is clearly a site of hope to guard against brutalisation and to nurture care. In 1927, Gramsci was charged with further offenses, moved from internal exile to prisons in Milan and Rome, and in 1928 sentenced after a show trial to 20 years, with the prosecutor infamously claiming "We must prevent this brain from functioning for twenty years" (Buttiegieg, 2011, p. 88). In this the authorities failed. Gramsci, despite severe illness, loneliness, insomnia, depression, and losing all his teeth, applied himself to study and writing with formidable organisation and energy and the groundbreaking *Prison Notebooks* remain a source of insight to this day.

Gramsci used reading, writing and conversation to work through, in a very detailed manner, issues which he thought the conditions of imprisonment allowed him to study. He developed plans for a multifaceted and coherent project of study and investigation. In January 1929 Gramsci obtained permission from the prison authorities to write in his cell, and in February on the opening pages of the first of his Prison Notebooks, he listed the main topics he intended to study. The list is illuminating, detailed, both wide-ranging and highly focussed. As a curriculum it deals with history, literature, economics and sociology. The themes in history he proposes to study are the theory of history and historiography, the development of the Italian bourgeoisie to 1872, the formation of Italian intellectual groups, and the history of language. The issues of literature that concern him are the reasons for the success of popular serials, the treatment of the Epicureans by Dante in the *Divine Comedy*, the concept of folklore, and the circulation of different types of periodicals. His focus on politics concerns the origins and development of Catholic Action in Italy and the popular writings defending authoritarianism by the Catholic priest, Antonio Bresciani. His interest in sociology centres on his experiences of prison life. In thinking about economics he wants to investigate the southern question in Italy, the composition and emigration of the population of Italy, and Fordism in America (Gramsci, 2011a, p. 99). This is a broad programme, ranging widely across periods, disciplines, the general and the particular. In a letter in 1929 to Antonio Sanna, a Communist comrade serving a long sentence for anti-Fascist activity, Gramsci wrote of his approach to study, reading even the most random books "with a purpose" and using the prison library "to extract blood from a stone" (Buttigieg, 2011, p. 15). "Every book, especially if it deals with history, can be worth reading. In every awful book one can find something useful..." (quoted in Buttigieg, 2011, p. 16). We see here a space of education as a terrain of self-instruction with sequenced frameworks, engagement with how to understand the present, and reflection on what is useful. The blood from the stones evokes a symbol of hope, resonating with Louise Michel's red scarf.

Gramsci and his fellow prisoners organised to engage in discussion during exercise, with Gramsci sometimes directing discussion to the themes he was studying. In his letters and Notebooks we have fragmented portrayals of these prison seminars and discussions with people who think differently, but always oriented to understanding and knowledge as an engagement with hope. Gramsci also wrote in detail to his wife about the education of his two sons (Gramsci, 2011b). Because his prison letters were censored, and because, one may surmise, of his need to shield from the view of the authorities the level of discussion amongst prisoners, we only have glimpses of the educational practices of the prisoners. They emerge in the lists of books Gramsci orders, what he sometimes describes as the "zigzag" of his thoughts, in his reflection on how study helps calm him and allows him to transcend "those vulgar and banal states of mind that are called pessimism and optimism" (Gramsci, 2011b, p. 299). He wishes to synthesize and overcome those two emotions. In a letter to his younger brother, Carlo, he likens his long term of imprisonment to the mental state his brothers experienced as a soldier during World War 1, and the stoicism they had to cultivate:

> I'm a pessimist because of intelligence, but an optimist because of will. In all circumstances I think first of the worst possibility in order to set in motion all the reserves of my will and be in a position to knock down the obstacle. I have never entertained any illusions and I have never suffered disappointments. I have always taken care to arm myself with an unlimited patience, not passive, inert, but animated by perseverance. (Gramsci, 2011b, p. 289)

I read this as an articulation of hope, not detached from an appreciation of what Gramsci calls the serious 'moral crisis' of today, but rooted in comparison with the past and reflection on the mental capacities he has to confront the present. He evokes it expressing a similarity, a kind of equity with what his brothers had experienced and had to confront. Part of the hope associated with equity as an educative space seems to be this reaching out for what connects people, drawing on some of the rigours of reflection. Education around equity and hope is not easy or instinctive, it is organised, detailed, highly critical, but also relational. In a poignant letter he wrote to his mother in December 1930 he remembers his time on Ustica as a kind of "paradise of personal freedom, compared to my condition as a prisoner" (Gramsci, 2011b, p. 367). But, he goes on to say that while he has lost his teeth, and no longer laughs with gusto as he used to, he has become wiser and 'enriched my experience of men and of things. He has not lost his "taste for life; everything still interests me", and while he says in dialect he can no longer "munch roasted beans" or fully taste the savour of life, he can imagine others doing so.

My last example is Robben Island in South Africa, where from the 1960s to 1991 anti-apartheid activists were imprisoned under most brutal conditions.

The autobiographies of a number of political prisoners, most notably Nelson Mandela, the most famous, attest to the formidable educational programme the prisoners put in place despite the racism, the viciousness, and explicit denial of any of the qualities of kindliness or encouragement we sometimes associate with education. In Mandela's autobiography he describes the prisoner organisation through which they established what they called the University of Robben Island, with prisoners becoming "our own faculty, with our own professors, our own curriculum, our own course" (Mandela, 1994, p. 556). They developed Syllabus A, to understand the history of the liberation struggle, the form, features, and strategies used by different groups, and what theories like Marxism or socialism could contribute to understand South African conditions (Mandela, 1994, pp. 556–557). A number of Robben Island memoirs describe the classes that took place while prisoners were digging lime at the quarry. Fikile Bam, a prisoner on Robben Island between 1964 and 1975, outlined the organisation that underpinned this:

> Just about anybody who had a degree or any form of education was allocated a subject to teach. Every morning…before going to work, the teachers would come together quickly and discuss their programme for the morning as to which periods would follow … So there was always movement when you got to the workplace, little groups assembling in different places and you knew there were classes in progress. (Quoted in Lodge & Nasson, 1991, p. 301)

Other prisoners recount the vibrant atmosphere of symposiums on international relations, science, the energy crisis, and the world education crisis (Desai, 2014, p. 74). The organisation resonates with the school Gramsci helped organise on Ustica. There are accounts of prisoners who could read helping to make books out of cement bags for those who could not, of those who had education organising classes at the appropriate level for those who had primary, secondary or degree level education, and giving structured lessons after they returned from work, reaching across the ANC/PAC divide (Desai, 2014, pp. 26–27). Mandela describes the educative materials taken clandestinely to the general, non-political prisoner on Robben Island, and the dialogues that unfolded with questions posed from direct experience, and requests for simplification to the abstractions (Mandela, 1994, pp. 556–557). He also discusses the engagements with the new perspectives informed by black consciousness, brought by a younger generation of prisoners in the 1970s.

From other memoirs of Robben Island we have accounts of how prisoners studied for multiple degrees and observed an intense quiet during study periods at night (Desai, 2014, p. 2). Prisoners who were studying could not give books to those who were not enrolled, but they organised to keep and distribute books, transcribe those they borrowed from university libraries, sometimes staying up all night to do so. These handwritten works were circulated clandestinely.

The curriculum of Robben Island was not just about history, politics or economics. There were readings and performances of plays from Shakespeare and Sophocles, which a number of prison autobiographies describe as revelatory, because particular phrases, characters and scenes were so resonant (Desai, 2014; Kathrada, 2005; Mandela, 1994; Soudien, 2015). There was a choir and a choirmaster. Prisoners organised and petitioned for the right to play and watch football, although many were not very fit, or particularly good sportsmen. The experience of the campaign across PAC/ANC/BCM lines, the establishment of football clubs on the Island with chairs, secretaries, goals, and rules, all were seen as building some of the organisational insights necessary for a time beyond imprisonment (Korr & Close, 2008, p. 61).

Mandela formulated ideas about nurturing a vision of equity, focusing on hope. These themes thread through much of his writing and the speeches he made before and after his time on Robben Island. A letter to his former articled clerk, Douglas Lukhele, written while he was on Robben Island in 1970, makes an explicit connection between thoughts, freedom, education, equality and a challenge to unjust institutions.

> To put it quite bluntly, Duggie, it is only my flesh and blood that are shut up behind these tight walls. Otherwise I remain cosmopolitan in my outlook; in my thoughts I am as free as a falcon. The anchor of my dreams is the collective wisdom of making as a whole. I am influenced more than ever by the conviction that social equality is the only basis of human happiness… It is on these issues that my thoughts revolve. They are centred on humans, the ideas for which they strive; on the new world that is emerging; the new generation that declares total war against all forms of cruelty, against any social order that upholds economic privilege for a minority and that condemns the mass of the population to poverty and disease, illiteracy and the host of evils that accompany a stratified society. (Mandela, 2010, pp. 182–183)

Discussing freedom and justice with Kanak pupils were themes that gave Louise Michel hope. Developing the mental discipline to understand the historical conditions of inequality, and taking care of other prisoners nurtured hope for Gramsci, and Mandela's image of himself as the wandering falcon, trying to gain an oversight of humans struggling, partly through ideas and literacy, for social equality, places, breadth of vision serve as a key facet of hope.

In all these three examples—Louise Michel working with the Kanaks on New Caledonia, Gramsci and his fellow prisoners talking of books and ideas, while walking beneath the gaze of hostile gaolers, and the organised engagement with politics, Shakespeare and football on Robben Island—we see the education terrain, be it a school, a prison exercise yard, a cell, or a lime quarry, as a space of hope. We see a reaching across difference: Louise Michel negotiated across languages, cultures and political aspirations with the Kanaks, symbolically tying her red scarf to connect them. Gramsci engaged through the format of the school on Ustica, in letters about how to study, in reading, writing, discussion and dialogue with people who held different views to his own—Anarchists, socialists, Communists from different wings of the Party—seeking to draw a nourishing blood from the harsh stones of the prison. This same negotiation across difference between levels of education, and political perspective was a key thread in the Robben Island University. It was guided by a notion to give a wider view, deepen the appreciation of time, listen to different voices. Mandela's image of himself as a falcon evoked a wish go to many places, many peoples, animated by a notion of equality, which closely evokes aspects of equity.

I have selected these three instances, because they do not romanticise what is possible in education. They evoke the harshness of imprisonment, the stress on human relations, the constant presence of vulnerability and the closeness of illness and death, the fragility of access to knowledge. These difficult engagements are as much part of the experience as the commitment, the living challenge to the injustice of the powerful institutions they confront, the reaching beyond the present, a struggling to make sense of the past, and a cherishing of hope for education linked to some distant future.

This resonates for me with Lauwerys' work with the inter-ministerial committee during World War 2, and his initiatives from 1945. The post-war period of Lauwerys' great energy in international educational gatherings, was, as much recent scholarship has vividly portrayed, a period that was chaotic and brutal. Many of the traumas of the recent past were confronted clumsily, often viciously, setting in train many problems that remain profound. But in what must have often been a dispiriting and troubling time to live through, Lauwerys does not ever seem to have lost hope for education or equality. In this he echoes Michel, Gramsci and his comrades, and the Robben Island prisoners. It is this feature of hope around ideas of equality, and the challenge to unjust institutions that I want to link with equity.

I want now to explore this aspect of equity reaching across difference and considering education as a space of difficult hope by people experiencing the hardest times. I want to consider critically how this interpretation of equity in education compares with other frameworks.

Equity is a slippery word, and equity in education a many-faceted concept. Groups of scholars use the term equity in education somewhat differently and I want to try to sort out and clarify some of the streams in this literature reflecting between the academic engagements and the practices on the island prisons I have sketched.

I want to begin with some definitional discussion of equity and I will return to this after some consideration of how equity has been used in work on education. One of the themes in discussion of equity in education concerns the relationship of what works and what matters in education policy and practice (Unterhalter, 2009a). Contrasts are sometimes drawn between the development of education systems which work, as evinced by some measurement of learning outcomes or other evaluations of efficiency linked with economic growth, political integration or health and well-being. This notion of what works is often counter-posed sharply with an evocation of what matters, which many authors links with processes of normative aspiration or reflection, fluidity, flux, uncertainty, and vulnerability. Sometimes this expresses the ways that people struggle to articulate what is they have reason to value, and how they understand their experience of being in the world.

I want to take this discussion between education in relation to what works and what matters and apply it to the terrain of education as a site of hope. The argument I want to make is that it is important to link what works with what matters. What works in my analysis should not be merely technocratic, but needs to be linked with practice, human located-ness, and what matters. However, what matters is not merely aspiration, a far off goal; it is also what is realised and made to work. Equity and hope appear to me important aspects of the connective tissue between these two nodes of education discussion.

The concept of equity in education has been discussed by an academic community of scholars, often centrally engaged with the contrast of what works and what matters in education. This theme is evident both in general policy studies in education and in comparative and international education. I want to distinguish four ways equity is used as a link idea in these analyses. Firstly there is a body of writing guided by principles, informed by some of the discussions in political philosophy regarding equity and equality, which stresses the significance of what matters, and singles out instances of this in practice to show that this can work, identifying some of the imperfections and areas that need further conceptual and practical engagement. This is the approach argued for in depth by Carlo Raffo who defines equity in terms of "the dynamics of educational fairness around young people's freedom to engage with valued educational capabilities" (Raffo, 2013, p. 10). Raffo links equity with agency in discussions of the capability approach, and shows how equity is a problem in many accounts of educational purpose. He distils a detailed framework for equity linked with purpose, quality and outcomes focusing on distribution and aspects of autonomy, presenting engagement with practice in the North-west of England. McCowan's (2016) article on higher education and equity is another example of this approach. He looks at equity in access to higher education, and defines equity in terms of fairness, discussing equality of opportunities for access in terms of three principles of equity—access, availability and horizontality of prestige between institutions. The discussion deploys a number of comparative moves, looking at how access and availability play out in Kenya, England and Brazil, drawing on international datasets, and generating the importance of horizontality between institutions as a feature of equity from an analysis of how inequalities persist.

Secondly there is an experiential engagement with the idea of equity, so that equity is associated with expanding access to education for groups who encounter particular kinds of discrimination, inequality and exclusion. This has been where much of the scholarship concerned with issues of race, gender, ethnicity, lack of citizenship, and disability cluster. Much of this writing starts with experiences of inequality, and is rightly critical of education systems and practices which reproduce or fail to confront inequalities in the wider society. This body of scholarship notes what fails to work in education, judging failures against a standard of equity, sometimes loosely defined, linked with equitable access, equitable participation, or aspects of outcome which change intergenerational inequalities. HadJar and Gross' (2016) collection poses the question from the point of view of the education system looking at the ways social relationships form education systems to shape inequalities across different axes, looking at the links between macro, meso and micro levels of engagement. In understanding how inequality works, they chart a terrain through which moves for equality would need to be put in place, and they utilise comparisons both of large multi-country datasets and small selected contexts in order to develop their analysis. The conclusion (Almendinger, 2016) distils some implications of what underpins equality and what might comprise some facets of equity. These are inclusive access, learning for life in ways that engage with contemporary problems, and connecting relevant actors in planning and evaluation. This distillation of equity evokes aspects of what works and what matters, and suggests equity happens at many different levels.

Thirdly there is a practice version of equity. I see this exemplified in Abdi and Richardson's (2008) collection of critical pedagogy in practice, where the authors show educational equity working for individuals or small groups, challenging the frameworks presented by colonialism, exclusionary forms of democracy or education systems that fail to recognise, for example, the conditions of indigenous girls in Canada, Aboriginal children in Australia, or the lived experience of postcolonial citizens in Africa. These accounts show how much and how deeply inequality is inscribed at the institution or system level, and how fragile the initiatives that challenge it often are.

Lastly there are definitional engagements with equity in education, teasing out the implications of different meanings, using practice to exemplify the semantic flexibility of the term, but applying it allusively rather than descriptively to real historical settings. My own initial discussion of the semantic history of equity took this form (Unterhalter, 2009b). I drew out three different meanings of the word equity which appear in English at different periods. There is an initial meaning expressing the walking with the powerful and angry, which I quoted at the beginning from Wycliff's translation of the Book of Malachi and which comes from an engagement with ideas, feelings and experience. There is a slightly later meaning associated with forming equity courts, which stood above the courts of church and nobles and which expresses equity as encoded in institutions. There is a third meaning of equity linked with money in the 18th century, which draws out some of its dynamism, fluidity and association with investment and exchanged.

Drawing on these three meanings of equity I distinguished for education what I called equity from the top, the middle and the bottom. The argument I made was that it was necessary for all these levels or sites of equity to articulate. I made a selective use of examples, deploying what I have since come to characterise as a form of reflexive comparative education, considering parts to illuminate the whole, rather than the rigorous system led comparisons that are so evident in much policy discussion (Unterhalter, 2014). This reflexive comparison of parts, drawing on biographies to illuminate a larger whole is something I have attempted to do in this discussion.

One of the problems with an approach to faceting the meaning of equity is that the word, like a number of others which denote value—efficiency, empowerment, evidence—can be re-inscribed with meanings different from those originally formulated. Indeed equity can be found linked with growth, to argue for aspects of austerity, marketisation, or the dismantling of processes of participation (Unterhalter, 2017). This semantic hollowing out in which selective use of comparative examples is often deployed, is one reason I have wanted to ground this chapter in trying to understand equity, linked with aspirations of justice, freedom, equality and hope by people who challenged unjust institutions. I want to set these lived examples against uses of the word equity as a superficial cover for education policies that do not share a notion of what matters.

We see here a number of different approaches to engaging with different facets of equity, and deployment of quite established approaches to comparison (for example by McCowan or the contributors to the Hadjar volume) and quite allusive meanings, for example drawing on critical pedagogy as exemplified in the contributions to Abdi and Richardson's collection or those of reflexive comparison I have suggested. Raffo provides us with an educational equity toolkit for use in schools and some experiences with using it will need to be documented.

In linking equity with a difficult terrain of education, I want to suggest that there is not one single approach to comparative method that is required, but rather to keep the orientation of equity emerging from concerns with justice, equality and challenges to the hierarchies and exclusions of power.

In concluding this discussion I want to pose some critical questions regarding this academic sorting game and the world we live in, marked by so many injustices and inequalities. How far does all this classification and analytical distinction around equity take us, and do our insights regarding comparative and international education give us any particular vantage point? We invest in education great aspiration to develop knowledge, skill, and understanding; connect across social, economic, political and historical divisions; and challenge unjust power. Like democracy, the education systems, practices and institutions we have are highly imperfect. Yet they continue to be for many of us, as they were for Michel, Gramsci, Lauwerys, and Mandela, sites of hope. Does equity take us further mitigating some of the imperfections? And how much further is good enough? What supplementary concepts can help anchor equity in education in difficult times? Given the enormity of the problems that confront us what direction is useful in the study of equity and education?

I think some of the academic work I have cited does help deepen our insight and there is enormous scope for more. In arguing for this I want to return to the accounts of Louise Michel, Gramsci and the Robben Island prisoners doing equity in education against the odds, building equity through practice in places that are deeply marked by the inequalities of the societies around them, yet in those places people use education as a form of opposition which challenges the prison power structures, and the inequalities they inscribe. They are doing what I have called equity from below. They were not unique in doing this, as there are many accounts of schools, universities, or adult education projects which establish themselves to challenge injustice through education practice.

What can we draw from the accounts of the island prisons I have cited to understand contemporary times of austerity, inequality and upheaval? All the education projects of the political prisoners suggest building equity against the odds, challenging a brutal power, in places carved out of harsh conditions. They seem particularly resonant in helping us to distinguish some of the practices and processes that may help to support the concept of equity in education to remain both rooted in ideas about justice, equality and knowledge, and also able to take multiple routes through fragmented experiences and across differences in a world that does not care much for the hope the concept offers. Indeed it often uses equity or meritocracy as a myth to justify the continued power of those who have so much at the expense of those with little or nothing.

One question that has interested me in researching the three different instances of political prisoners using education as a space of hope is what minimum conditions must exist for political prisoners to engage in the kinds of educational practices I have outlined. They have deprivations, harsh conditions, abusive jailers, and long stretches of time cut off from people who they care for, but they do have access to books, imaginative worlds, and moments of association with other prisoners. When there are deprivations they often strategise to redistribute books or ideas. The islands where they are held are cut off, but not completely. Messages in various guises get through. They have very powerful frameworks of meaning making, given by their political experience which help them respond to the cruel places they are condemned to live. These frameworks were given by the commune and aspirations for gender equality and women's rights for Louise Michel, through the experience of Communist Party and systematic study of history for Gramsci, and through an appreciation of the history of anti-apartheid opposition in South Africa for the Robben Island prisoners. All three groups are very firmly rooted in a particular framework of meaning, and, while they examine this critically, they have a starting point, which anchors them and their education project in relation to what matters. All three also have an aspiration point, be it delineated conceptually, experientially, or politically. What matters is not static, but moves across an arc of practice. This and the sociability of the educational practices and the human relationships that work, that reach across difference, listen to others, try to position knowledge sequentially, actively, critically, emotionally or imaginatively all seem to be key facets of the modalities of equity and hope. In the three accounts of the education projects on the island prisons these moves offer some niche of protection against the humiliations and denials of humanity.

Thus what works is the attempt to put equity and hope into practice. There are many failures, losses, disappointments, deprivations and false starts, many attempts to deceive the prisoners, isolate or undermine them. I do not have illusions that the many-faceted notion of equity in education is the only idea to guide contemporary hard times, but it is an idea with some potential to confront unjust institutions, and a deep history, animated by hope.

ACKNOWLEDGEMENTS

The author would like to thank: Stephen Carney (Roskilde University, Denmark), Bob Cowen (UCL Institute of Education, England), Richard Crawford, Emily Henderson (University of Birmingham, England), Holly Henderson (University of Warwick, England), Tristan McCowan (UCL Institute of Education, England), Amy North (UCL Institute of Education, England), Donatella Palomba (Rome Tor Vergata University, Italy) and Michele Schweisfurth (University of Glasgow, Scotland).

NOTE

[1] This chapter was originally developed as the Joseph Lauwerys Memorial Lecture, delivered at the CESE Conference, May 2016, Glasgow.

REFERENCES

Abdi, A. A., & Richardson, W. G. (Eds.). (2008). *Decolonizing democratic education: Trans-disciplinary dialogues*. Rotterdam, The Netherlands: Sense Publishers.

Albright, A. (2016, May 22). Children caught in humanitarian crises cannot wait for education. *World Humanitarian Summit*. Retrieved July, 2017, from http://blog.worldhumanitariansummit.org/entries/children-caught-in-humanitarian-crises-cannot-wait-for-education/

Allmendinger, J. (2016). Good and bad education systems: Is there an ideal? In A. Hadjar & C. Gross (Eds.), *Education systems and inequalities* (pp. 321–334). Bristol: Policy Press.

Buttigieg, J. (2011). Introduction and chronology. In A. Gramsci (Ed.), *Prison notebooks* (pp. 1–94). New York, NY: Columbia University Press.

Desai, A. (2014). *Reading revolution: Shakespeare on Robben Island*. Chicago, IL: Haymarket Books.

Gramsci, A. (2011a). *Prison notebooks* (Vol. 1). New York, NY: Columbia University Press.

Gramsci, A. (2011b). *Letters from Prison*. New York, NY: Columbia University Press.

HadJar, A., & Gross, C. (Eds.). (2016). *Education systems and inequalities: International comparisons*. Bristol: Policy Press.

Halls, W. (2004). Lauwerys, Joseph Albert (1902–1981). In *Oxford dictionary of national biography*. Oxford: Oxford University Press. Retrieved July 16, 2017, from http://www.oxforddnb.com.lib.exeter.ac.uk/view/article/31336

Kathrada, A. M. (2005). *A free mind: Ahmed Kathrada's notebook from Robben Island*. Johannesburg: Jacana Media.

Korr, C. P., Korr, C., & Close, M. (2008). *More than just a game: Football v apartheid*. London: HarperCollins.

Lauwerys, J. (1944). National integration and education. *The New Era, 25*(2), 21–22.

Lauwerys, J. (1945a). Nationalism and internationalism in education. *The New Era, 26*(4), 71–72.

Lauwerys, J. (1945b). Summing up. *The New Era, 26*(9), 220–222.

Lodge, T., & Nasson, B. (1991). *All, here, and now: Black politics in South Africa in the 1980s*. Cape Town: New Africa Books.

Maclellan, N. (2004). *Louise Michel*. Melbourne: Ocean Press.

Mandela, N. (1994). *Long walk to freedom: The autobiography of Nelson Mandela*. London: Little Brown.

Mandela, N. (2010). *Conversations with myself*. London: Macmillan.

McCowan, T. (2016). Three dimensions of equity of access to higher education. *Compare: A Journal of Comparative and International Education, 46*(4), 645–665.

McLean, M. (Ed.). (1981). *Joseph A. Lauwerys: A festschrift.* London: University of London Institute of Education Library.

Michel, L. (1981). *The Red Virgin: Memoirs of Louise Michel* (B. Lowry & E. Gunter, Ed. & Trans.). Alabama: University of Alabama Press.

Raffo, C. (2013). *Improving educational equity in urban contexts.* Abingdon: Routledge.

Soudien, C. (2015). Nelson Mandela, Robben Island and the imagination of a new South Africa. *Journal of Southern African Studies, 41*(2), 353–366.

UNESCO. (2015, June). *Humanitarian aid for education: Why it matters and why more is needed* (UNESCO EFA Global Monitoring Report, Policy Paper No. 21). Retrieved from http://unesdoc.unesco.org/images/0023/002335/233557E.pdf

Unterhalter, E. (2009a). Translations and transversal dialogues: An examination of mobilities associated with gender, education and global poverty reduction. *Comparative Education, 45*(3), 329–345.

Unterhalter, E. (2009b). What is equity in education? Reflections from the capability approach. *Studies in the Philosophy of Education, 28*(5), 415–424.

Unterhalter, E. (2014). Walking backwards to the future: A comparative perspective on education and a post-2015 framework'. *Compare, 44*(6), 852–873.

Unterhalter, E. (2017). A review of public private partnerships around girls' education in developing countries: Flicking gender equality on and off. *Journal of International and Comparative Social Policy, 33*(2), 181–199.

Elaine Unterhalter
UCL Institute of Education
London, England

MASAKO SHIBATA

2. HOLOCAUST EDUCATION IN TRANSITION

A Transnational Perspective

INTRODUCTION

It has been a remarkable phenomenon over the past few decades that a number of national governments and state leaderships have issued formal apologies in an attempt to correct political and social injustices committed in the past. These have been offered to victims who suffered from unequal and often inhumane treatment by state authorities because of their political creeds, religious faiths or racial origins. Regardless of the time of the wrongdoings—some were done in the remote past and others quite recently—offering such apologies has become a common phenomenon around the world. In some cases, apologies resulted in reconciliation with the victims, and in others it did not. These differences notwithstanding, policy makers in the educational arena have followed suit. Correcting the interpretations of past injustices is reflected in the ideas and practices of education, notably history education. In teaching history, the conceptions of equal rights and basic human rights have become weightier than ever.

Given this new trend in the history of modern states, this chapter looks at changes in the political and educational treatment of the Holocaust, which stemmed from centuries-long racial and religious discrimination against European Jewry. For about half a century after 1945, the mass murder of six million Jews was largely viewed as a brutal undertaking by Nazi Germany. During the post-war period while appreciating West Germany's self-critical policy of *Vergangenheitsbewältigung* (overcoming the past), its neighbouring countries remained somewhat aloof from the crimes of the Holocaust. However, from the 1990s onwards, a number of those countries began to interpret and teach this history as part of their national history, by suggesting their overt or covert involvement in the genocide.

This chapter examines the changes in the teaching of Holocaust history in Europe, and positions this in relation to attempts elsewhere to atone for past injustices. It is argued that the attempt to address or at least acknowledge past injustices should be seen in relation to heightened commitments to equity and human rights in the context of post-Cold War pacifist-inclined international relationships. Particularly in Europe, the subsequent regional unification generated a momentum for building societies within which history is constructed afresh in the form of collective memory based on shared European values. Further, it is argued that the conventional nation-state framework of history interpretation has been transformed to a wider scope of the perception of the Holocaust as a universal theme for human rights. Lastly, and not least, this transformation has gone through a long process of Holocaust education, which was facilitated by the deliberate policy of the government of West Germany for amending historical injustices.

To unfold these arguments, the chapter explores changing notions of equity in a globalising context, viewing this as a recent phenomenon. I then move on to a detailed account of the changing way in which Holocaust history is treated in Europe, illustrating the argument with examples from France, Sweden and Britain.

NEW NOTIONS OF EQUITY

Collective memory has trends. It is socially constructed, reflecting the dominant discourses of society (Halbwachs, 1989). In principle, collective memory is differentiated from 'objective' history. In reality, the history construed by elites in society largely shares the elements of collective remembering, and often becomes compatible with it (Burke, 1997; Wertsch, 2002, p. 20). Official interpretations of historical events are inseparable from, or often the direct reflection of, collective memory. Thus, the perception of national history is transformed along with the metamorphosis of society.

Without question, collective memory is not a collection of individuals' memories. In the cases of historical incidents of injustices, the memories of individual victims are sometimes alienated from collective memory, affected by the 'public' interest of a concerned society. More often than not, this discrepancy results in the exposure of victimhood to political whims, and the trivialisation of it. Such cases can be found in East Asia where the settlement of WWII in the region was left more ambiguous than in Europe. For example, the Nanjing Massacre had deliberately been downplayed in history education by the Chinese government during the period of nation building. However, the death of Mao Zedong and the subsequent rise of Deng Xiaoping brought about a radical policy in this area (Mitter, 2003). In the cases of Hiroshima and Nagasaki, the stories of the victims of atomic bombs were underplayed in Japanese education during the phase of national reconstruction, but became an important part of the collective memory of WWII, especially in the context of growing anti-nuclear movements.

At the same time, the official interpretation of past injustices, or the dark side of national history, are largely affected by public memory. Over the past few decades, such histories have drawn intensive political and academic attention. The leadership of countries which had been heavily involved in political and social inequity in the past began to review the traditionally and broadly accepted perceptions of the past injustices. Often, they offer official apologies and compensation to the victims. Such tendencies are observable in many international contexts. Even though official apologies have not always resulted in final reconciliations with the victims, examples are many.

Whilst the French presidential apology in 1995 for the deportation of Jewish residents to Nazi 'death camps' during WWII was a symbolic one, another apology to Holocaust victims was offered by the Swiss government in 1997, along with a five-billion-dollar compensation for the property loss incurred by victims through Swiss banks. This is a remarkable example, as it demonstrates the unspoken guilt of so-called 'Holocaust bystanders' in a war-time neutral state. In Asia, the Japanese Prime Minister Tomiichi Murayama stated in an official speech in 1995 his 'deep remorse' and 'heartfelt apology' to the victims of Japan's aggression during the war and colonial rule.[1] Changing notions of equity and justice could also be viewed as the reason for addressing much older cases of exploitation. For example, the Australian government acknowledged its policy of discrimination imposed on indigenous people, with the Prime Minister Kevin Rudd communicating this apology via a televised speech to the population in 2007. In the United States, another traditionally multi-ethnic society, the state of Oklahoma admitted in 2001 the guilt of its legislature during the Tulsa Race Riot of 1921, and its treatment as a 'myth' was subsequently modified in educational materials.

The sequence of those official apologies can certainly be understood as political and social movements. Barkan and Karn (2006) view such movements as a tendency in recent political discourse particularly after the end of the Cold War, and argue that this new political vigour is driven by the long-term tactics of the individual governments for constructing more mutually prosperous political and economic relationships in their region and at the world-level. One could argue that effective processes of reconciliation between victims and perpetrators rest largely upon the political leadership and moral courage of both sides, especially of the latter (Feldman, 2014, pp. 12–17). In addition, there has been a growing and global public awareness of the notion of 'crimes against humanity', which has legitimised the claims of victims and thus given them effective political and educational means of action (Barkan, 2000; Bekerman & Zembylas, 2012, p. 82). Importantly, moreover, as political, economic and cultural globalisation intensifies in the post-Cold War world, it has become inevitable for most governments to institute more liberal policies to deal with the growth in number of 'minorities' and their larger political representation in multi-ethnic and multi-cultural society. This is particularly observable in those European countries which face internal and external criticisms about their religious and racial intolerance in the post-colonial and post-war eras (Howard-Hassmann & Gibney, 2008). Those countries have gone through a long process before embracing Holocaust history in the new notions of national history and a universal theme of human rights.

HOLOCAUST EDUCATION AS A UNIVERSAL THEME
FOR HUMAN RIGHTS: ITS LONG PROCESS

The Holocaust as an educational theme is a relatively new initiative in public schooling. Many years after the Nuremberg Trial, it has now become a kind of archetype in teaching human morality and equity inside and outside Europe. What gave the Holocaust such a universal value is the well-known accounts of the distinctiveness of this institutionalised genocide, i.e. the totality of intent and the means employed, such as the state bureaucracy, technologies and the systematic management of a modern nation state (Bauman, 1989; Eaglestone, 2004).[2] With no precedent or an adequate analogy, this watershed event has received iconic status concerning morality in human history (Young, 1988). Because of, and ironically in spite of, its distinctive nature, the Holocaust gained universal application.[3] Especially since the end of the Cold War, the Holocaust literature has 'mushroomed', and Holocaust studies seem to have become a paradigm in an academic discipline (Stone, 2010). David MacDonald (2008, p. 16) suggests that the Holocaust, as it is spoken of today, is largely "a retrospective construction". In other words, this has not been a common phenomenon throughout the post-war period. Both victims and perpetrators have devoted effort to passing on for posterity a full account of this period: a process that has been long and shaped by struggle.

Even in Israel, Holocaust education did not come into the political or public spotlight immediately after the War. In the process of its national building, the Holocaust had not been taught until its first appearance in the curriculum in 1954 (Porat, 2004). Even here, its treatment was not lengthy, mirroring other war-time events such as the battle in Stalingrad. While the foundation of Yad Vashem was decided by the Knesset in 1953, the political treatment of this national Holocaust memorial museum was minor in terms of the size and the location. It was a policy of Ben-Gurion and his followers to spotlight more heroic stories about the war-time Jews rather than their victimhood. From the 1960s, however, Holocaust education was becoming the central theme in Israeli politics, largely emboldened by the dramatic impact of the Eichmann Trial in 1961 and the following Arab-Israeli conflicts, especially the attack on Yom Kippur in 1973. A textbook in the 1980s, for instance, devoted over 450 pages on Holocaust narratives, twenty times as sizable as in the 1960s (Porat, 2004, pp. 626–630). In 1979, this history became a compulsory subject in upper secondly education, and the Knesset Committee of Education and Culture prepared a bill for all Israeli students to be educated "on consciousness of the memory of the Holocaust and Heroism" (Porat, 2004, p. 630, 2010).

In Europe, the development of Holocaust education was similarly far from linear. Soon after the war, so-called peace education was advocated by UNESCO, and education of humanity, equality and moral solidarity was stressed. History education was specially valued to enhance international understanding. Alongside this development, the International Textbook Research Institute was established in Braunschweig in West Germany on the initiative of Georg Eckert. The country's national agenda of *Vergangenheitsbewältigung* was a direct reflection of this awareness of the potential of history education. Since its introduction, the policy has been one of the most important national political as well as educational schemes in West Germany.

From the 1960s, collective memory of the National-Socialist past grew among the public. The student movement and its leadership by intellectuals had a vital impact on the ways in which the country coped with this dark side of national history (Kattago, 2001; Wiedmer, 1999). The political leadership of West Germany, notably Chancellor Willy Brandt (1969–1974) and President Richard von Weizsäcker (1984–1994), garnered the backing of public opinion in favour of the national policy for war-time history. From this period, the Holocaust came to be highlighted in public education in West Germany, with substantial space allocated to its history in school textbooks. This was not limited to history, however, but also encompassed political education and special learning materials. By the 1980s, though, Holocaust education in Germany had become 'routinised' or 'fragmented' (Kansteiner, 2006). Participants of study visits to Holocaust memorial sites, e.g. Auschwitz, had become fewer in number (Vocke, 2009). As the national unification of Germany progressed, there was a sense in which the nation should cease to be "punished" by the international community for its earlier atrocities (MacDonald, 2008, p. 25). It is ironic that the post-war national policy for racial tolerance has made Holocaust education carry weaker connotations of 'national history' then in contemporary multi-ethnic classrooms.

In the process of Holocaust history becoming a universal theme for human rights education, approaches to the history of this period have also changed. Inside and outside the school, the representation of Holocaust victims has become multi-dimensional by including so-called 'forgotten victims' such as the Romanies and homosexuals. History museums too began to value 'active understanding', i.e. providing students with seminar rooms for discussion rather than with conventional guided tours (Dietzfelbinger, 2007). Instead of instilling into children conventional judgements and criticisms about the Nazi regime, the focus now is on in-depth understandings about the fragilities of democracy, the importance of public courage against violence and the consequences of hatred against 'others' (Prölß-Kammerer & Oschmann, 2010). Here, the portrayal of 'perpetrators' has become complex as well. In history textbooks, for example, the Allied bombing of civilians in Hamburg and Dresden has become a stable feature in the curriculum. Shifts in historiography from narratives around the theme of nation-state to broader attention to 'everyday life' or 'ordinary people'—illustrated in the work of Christopher Browning (1992), Daniel Goldhagen (1996) and Claus Leggewie (1998)—also modified the earlier simplistic dichotomy of victim versus perpetrator in understanding the history of the war. In the field of public culture such as film, war-time Germans can now be presented from the perspective of victimhood.[4]

DEVELOPMENT IN NEIGHBOURING COUNTRIES

Whilst Germany's dedication to Holocaust education was deep, its neighbouring countries had long adopted a so-called bystanders' approach to Holocaust history. Regional studies on the history were lacking or did not progress. What is called the 'Auschwitz Syndrome', a somewhat inevitable concentration of academic and public interest in key symbols of the history, has been suggested as a reason for the dearth of interest (Stone, 2010, p. 90). The collapse of the communist regimes in East Europe, where anti-Semitism had traditionally been strong, certainly widened the geographic scope of studies on the theme. There, until the end of the Cold War, Holocaust education had long been taboo (István, 2013; Ludvikova, 2008; Mink, 2013). In the countries of post-war West Europe as well, the innocence of one's own people was proclaimed, while guilt was fixed on Germany (Uhl, 2006). However, as Europe became a more unified political, economic, cultural and educational sphere, memory of the Holocaust began to be shared by people in the region. The chapter examines three examples which have shown differing degrees of attachment to Holocaust history.

France, an Immediate Neighbour

The origin of Holocaust studies in France was early and traceable to an underground project for documenting anti-Semitic persecutions during the German occupation. Born in Grenoble, the project led to the creation of a memorial site for the Jewish martyrs in Paris in 1956, which eventually brought about the Mémoire de la Shoah inaugurated by President Jacques Chirac in 2005.

This Holocaust museum now functions as a centre for Holocaust education for school children and teachers, prior to the eventual study of the latter in Auschwitz and Yad Vashem. For schools outside Paris, La Maison d'Anne Frank en France provides exhibitions on the theme throughout the country in collaboration with teachers, especially younger ones (Laureau, 2010). In public schooling, learning about the 'Shoah' has become obligatory (Francapane, 2012) and since 2002, and framed as a crime against humanity, it has become firmly installed in the school curriculum in France. In 2006, a joint group of French and German historians and educators announced their publication of a common history book on the post-1945 era.

As mentioned earlier, the development of such Holocaust education in France is an expected outcome of Chirac's official acknowledgement of 'collective fault' regarding the Holocaust under the Vichy regime. This acknowledgement was delivered at the 53rd anniversary of the Vél' d'Hiv incident of 1942.[5] In France, as in Romania, Slovakia, Croatia and the Baltic States, the war-time persecution of Jewish people had indigenous roots, which had coincided with a longer tradition of anti-Semitism (Stone, 2010, p. 6, 2012, p. 13). The impact of Chirac's apology was significant enough to impair the post-war Gaullist 'myth' that the majority of the wartime French people were dissidents against the Nazis, and the collaboration of the Vichy regime with them was a deviation in a political interregnum. After a few decades of 'quietism' during the presidencies of Georges Pompidou (1969–1974) and Valéry Discard d'Estaing (1974–1981), the popular myth was gradually eclipsed. François Mitterrand's Vichy past was also unveiled. The trials of

Vichy bureaucrats in the 1990s strengthened public anger about the earlier political and educational treatment of Holocaust history in the country. After Chirac's apology, official measures followed suit for economic reparation for Jewish victims and for more comprehensive education about Holocaust history.

Pedagogically speaking, it is often argued that the most effective method of teaching the gravity of the events to students is to make them identify themselves with particular victims (Cowan & Maitles, 2017). In this sense, President Nicolas Sarkozy's curriculum reform should have been successful. In 2008, Sarkozy tried to revise the school curriculum by introducing a new programme for every fifth grader to learn the personal life story of one of the 11,000 French children of Holocaust victims. He said that "Nothing is more moving for a child, than the story of a child his own age, ... who, in the dawn of the 1940s, had the bad fortune to be defined as a Jew" (Sciolino, 2008). In reality, this policy of focusing on victims was regarded by critics as an attempt of turning people's eyes away from the Vichy past (Sciolino, 2008). Above all, this 'personalisation' of Holocaust history imposed on children was criticised as a deliberate attempt to insert a Christian-inclined 'spirituality' in history education. Nonetheless, as the Franco-German partnership became mature, Sarkozy and the German Chancellor Angela Merkel jointly dedicated a de Gaulle memorial in 2008, with her emphasis on 'historic responsibility' (Feldman, 2014, p. 111). In sum, because of the relatively deep involvement of France in the wartime Jewish persecution, the positioning of Holocaust history as such seems to be weightier than ever in the education of French national history. According to the historical processes, Holocaust education in France has developed hand in hand with its reconciliatory relationship with its immediate neighbour Germany towards the successful integration of post-war Europe.

Sweden, a Bystander

Changes in Holocaust education in Sweden are largely driven by personal engagement in the national leadership. While stories about the courageous rescue of Hungarian Jews by Raul Wallenberg or 'white busses' were prominent, Holocaust education remained underdeveloped until the onset of special programmes initiated by Prime Minister Göran Persson (1996–2006). In a war-time neutral state, public memory had been separated from history. Despite the fact that Sweden had maintained its political neutrality throughout the war, its actual policy toward Nazi Germany was more benign than other neutral states, e.g. granting railway use to the *Wehrmacht*. After the *Anschluß* and the *Kristallnacht* of 1938, the Swedish foreign office tried to prevent the influx of Jews, until it came to recognise Norwegian victims of the Final Solution (Kvist, 2000). Such ambiguous attitudes towards Nazi crimes became a basis of 'Swedish guilt discourse', which eventually led to the development of Holocaust education as a national programme (Persson, 2000; Selling, 2011).

The social democratic Premier started 'Living History' campaign in 1997 to promote the greater awareness of the Swedish populace about the values of tolerance, democracy and equal rights through learning about the Holocaust. In his view, the people had long lived in ignorance of the history, and were unable to link it with their own national history. Based on a parliamentary decision, the Living History Forum was founded in 2003 in the capital to enlighten the people about the Holocaust as a starting point of valuing equal rights of all people. The publicly funded researchers compiled a book, *Tell ye your children...: A Book about the Holocaust in Europe 1933–1945*, which was given free of charge to all households throughout the country. Altogether 1.3 million copies were distributed in seven language versions, i.e. in Swedish, English, Finnish, Persian, Spanish, Turkish and Arabic (Franck, 2010). The title of the book is based on a quotation from the Bible: "Hear this, ye old man, and give ear, all ye inhabitants of the land. Hath this been in your days, or even in the days of your fathers? Tell ye your children of it, and let your children tell their children, and their children another generation" (Bruchfeld & Levine, 2012, p. 4).

Over time, the Living History Forum has changed its initial aim of fighting against racism and anti-Semitism to advocating universal democratic values, and collaboration in Holocaust education and research was extended internationally (Selling, 2011). In 1998, Persson collaborated with the British Prime Minister Tony Blair and the US President Bill Clinton to establish a Task Force for further international cooperation in the new millennium.[6] At the first conference of the Stockholm International Forum on the Holocaust in 2000, 46 governments signed the Stockholm Declaration, advocating for "international support for combating racism, anti-Semitism, ethnic hatred and ignorance of history". It asserts that "[t]he unprecedented character of the Holocaust will always hold universal meaning" (Government of Sweden, 2006, p. 23). Kofi Annan, a participant in a series of the Forum conferences, delivered a historic speech on the 60th anniversary of the liberation of Auschwitz, becoming the first Secretary-General of the United Nations to talk officially about the history. As a result, UNESCO expanded its budget and personnel for a global development of Holocaust education (Francapane, 2012). In sum, the perceived distant attachment of Sweden to the Holocaust is reflected in its treatment of the history in education as part of the broader focus on human rights.

Britain, a Distant Neighbour

The Holocaust has received special treatment in British history education. Within and beyond the National Curriculum, said the House of Commons Education Committee, "[t]he Holocaust stands apart from other historical events" (House of Commons Education Committee, 2016, p. 3). In history education, WWII is certainly a prime theme in the modern period along with WWI. Generally speaking, history textbooks demonstrate the portrayal of the wars with colourful illustrations of military operations in major theatres and perseverance on the British home front. Beside those standard illustrations, substantial pages are spared for special sections or even a whole chapter about Nazi Germany and the Holocaust, while other controversial war-time atrocities are treated modestly (Shibata, 2008).

Unlike France, Britain had fought Nazi Germany throughout the war, and actually accepted Jewish escapees from the continent.[7] The Holocaust, as part of national history, is talked about via heroic stories such as the *Kindertransport* and the liberation of Bergen-Belsen. At the same time, history downplays other key events such as the radical shift in immigration policy after the *Anschluß* aimed at limiting probable Jewish migration into the country and the government's refusal of requests from Jewish underground lobbies to bomb the Budapest-Auschwitz railway link (Romain, 1999; Rubenstein, 1996). The perception of WWII as a 'good war' certainly made the collective memory of the war in Britain more positive relative to neighbouring countries. Such views of the war and the Holocaust also prevail outside the school. In Britain, museums undergo evaluation by the Research Centre for Museums and Galleries, and their educational functions are subject to social accountability and certain adjustment to the school curriculum (Hooper-Greenhill, 2007). Unlike war-related museums, in the former Axis countries, Imperial War Museums (IWM) in Britain display little gloom. There, children can interact with displayed fighter planes and commander radios. On the other hand, the IWM in London dedicates a whole floor to 'The Holocaust Exhibition' and 'Crimes against Humanity'.

Research on the Holocaust also demonstrates remarkable intellectual development. New governmental initiatives are added to the conventional treatment of Holocaust history in British education. A wide range of academic disciplines is adopted for research on the theme at the Holocaust Research Centre since its establishment in 2000 at Royal Holloway, University of London. The Centre for Holocaust Education at UCL, Institute of Education (CfHE) started in 2008 as the only research institution which offers professional schemes for actual classroom teaching of the history. The government funded the CfHE with £500,000 (House of Commons Education Committee, 2016, p. 9). There, new approaches to Holocaust education can also be found in a cross-curricular methodology that is extended to the field of religious education and citizenship. Based on this substantial public fund, programmes for innovative teaching methodologies are created and expanded throughout England. Overnight seminars or study visits to Poland are prepared for selected schools every year (UCL Institute of Education, 2015). Behind this initiative, there is the government's intension of promoting tolerance and equality of people in the multi-ethnic society. This viewpoint is demonstrated by the speech of Tony Blair on the Holocaust Memorial Day ceremony first held in Britain in 2000. For the day, the Department for Education and Employment prepared an 'Education Pack', which included materials about the genocides in Rwanda and Bosnia along with a major focus on the Holocaust (Cesarani, 2001). Holocaust education in Britain tends to entail a broader theme of human rights, and, in contrast to France, connotes less attachment to its history.

CONCLUDING REMARKS

Many Holocaust researchers say that the history of this period has finally become prominent, in large part due to the end of the Cold War. It is now perceived that the

Holocaust was and is part of European and human history. New developments in Holocaust education in unified Europe show this perception half a century after the end of WWII. As seen above, there have been long processes until this stage.

Firstly, the longstanding history policy of the government of West Germany was certainly an important basis and driving force of the development. The educational policy and practices raised political awareness about, and public interest in, the event inside and outside the country. Behind the policy, there was increased political, economic and social representation of the Jewish people around the world, notably in the Middle East and North America. New generations in the state leadership altered conventional historical views; a situation that can be seen in all three cases.

Moreover, changes in historiography modified the theoretical framing of Holocaust narratives. New broader perspectives of historical interpretation, the role of ordinary people, bystanders and sympathisers came to be illuminated, and added new actors to Holocaust education. It is now a widely accepted account that the war-time persecution of Jews took place not only in Auschwitz or 'famous' concentration camps, but also in people's neighbourhoods in Europe. The orthodoxy of a simplistic dichotomy of victim versus perpetrator is in question. At the same time, Holocaust education in countries like Sweden and Britain, which could be argued to have had a less direct involvement in the history than France and above all Germany, tends to treat the event in terms of broader themes of human rights and equity.

Lastly, the end of the cold war was crucial to a paradigm shift in collective memory. It affected not only Holocaust education but also the amendment of the other historical injustices as mentioned earlier. The dissolution of the bipolar mechanism of the Cold War brought about a new political vigour for seeking mutual prosperity of nations. The governmental remedy of past injustices worked well for this purpose. In most cases studied above, the policy of apology seems to have thrived positively. Above all, in the European context, the collapse of the communist regimes in East Europe led to a revision of traditional anti-Semitism in the continent and the history of the Holocaust as a whole. The post-war unification of Europe, driven by the Franco-German leadership, was an essential background particularly for Germany's neighbours to confront the Nazi past differently from earlier periods. In Europe, where nations have shared distinct civilisational values (Habermas, 2004), Holocaust education seems to develop as a supra-national agenda. At the same time, as societies in Europe are becoming more multi-ethnic and multi-cultural, renewed notions of national identity will and do carry different connotations of Holocaust history as 'national history'. This can be seen in the case of Germany.

ACKNOWLEDGEMENTS

The author would like to express special thanks to following people for their cooperation in interview. Institutional affiliation is based on the day of the interview:

1. Dietzfelbinger, E. (4 August 2007). Dokumentation Centre, Nuremberg, Germany.
2. Francapane, K. (30 January 2012). The Division of Education for Peace and Sustainable Development of UNESCO, Paris, France.
3. Franck, E. (19 August 2010). The Living History Forum, Stockholm, Sweden.
4. István, N. (14 March 2013). Holocaust Memorial Center, Budapest, Hungary.
5. Laureau, C. (3 December 2010). La Maison Anne Frank en France, Paris, France.
6. Ludvikova, M. (18 August 2008). The Education and Culture Centre of the Jewish Museum, Prague, Czech Republic.
7. Porat, D. (14 June 2010). Hebrew University, Jerusalem, Israel.
8. Prölß-Kammerer, A. & Oschmann, J. (21 January 2010). DoKuPäd, Nuremberg, Germany.
9. Vocke, U. (28 July–1 August 2009). Theodor-Heuss-Gymnasium, Wolfenbüttel, Germany (during its study visit to Cracow and Auschwitz/Birkenau).

NOTES

[1] Unlike a number of other WWII-related official apologies, the Japanese case did not bring about lasting reconciliation with the victims, revealing 'the difficulty of translating the western rhetoric of apology into terms of consistent with non-Western culture' (Barkan & Karn, 2006, p. 7).

[2] Cf. Stone (2010, p. 126) who argues that Bauman's account merely shows the transmittal process of the mass murder, and does not actually illuminate the real driving force of it.

[3] Bekerman and Zembylas (2012, p. 162) point out that "only when the commemoration of the Holocaust is free from ideology and Zionist/Israeli co-operation can it become 'universal'... and only then it can gain its critical symmetry/asymmetry with other catastrophes. Otherwise, the Holocaust will continue to be submitted to the will of nationalism (the same power that created it) and will not be made available to all humans".

[4] A recent example is a Danish-German film, *Under sandet* or *Land of Mine* (2015) which pictures the ill-treatment of underage German POWs by the Danish authority immediately after the war. It questions the conventional judgement about 'victims'.

[5] A document of the Wannsee Conference of 1942 shows that initially 865,000 Jewish residents in France were the target of the Final Solution, of which 165,000 lived in the German-occupied territories (Wannsee, 2015, p. 148).

[6] Twenty-four states joined it: Argentina, Austria, Belgium, Croatia, the Czech Republic, Denmark, France, Germany, Greece, Hungary, Israel, Italy, Latvia, Lithuania, Luxembourg, the Netherlands, Norway, Poland, Romania, Slovakia, Sweden, Switzerland, the UK and the US.

[7] Like Sweden, Britain was classified in the 'secondary' category in the Final Solution, and initially had 330,000 Jewish residents as its target within the country (Wannsee, 2015, p. 148).

REFERENCES

Barkan, E. (2000). *The guilt of nations: Restitution and negotiating historical injustices.* New York, NY: W.W. Norton & Company.
Barkan, E., & Karn, A. (2006). Group apology as an ethical imperative. In E. Barkan & A. Karn (Eds.), *Taking wrongs seriously: Apologies and reconciliation* (pp. 3–30). Stanford, CA: Stanford University Press.
Bauman, Z. (1989). *Modernity and the Holocaust.* Cambridge: Polity Press.
Bekerman, Z., & Zembylad, M. (2012). *Teaching contested narratives: Identity, memory and reconciliation in peace education and beyond.* Cambridge: Cambridge University Press.

Browning, C. R. (1992). *Ordinary men: Reserve police battalion 101 and the final solution in Poland.* New York, NY: Harper Collins.
Bruchfeld, S., & Levine, P. A. (2012). *Tell ye your children… A book about the Holocaust in Europe 1933–1945.* Stockholm: Regeringskansliet.
Burke, P. (1997). *Varieties of cultural history.* Cambridge: Polity Press.
Cesarani, D. (2001). Holocaust make it incomparable and inoperative for commemorating studying and preventing genocide? Britain's Holocaust memorial day as a case study. *Journal of the Holocaust Education, 10*(2), 40–56.
Cowan, P., & Maitles, H. (2017). *Understanding and teaching Holocaust education.* London: Sage Publications Ltd.
Eaglestone, R. (2004). *The Holocaust and the postmodern.* Oxford: Oxford University Press.
Feldman, L. G. (2014). *Germany's foreign policy of reconciliation: From enmity to amity.* Lanham, MD: Roman & Littlefield.
Finney, P. (2011). *Remembering the road to world war two: International history, national identity, collective memory.* London: Routledge.
Goldhagen, D. (1996). *Hitler's Willing executioners: Ordinary Germans and the Holocaust.* New York, NY: Alfred A. Knopf.
Government of Sweden. (2006). *Stockholm international forum conferences (2000–2004).* Retrieved November 29, 2016, from http://www.government.se/contentassets/66bc8f513e67474e96ad70c519d4ad1a/the-stockholm-international-forum-conferences-2000-2004
Habermas, J. (2004). *Der gespaltene westen.* Berlin: Suhrkamp.
Halbwachs, M. (1989). *Shugo-teki kioku* [On collective memory]. Tokyo: Kohrosha.
Hooper-Greenhill, E. (2007). *Museums and education: Purpose, pedagogy, performance.* London: Routledge.
House of Commons Education Committee. (2016). *Holocaust education: Second report of session 2015–2016.* London: The Stationery Office Limited.
Howard-Hassmann, R. E., & Gibney, M. (2008). Introduction: Apologies and the west. In M. Gibney, R. E. Howard-Hassmann, J.-M. Coicaud, & N. Steiner (Eds.), *The age of apology: Facing up to the past* (pp. 1–9). Philadelphia, PA: University of Pennsylvania Press.
Kansteiner, W. (2006). Losing the war, winning the memory battle: The legacy of Nazism, world war II, and the Holocaust in the federal republic of Germany. In R. Lebow, W. Kansteiner, & C. Fogu (Eds.), *The politics of memory in post-war Europe* (pp. 102–146). Durham, NC: Duke University Press.
Kattago, S. (2001). *Ambiguous memory: The Nazi past and German national identity.* Westport, CT: Praeger.
Kvist, K. (2000). A study of antisemitic attitudes within Sweden's wartime utlänningsbyrån. *The Journal of Holocaust Education, 9*(2–3), 199–211.
Leggewie, C. (1998). *Von Schneider zu Schwerte: Das ungewöhnliche leben eines mannes, der aus der geschichte lernen wollte.* München: Carl Hanser Verlag.
MacDonald, D. B. (2008). *Identity politics in the age of genocide: The Holocaust and historical representation.* London: Routledge.
Mink, G. (2013). Institutions of national memory in post-communist Europe: From transitional justice to political use of biographies (1989–2010). In G. Mink & L. Neumayer (Eds.), *History, memory and politics in central and Eastern Europe* (pp. 155–170). New York, NY: Palgrave Macmillan.
Mitter, R. (2003). Old ghosts, new memories: China's changing war history in the era of post-mao politics. *Journal of Contemporary History, 38*(1), 117–131.
Persson, S. (2000). Folke Bernadotte and the White buses. *The Journal of Holocaust Education, 9*(2–3), 237–268.
Porat, D. A. (2004). From the scandal to the Holocaust in Israeli education. *Journal of Contemporary History, 39*(4), 619–636.
Romain, G. (1999). The Anschluss: The British response to the refugee crisis. *The Journal of Holocaust Education, 8*(3), 87–102.
Rubenstein, R. L. (1996). Holocaust and holy war. *The Annals of the American Academy of Political and Social Science, 548*(1), 23–44.

Sciolino, E. (2008, February 16). By making Holocaust personal to pupils, Sarkozy stirs anger. *New York Times*. Retrieved October 24, 2016, from http://www.nytimes.com/2008/02/16/world/europe/16france.html

Selling, J. (2011). Between history and politics: The Swedish living history project as discursive formation. *Scandinavian Journal of History, 36*(5), 555–569.

Shibata, M. (2008). Dainiji-sekaitaisen ni kansuru Doitsu no chutogakko rekishi-kyokasho chosa: Igirisu tono hikaku kentou [Research on the treatment of world war II in secondary school history textbooks in Germany: A comparison to the case of England]. *Area Studies Tsukuba, 30*, 55–82.

Shibata, M. (2011). Hakubutsukan ni okeru dainiji-sekai-taisen no tenji to rekishi-kyoiku [Museum exhibitions on world war II and history education]. *Journal of International and Advanced Japanese Studies, 4*, 31–42.

Shibata, M. (2014). Time, location and identity in WWII-related museums: An international comparative analysis. In L. Vega (Ed.), *Empires, post-coloniality and interculturality: New challenges for comparative education* (pp. 59–74). Rotterdam, The Netherlands: Sense Publishers.

Stone, D. (2010). *Histories of the Holocaust*. Oxford: Oxford University Press.

UCL Institute of Education. (2015). *Beacon schools in Holocaust education*. London: UCL Institute of Education.

Uhl, H. (2006). From victim myth to co-responsibility thesis: Nazi rule, world war II, and the Holocaust in Austrian memory. In R. N. Lebow, W. Kansteiner, & C. Fogu (Eds.), *The politics of memory in post-war Europe* (pp. 40–72). Durham, NC: Duke University Press.

Wannsee kaigi kinenkan [Gedenk- und Bildungsstätte Haus der Wannsee-Konferenz]. (Ed.). (2015). *Holocaust no rekisi [Die Wannsee-Konferenz und der Völkermord an den europäischen Juden. Katalog der ständigen Ausstellung]*. Yokohama: Shunpusha.

Wertsch, J. V. (2002). *Voices of collective remembering*. Cambridge: Cambridge University Press.

Wiedmer, C. (1999). *The claims of memory: Representations of the Holocaust in contemporary Germany and France*. Ithaca, NY: Cornell University Press.

Young, J. E. (1988). *Writing and rewriting the Holocaust: Narrative and the consequences of interpretation*. Bloomington, IN: Indiana University Press.

Masako Shibata
Graduate School of Humanities and Social Sciences
University of Tsukuba
Tsukuba, Japan

LIZ JACKSON

3. IMPLEMENTING MULTICULTURAL CURRICULUM FOR EQUITY

Islam in Hong Kong Education

A Special Administrative Region of the People's Republic of China ('China') since 1997, Hong Kong has continuously faced questions related to its cultural and social orientation. There are historical and demographic connections at the national level to China, while Hong Kong also has a cosmopolitan and multicultural identity, reflected in its British colonial political traditions from before the handover, and captured in its self-proclaimed status as 'Asia's world city'. At the same time, Hong Kong society features multipronged intergroup social tensions today. Recent Chinese immigrants to Hong Kong often experience prejudice and discrimination, while other cultural and ethnic minorities' needs for equal rights, fair political representation, etc., have been repeatedly overlooked (Kapai, 2015; Unison, 2012). Social stigma is a likely factor in inequitable treatment of cultural and ethnic minorities in society. In a 2012 survey, over one-third of Hong Kong resident participants expressed they would not want ethnic minority residents in their neighbourhoods, while over half indicated they did not want ethnic minorities in their personal lives (Unison, 2012).

Improving perceptions of social and cultural diversity within Hong Kong is fundamental to enhancing equality and human rights there in the future. Though the importance of multicultural education is referenced by the Hong Kong government, research has indicated that the implementation of multicultural curriculum in schools is incomplete, sometimes reinforcing rather than challenging stereotypical, negative views of internal diversity in society (Jackson, 2017a; Unison, 2012). Past research has considered as well how Hong Kong schoolteachers feel ill equipped in managing diversity in the classroom, and how local ethnic minorities and minority religions are often inaccurately represented in textbooks and other curricular resources (Hue & Kennedy, 2014; Jackson, 2015, 2017a). However, people do not only learn attitudes about diversity in equity in schools, but also from other informal educational venues, such as from family and peers, and news media.

In this chapter I consider holistically the implementation of multicultural education for greater equity within Hong Kong, taking as one case in point education related to Islam and Muslims. Studies in urban cultural anthropology (Law, 2015; O'Connor, 2012) provide strong evidence that this religion is particularly poorly understood among Hong Kong people, to the detriment of local Muslim communities as well as the rest of the members of Hong Kong as a liberal, pluralist society. As the next section shows, this inequity has to do with issues related to religion, and the relationship between racial, national, and religious identity in Hong Kong legal practice. After discussing the theoretical approach to multicultural education for equity that is taken here, the chapter then examines what Hong Kong people are likely to learn about Islam and Muslims in their society within and outside schools, focusing on relevant curriculum resources, teachers' classroom experiences, and news media. This chapter argues that despite government attention to multiculturalism as a remedy for prejudice reduction in society, a one-sided pattern of representation of Muslims and Islam found across educational platforms (both formal and informal) can serve as a barrier to Hong Kong people effectively understanding this religion and community. The chapter concludes with brief recommendations for enhancing multicultural education for societal equity in Hong Kong's future.

RELIGION AND ISLAM IN HONG KONG

Of relevance in examining inter-religious education in Hong Kong are the distinctive attitudes toward religion commonly found among Hong Kong's people. International polls of religious identification portray Hong Kong as a relatively irreligious society. The 2012 Gallup poll indicated that 38 percent of Hongkongers identified as religious, while 51 percent identified as not religious, and 9 percent as atheists (quoted in Bosco, 2015). Yet as Bosco (2015) observes, traditional conceptualisations of religion tend to focus on formal religious organisation, using Christianity as a model. Meanwhile, many Hong Kong people (self-)identify more informally as superstitious, demonstrate belief in ghost stories, and follow traditional practices related to ancestor worship and obtaining good luck. Thus, typical religiosity in Hong Kong is better understood as "diffused" (Yang, 1961), as the concept of organised religious community is not particularly helpful or relevant for understanding local experiences (see also Lagerwey, 2010).

Christianity and Islam are both growing religions in Hong Kong today, making up 12 percent and 3 percent of the local residential population, respectively (Formichi & O'Connor, 2015). Yet due to Hong Kong's British colonial heritage and the related role given to churches and Christian organisations in local educational and social development in the early twentieth century, Christianity tends to be perceived as a local phenomenon, in contrast with Islam (Leung & Chan, 2003). For instance, in a discussion on the development of a mosque in Hong Kong in 2001, one resident expressed concern that "We don't understand the culture of Islam...If the Christians and Catholics wanted to build a church, it is not a problem because they are locals" (Hong Kong Human Rights Monitor, 2001; quoted in Law, 2015; see also Mathews, 2011). Despite the fact that a significant part of the Hong Kong Muslim residential community is local and Chinese, this group is overlooked by such attitudes, while Islam is conflated with non-Chinese and foreign segments of the society (Law, 2015; Formichi, 2015; see also Berlie, 2004).

One factor in such confusion about religious and ethnic identity in Hong Kong is the longstanding conflation of religion, nationality, and race and ethnicity in the society's legal system (Kapai, 2015; Formichi, 2015). Religious groups have political representation in one sub-sector of the Hong Kong Election Committee. And Hong Kong's Racial Discrimination Ordinance is supposed to address issues of discrimination based on various social differences, including religion. Yet as Formichi (2015) notes, religious discrimination as distinct from racial discrimination is neglected in the ordinance, which is seen as problematic to most grassroots ethnic minorities in Hong Kong. Religious discrimination can only be challenged as a form of racial discrimination, when the situation involves people of different racial groups (Kapai, 2015). In legal practice, racial difference is required for any charge of discrimination, while (to further complicate things) race/ethnicity is typically ascribed by nationality. Thus, a Muslim who is classified as white nationally and racially would be unable to claim religious discrimination if the discrimination is not based on their status as white, while Chinese Muslims may not be able to charge discrimination by other Chinese Hong Kong people based on religion rather than race (Formichi, 2015).

Such legal practices stemming from "the colonial legacy of classifying populations according to ethnicity, and of culturalising such identities by attaching religious attributes to them" are in need of challenge and reflect Hong Kong institutions' lack of appreciation for complexities of multicultural identity (Formichi, 2015, p. 29). Indeed, racialisation of national and civic identity categories and reliance upon highly problematic ascriptions of cultural norms and "blood relation" loyalty are lingering challenges to multicultural education in Hong Kong today as well (Jackson, 2017b). Despite compelling reasons for treating race in social science and social theory as socially constructed rather than as essential or natural categories, much educational and social discourse in Hong Kong continues to connect race and ethnicity in a deterministic fashion to people's culture, personality, ability, and beliefs (Jackson, 2017b). While perhaps connected in part to social aims of cultural integration of Hong Kong people with China, this racial essentialism also obscures significant ethnic and cultural diversity within Hong Kong and China, even among 'Chinese' people, as this category too is more complex, linguistically, culturally, ethnically, and so on, then one might imagine at first glance. It is no surprise in this context that efforts toward multicultural education in Hong Kong are incomplete, as prevalent attitudes about religion and race in the society more broadly remain simplistic and problematic in relation to the purposes of appropriately recognising social difference.

MULTICULTURAL EDUCATION THEORY AND PRACTICE

The term 'multiculturalism' can be used to refer to a wide variety of theories and practices with diverse implications for education. The term was not commonly used before the late-twentieth century, though most modern societies have featured various kinds of diversity for much longer, owing to the international movement of peoples and colonialism, and now to globalisation processes. The earliest forms of multicultural education were assimilationist in nature, equipping people, particular minorities, to adapt to majority cultural norms of society (Jackson, 2014; Banks, 1993). That ethnic minorities experienced inequity, injustice, or discrimination was not considered significant in such contexts, including Hong Kong for most of its history. Pluralist multicultural discourse, on the other hand, emphasises positive recognition of diversity in society, and the interests of minorities and to society in preserving and appreciating ethnic, cultural, and other differences. Discrimination, inequity, and lack of acceptance in society are seen as problems in this view, which requires educating all members of society to work well together and develop positive understanding of each other's cultures, lifestyles, and views.

Today this pluralist orientation toward multiculturalism can be found in the objectives of educational authorities around the world, including in Hong Kong education. In particular, the importance of learning to recognise multicultural diversity with less prejudice undergirds several objectives of the Hong Kong subject Liberal Studies. Liberal Studies became part of the curriculum in 2009 and is the only compulsory subject in senior secondary education (grades 10–12) apart from Chinese language, English language, and math. Germane to the needs for multicultural education in Hong Kong, this interdisciplinary subject aims to help students "appreciate and respect diversity in cultures and views in a pluralistic society", "assess the impact of reform and opening-up [of] China", recognise the impact of globalisation on individuals and communities, and "demonstrate an appreciation for the values of their own and other cultures, and for universal values, and be committed to becoming responsible and conscientious citizens" (CDC, 2007/2014, pp. 5–6). Though it was controversial at its start and remains so, particularly since the recent youth-led Occupy movement of 2014–2015 (Jackson & O'Leary, 2016), Liberal Studies remains as an examined part of the curriculum required regular entrance in local higher education.

Where pluralist education for multicultural recognition has been seen to prevail, additional dilemmas occur, however. These have to do primarily with the highlighting of differences in multicultural education over all else. Critical multiculturalists have argued that "difference" itself should also be socially deconstructed in such cases (McCarthy, 2003). Despite the Hong Kong government's conflation of religious and racial identity (as one example), no culture is a monolith, but cultural communities are diverse and dynamic themselves. When culture is conflated with race or ethnicity, and prioritised above all else (as is often the case, given concerns with racism that undergirded much early pluralist work), the educational implications are also problematic. As suggested in the previous section, to claim there is a white culture or African culture, for example, is as much a political statement in the classroom as it is a sociological or anthropological claim (Ravitch, 1990), given the limitations and challenges to this view (that is, the diversity of lifestyles, practices, beliefs, and more, within such categories). Some have objected further to the idea that one should be recognised in education and society particularly for a marginalized status, which can be damaging for people who want to be recognised equally and as individuals despite their particular forms of ascribed social difference (Appiah, 1994).

Relatedly Ahmed (2010) notes how in contemporary multicultural societies which positively recognise difference at the surface level, discrimination is regarded in common social discourse and reflected in institutions as an anonymous, mysterious force, as the societies identify as nonracist and nondiscriminatory and few individuals identify as hateful toward diversity. The only people who are seen as connected to ongoing injustice in this so-called post-multicultural era are its victims and other witnesses who still observe it, who become akin to the authors of discrimination where structural injustice continues while open racists cannot be easily identified. As Ahmed discusses, "[b]ad feeling thus originates with the migrant who won't let go of racism as a script that explains suffering" (2010, p. 143). "Different" individuals thus become a "sore point" for a community that apparently celebrates diversity, and a sense of soreness gets attributed to the "migrant" (Ahmed's word) him- or herself (2010, p. 141). Although the source of the migrant's suffering may be structural and reflected in practices of institutional racism and other practices maintained and enacted by and for the benefit of majority members of society, by observing and not denying experiences of racism and related discrimination and inequity, the "melancholy migrant" is seen to cause the community to suffer.

These perspectives also find resonance in social and educational experiences in Hong Kong. Despite the vast diversity of Muslims (even within Hong Kong) as a growing dynamic, global community crossing lines of ethnicity, race, language, cultural, political ideology, and more, a traditionalist form of multiculturalism can homogenise such a group identity in deceptive rather than accurate ways, framing Muslims simply as conservative and traditional (or fanatical or terroristic), for instance (Jackson, 2014). Even an education that aims to teach positive recognition cannot do justice to such large-scale religious community within a brief lesson. In Hong Kong, O'Connor (2012) notes, for instance, that some Muslim children learn different lessons about their religion at their (religiously and culturally more diverse) schools versus their mosques, given the tendency to reduce complexity in pluralist multicultural education. Formichi's examination of religious discrimination in Hong Kong (2015) also underscores the way that Hong Kong society does not view religion as a distinct factor of discrimination in society, preferring to lump religion together with race in such cases, in contrast to the experiences of grassroots ethnic minorities. Such minorities, who contradict normalised societal attitudes by their very existence, represent a sore point, identifying and thus actively reflecting a challenge, in a society viewed by its elites as sufficiently tolerant with regard to religion and other forms of cultural difference. The next sections consider these challenges more systematically for Hong Kong (formal and nonformal) education.

ISLAM IN HONG KONG EDUCATION: OVERVIEW

In line with Hong Kong's self-understanding as a relatively irreligious society, religious education for learning about diverse religions is not prioritised in the schools (Lee, 2001). As I discussed previously (Jackson, 2015):

> This lack of formal religious education emphasis in Hong Kong is reflected in the guidelines developed by the Education Bureau for teaching about religion and related topics in schools. The curriculum guide provided for teaching comparative religious education…dates back to 1999. The document has significant inaccuracies. For instance, it describes Jews as Israelites and lists them as Christian believers (CDC, 1999, p. 24). It discusses Islam apparently interchangeably with 'Islamism' (CDC, 1999, p. 33). As 'Islamism' usually refers to a political ideology related to Islam rather than the religion generically, it is problematic for the text to claim for instance that, "Islamism is a world-wide religion…" (CDC, 1999, p. 33). It seems unlikely that any Muslim individuals or groups assisted in developing the guide.

Other curricula in Hong Kong that may provide any form of religious education include "Ethics and Religious Studies", which is heavily oriented to ethics and otherwise highlights Buddhism or Christianity (CDC, 2007), and "Personal, Social and Humanities Education", a lower-level course that encourages students (in part) "to respect…different religious backgrounds" (CDC, 2002; Jackson, 2015).

The main part of Hong Kong education that includes education about religion within a pluralist multicultural orientation is the previously mentioned subject of Liberal Studies. As described above, understanding and appreciating diversity, including religious difference, is emphasised in the curriculum guidelines for the subject (CDC, 2007/2014), while modules on "Hong Kong Today", "Modern China", and "Globalisation" emphasise social studies orientations, comprising half of the content of this major (mandatory and examined) course. The next sections of this chapter examine how Islam is taught about in this subject. The first considers the content of the planned curriculum via an analysis of textbooks. Next, implementation is considered with reference to teachers and pre-service teacher education students' experiences. Finally, mainstream media is also examined, as a likely used resource for teaching in Liberal Studies and other subjects (indeed recognised and recommended by the Hong Kong Education Bureau for classroom use), and as a powerful kind of alternative education that informs Hong Kong youth as well as adults today with regard to difference in society (Jackson & Nesterova, 2017).

Islam in Liberal Studies Textbooks

As part of a larger study of multiculturalism in Liberal Studies (Jackson, 2017a), my research team obtained and analysed all available Liberal Studies textbooks (28 in total) published between 2009–2014. Text was coded using parallel content analysis to ensure reliability, with coding focused on the context, content, and connotations of references to diversity. A subsequent check of reliability asked practicing teachers to also code select text extracts, and this exercise demonstrated that the researchers and teachers interpreted textbook information in highly similar ways. Similar procedures were used to code and analyse mainstream media sources focused on diversity, including articles from 2009–2015 published by major Hong Kong news sources *Apple Daily, Oriental Daily*, and *South China Morning Post*, given that the Education Bureau recommends the use of mainstream news clippings as reference materials for teaching in Liberal Studies.

The textbooks typically contained few references to religion, apart from listing religion as one of a handful of categories that one should not discriminate with regard to, such as in these excerpts:

> According to the United Nations, the definition of human rights is those "rights humans are born with". It includes personal freedom and political and social rights. Different people in the world should enjoy these rights and not be restricted by nationality, ethnicity, skin color, gender, sexual orientation, political views, religious belief, or social status. (Ngai, 2013, p. 112)

> Frequent interactions have gradually led to common beliefs and visions such as peace, friendship, equality, freedom, democracy, human rights, etc. Because the general public, regardless of religious belief, ethnicity and nationality, agree with those commonly held and praised values, these values are called "universal values". (Chu, Ho, Leung, & Cheung, 2014, p. 7)

Textbooks most frequently mentioned religion in Hong Kong indirectly, through images of temples, or by referencing religious community organisations (most typically Christian missions) who do good works for socioeconomically disadvantaged group. The religious make-up of Hong Kong is never discussed. "Hong Kong Today" (Ng, Wong, & Wong, 2010, p. 245) comes closest, emphasising a pluralistic orientation wherein tolerance and acceptance is assumed, yet placing witnesses of religious discrimination as outliers to the prevailing view:

> Taking religion for example, different religions coexist in Hong Kong, including Catholicism, Christianity, Buddhism, Islam, and Sikhism… Although Hong Kong residents have different religious beliefs, religions respect each other. Religious conflicts never happen…Hong Kong residents respect different cultures, and give communities the right to be heard, enabling Hong Kong to be a multicultural society and maintain stability. (Translation from Chinese)

In direct contradiction to this orientation, many of the texts have 1 or 2 references to Muslims facing challenges in Hong Kong in relation to (seemingly *due to*) their divergent practices from majority norms. Often these are cryptic references, and may explore legal or structural challenges experienced by Muslim ethnic minorities (Chinese Muslims are not visible in the texts). These references are problematic as well in some of the overgeneralisations they make about Islam in Hong Kong. As one text states:

> Although the Hong Kong lifestyle affects obedience to Islamic dogmas (such as believers have to pray five times a day, women need to use headcovers all the time, they are forbidden to cook pork, etc.), their freedom of religion is not deprived. Karim says that the Hong Kong government does not intervene with the freedom of religion. He can preach outdoors and sometimes even the police will actively help maintain order. (Hui, 2009, p. 152; Jackson, 2015, p. 48)

Although this excerpt does not have as its aim to educate students specifically about Islam or Muslims in Hong Kong, it plays a problematic role with regard to religious understanding. As mentioned above, there is a tendency to conflate and homogenise diverse experiences in multicultural education, as reflected in this extract. For instance, hijab is not universally practiced and Muslim women do not "need to use head covers all the time". The extract also hints at Muslims being disorderly or needing police attention, signalling difference as risky and potentially inharmonious in this case. It is not clear how Hong Kong lifestyles intersect in a contrary way with Muslim identity, while Muslims are positioned here as problematic against a neutral or good backdrop.

As Formichi found with regard to legal practice in Hong Kong, the Liberal Studies textbooks also subtly connect ethnic minority identity with religiosity. One text notes that ethnic minorities "may face disputes and conflicts due to their different race, appearance, skin colour, language, living habits and religious beliefs as compared to local Chinese, [which] makes it more difficult for them to establish their identity as Hong Kong people" (Hui, 2009, p. 102). Later, the same text suggests that students can learn about ethnic minorities by reading *Colors of Hong Kong*, to "understand our neighbours free from the influence of skin colour, race and religion" (Hui, 2009, Book 2, p. 153). As religious identity is only reflected in relation to ethnic minority experiences in Hong Kong, this approach regards Hong Kong as irreligious and religiosity as a form of difference under the umbrella of racial or ethnic diversity from being Chinese.

There are also many negatively connoted representations within further references to the religion. Although not focused on Muslims in Hong Kong, numerous discussions show Islam as clashing with modernity and/or Western civilisation. As Hong Kong is described frequently in the texts as an "East-meets-West" culture (while Muslims are framed as possibly disorderly) references to Islam clashing with Western civilisation may be read to imply Islam as problematic in Hong Kong. Discussions of Islam as a source of cultural clash against an apparently good or neutral backdrop refer to terrorism and to Muslim women's rights. Reflecting nearly one-fourth of coverage related in any way to religion in the texts, these references reflect the negative cultural attitudes students may develop toward Islam through Liberal Studies. For example, one booklet for "Globalisation" (Ngai, 2010), states:

> There has been a revival of Islamic fundamentalism in Islamic countries in recent years. Fundamentalists emphasise that when their religion is under threat, they must embrace classic Islamic rules. As there is a concept of jihad (holy war) in Islamic teaching, some extremists may use radical and violent means in order to counter Western Christian civilisation. (p. 96)

Simplifying Islam is damaging here for multiculturalist aims, as "holy war" is not the exclusive definition of *jihad*, which has often also been used historically to refer to other forms of righteous struggle and effort. An accompanying picture shows an unknown, angry-looking man, with the caption, "An Islamic extremist intimidates to launch a terrorist attack to revenge the invasion of Western culture". Homogenising Islam to refer to terrorism is hardly effective toward encouraging cross-cultural understanding.

In another discussion, Islam is compared to the West as civilisations in broad strokes, obscuring internal diversity within such large-scale social groups (Jackson, 2015):

> The social order of Islam is opposed to some prominent western values. For example, human rights, democracy and gender equality are incompatible with the Muslim religious doctrine. In Islam, it is not the individual and his free will that counts, but faith and religious struggle. (Wong, 2010, p. 51)

This text also provides an image of two women in *hijab*, with the caption, "In countries where people believe in Islam, female status is relatively low, which is opposed to the Western values of gender equality". This framing of Islam as dichotomous to the West discounts other views, such as that often Westerners (and other people with "Western values") and Muslims live side-by-side, and that women's rights and status are not rejected across diverse Muslim societies (while, on the other hand, gender equality has not been fulfilled across western/western-oriented societies). That Islamic dogma forbids democracy or human rights is also controversial and overly simplistic. This lack of specificity and complexity here bolsters an anti-Muslim view. This text also references *jihad*, stating that in 1948, "the Arabian countries denied [the proclaimed new state of Israel] and jointly declared 'Jihad' (Holy War) on Israel" (Wong, 2010, p. 134). This is not only highly negatively connoted toward Muslim-majority societies, positioning them as a major antagonist in World War 2 (in contrast with the benevolently framed United Nations), but it is also historically inaccurate: no such joint declaration of *jihad* was made, although the Arab League did reject the United Nations partition plan (Jackson, 2015).

The ban of *hijab* in French institutions is also discussed in a way that paints a broad picture of Islam versus West:

> Islamic full veil is regarded as a threat to the public safety, as those who have full veil cannot be identified easily. It also damages women's rights. The above ban is widely supported by the French public. However, Islamic women claimed that this would damage their dignity, rights and freedom. They also expressed

that the law will probably force them to stay at home. So, it is strongly opposed by the Islamic citizens. (Wong, 2010, p. 62)

Again, oversimplification can be seen, as Muslim women (and "Islamic citizens"—a problematic description that obscures citizenship and significance of being "Islamic" versus "Muslim") and the French public are portrayed inaccurately as homogeneous and ideologically monolithic and dichotomous camps in the debate. Taken as a whole, Muslims are portrayed as singular in culture, values, politics, and origin/ethnicity, and as sexist, patriarchal, and oppressive across texts. The discussion of Karim (mentioned in the outset of this section) is the only reference that might encourage appreciative interest or positive recognition, although it too is mixed in its social implications. The rest are likely to cause students to feel suspicious or offended by the religion in Hong Kong.

Liberal Studies Implementation

The Curriculum Development Council in Hong Kong discourages reliance on textbooks for teaching Liberal Studies, and recommends extensive use of supplementary sources, identifying a government-provided Web-based Resource Platform for Liberal Studies, among other media resources. However, in research by Wong, Chan, and Ho (2012), Liberal Studies teachers reported relying heavily on textbooks, which is particularly common early in a subject's history and among inexperienced teachers (Kaviani, 2007). Teachers continue to use the texts to provide students with background information, to satisfy expectations of students and parents, and as a source for learning activities (Wong, Chan, & Ho, 2012).

My research on multiculturalism in Liberal Studies obtained a further sense of teachers' views and use of textbooks and resources for teaching about religious education through the reliability exercise for interpreting textbooks for practicing teachers, and a questionnaire of final-year pre-service teacher education students' practicum experiences. The data from these sources reflect concerns of both groups regarding the quality and representativeness of texts for the purposes of inter-religious and multicultural education. One teacher participating in the reliability exercise observed that one text extract was discriminatory and "provided one side of the story", a common comment of most participants in interpreting the texts. When asked about their views about using textbooks, some teachers described it as their role to supplement textbooks by helping "readers…triangulate the things they read", while another conceded to personally having "a superficial understanding of ethnic minorities. Therefore it is hard to develop a deep analysis" with students (Jackson, 2017a).

The questionnaire of final-year Liberal Studies pre-service students focused on how much and how they taught about multicultural and inter-religious topics in their practicums. Of the 20 participants, 4 had taught something related to religious diversity or religious groups, and 2 of the 4 described it as difficult or moderately difficult. When asked what factors made it easier for them to teach, the student participants reported that the background knowledge of students was more helpful than the content of textbooks or the background knowledge of teachers (this may also be partly related to the student-centred orientation of the curriculum). During their practicums, half of the student teachers reported that they used textbooks for teaching Liberal Studies most days, although a handful used them never or once per month. In contrast, most felt they should use textbooks once per week at most. When asked about the quality of textbooks, most described it as "satisfactory", while 2 thought it was "good" and 5 described it as "marginal". They identified as weaknesses of the texts that they are lacking in criticality, though they saw strengths of the texts in their being organised, clear, and readable.

Islam in Hong Kong Media

The aforementioned government-sponsored website for supporting teaching in Liberal Studies contains hundreds of newspaper articles and related materials for studying Liberal Studies for teacher and student use. However, only one article included in the collection discusses diversity substantively: the case of an ethnic minority's legal challenge in Hong Kong. My study therefore also examined mainstream news media in Hong Kong more broadly as an informational and educational source. In *Oriental Daily* and *Apple Daily*, Hong Kong's two major Chinese-language newspapers, about 10 articles per year for the last several years (2009–2015) focused on issues of religious diversity. In *South China Morning Post*, Hong Kong's English-language newspaper, about twice that many articles were identified. Most of these sources had a negative tone, discussing problems religious and ethnic minorities "face".

Even *Apple Daily*, the most liberal source in overall orientation, included simplistic, damaging portrayals of Islam. One article focused on the challenges of Muslim girls in society: "although they study in Hong Kong, they cannot study together with boys", must give up their studies once married, and obey "oppressive traditional culture" (Chan, 2013). No Muslim woman in Hong Kong represents their views on the matter (Jacskon & Nesterova, 2017). An article entitled, "Ethnic Minorities in Tiu King Leng", claims that "to uphold the legacy", Pakistani children need to study the Quran every day; no explanation is given of the Quran or its "legacy". On two occasions, articles portray Islam in a more favourable light, although only brief explanations are given. One article details how a Pakistani boy found a wallet of money and gave it to the police. The boy was quoted saying that Islam teaches respect for others and their property (Lo, 2013). In "A 'Little Pakistan' in Kwai Chung", Lui (2013) discusses a mobile mosque that gathers Pakistani children to pray, calling it "a unique cultural characteristic in this public estate". Liu explains the meaning of praying for Muslim life and links Pakistani New Year to similar traditions in Chinese culture. As in the textbooks, coverage is mixed overall, yet highly simplistic regarding difference, seldom recognising any diversity within Islam or Muslim communities in Hong Kong or worldwide.

DISCUSSION

Multicultural social policy and education in Hong Kong faces many challenges in enhancing equity and nondiscrimination for Muslims in Hong Kong. Formichi's observations (2015) of the conflation of race, ethnicity, nationality, and religion in Hong Kong legal practices for nondiscrimination are echoed in educational materials, including textbooks and media articles, that oversimplify Islam as a monolith to the neglect of understanding Muslims in Hong Kong who are Chinese as well as Pakistani, Indonesian, etc. In relation, as critics of multicultural education have pointed out broadly, an education that simply aims to raise awareness of diversity without examining social complexity can misrepresent diversity in everyday life, failing to articulate real challenges involved. An education that portrays Islam stereotypically, as seen here in excerpts from textbooks and news media, can hardly help students appreciate neighbours and fellow residents in an effective way. Instead it is likely to echo and enhance already prevalent negative xenophobic views of differences, clashes, and more.

As Ahmed has noted (2010), there is also a tendency in post-multicultural environments, where people presume themselves to be nondiscriminatory and nonbiased, to frame minorities as the only actors in cases of social tension and experiences and observations of inequity. In this context, the texts reviewed in this chapter observe that Muslims experience challenges to belonging and to getting along in various contexts (France, the Middle East, etc.) including Hong Kong. Yet those non-Muslim actors involved in such challenges are faceless and inhuman, such that the challenges get attributed not to discriminating or prejudicial actors or entities, but to the differences of Muslims themselves. Texts state for instance that Hong Kong minorities' "different languages, lifestyles, skin colors…make it harder for them" so that "[a] sense of discrimination is created" (Ng, Wong, & Wong, 2010, p. 271). There are many references to cultural minorities in Hong Kong who "faced much discrimination" (Ng, Wong, & Wong, 2010, p. 276), "still face a certain level of discrimination" (Bak et al., 2013, p. 18); and are "sometimes viewed negatively [and] face discrimination" (Ngai, 2013, p. 306). Yet there are no references to who or what causes discrimination. Minorities experience and 'face' it without anyone or anything acting in a problematic way toward them. As individuals, the problems are bound only to the minorities. Though the culture clash view of social difference is highly problematic, as a performative text that encourages people to see cultural differences as threatening and yet which is hardly 'confirmed' on empirical and theoretical grounds (Jackson, 2014), students are likely to learn from these textbooks to see cultural diversity, intercultural mixing, and ethnic minorities in society as problematic, rather than recognise how prejudice, inequity, and discrimination operate, and may be bolstered (such as by anti-multicultural worldviews) in majority practices and norms.

This study thus indicates, first, that in order to teach effectively about Islam and Muslims in society, the textbooks for Hong Kong Liberal Studies are in need of revision, inspection and consultation in coordination with inter-religious educational specialists; or in need of disuse, or more critical use (for example, some teachers have found success in critically contrasting textbook information within a critical literacy approach to social studies; Kaviani, 2007). In line with recommendations also made by Unison (2012), more technical pedagogical skill and content knowledge related to diversity would also help teachers to feel more comfortable relying on their own knowledge or that of better resources. In relation, teachers would benefit from critical media literacy education in their professional preparation, as a skill they can also impart to students, who may learn imbalanced and unhelpful information about Islam not just from their formal curriculum, but also from the nonformal educational environment around them. Though this study did not consider the informal or hidden curriculum of schools, no doubt efforts could be made to systematically enhance this educational context as well in Hong Kong. These are relatively modest recommendations that would clearly help Hong Kong education enhance multicultural understanding of difference to improve experiences of Muslims in society.

CONCLUDING REMARKS

In Hong Kong, prejudicial, discriminatory, and xenophobic attitudes toward ethnic and cultural minorities remain commonplace as barriers to equity and social justice. Despite the prevalence of discourses of multiculturalism and nondiscrimination, various societal minorities' needs, challenges, and experiences remain poorly understood. This chapter examined the distinct case of Muslims in Hong Kong, including their treatment in society and in education, particularly multicultural curriculum that aims to ameliorate prejudice and intercultural ignorance. As discussed here, to claim inequitable treatment based on religious status one must identify racial and national interpersonal differences, as religion, race, and nationality are conflated in ordinary legal practices. Such social categories are also blurred in multicultural education in Hong Kong, which tends to lump ethnic and religious minorities together, painting Hong Kong people as irreligious and minorities as religious in broad strokes. A related challenge for multicultural education is the tendency to essentialise racial categories and stereotype differences. As seen here, Muslims in Hong Kong are portrayed as a monolithic community in textbooks and in other media sources, and the diversity of Islam is invisible. Also invisible are parties or agents who clash actively with Muslims, in Hong Kong or globally. Though references are made to cultural differences of Islam and West, the West is portrayed, as Hong Kong is, as multicultural, benevolent, and nonracist. Islam is reflected repeatedly as aggressor.

These messages contradict the goals of Hong Kong multicultural education, particularly in Liberal Studies, to help students appreciate, positively recognise, and better understanding diversity of peoples and views around them. Students are not likely to want to work with Muslims, in their classes or in society, if they regard them as problematic, anti-democratic, sexist, fanatical, anti-West, illiberal, and more. Yet nonsexist Muslims, Chinese Muslims, liberal Western Muslims, etc., are nowhere to be found; nor are peaceful Muslims living in Hong Kong or elsewhere, who are not 'facing' challenges every day. When it comes to Islam, the formal planned and informal curriculum of Hong Kong, inside and outside of schools, is more likely to enable prejudicial treatment than to enhance equity for Muslims, as discussed in this chapter.

In this context, a great deal can be done to improve multicultural education in relation to learning about Islam and Muslims. Liberal Studies textbooks are in need of revision, if they continue to be used (and it is likely that they will be), and teachers can also develop more skills and further content knowledge to impart to students, via the critical use of reference materials, including perhaps alternative information sources. For multicultural education to be implemented in such a way that social equity is enhanced, considering in depth the complexities of different individuals' experiences, rather than painting groups in broad strokes, is essential so that Muslims are not relegated to a status as 'bad guys' against a backdrop of a good, neutral, multicultural and nondiscriminatory society. Critically exposing how normalised social and cultural spaces can also be problematic, in a productive and constructive way, can also help students develop in schools to participate in society in ways that do not merely give lip service to multiculturalism and nondiscrimination, but also can identify and correct where the entrenchment of such well-intentioned discourses can go wrong.

ACKNOWLEDGEMENTS

This work was supported by the Research Grants Council, University Grants Committee of Hong Kong under Early Career Scheme Grant [758713]. The author would also like to thank Gordon Tsui for translation and research assistance.

REFERENCES

Ahmed, S. (2010). *The promise of happiness*. Durham, NC: Duke University Press.
Appiah, K. A. (1994). Identity, authenticity, survival: Multicultural societies and social reproduction. In A. Gutmann (Ed.), *Multiculturalism: Examining the politics of recognition* (pp. 107–148). Princeton, NJ: Princeton University Press.
Banks, J. A. (1993). Multicultural education: Development, dimensions, and challenges. *Phi Delta Kappan, 75*(1), 22–28.
Berlie, J. A. (2004). *Islam in China: Hui and Uyghurs between modernization and sinicization*. Bangkok: White Lotus Press.
Bosco, J. (2015). Chinese popular religion and Hong Kong identity. *Asian Anthropology, 14*(1), 8–20.
CDC (Curriculum Development Council). (1999). *Syllabuses for secondary schools: Religious education*. Hong Kong: The Education Department.
CDC (Curriculum Development Council). (2002). *Personal, social and humanities education: Key learning area curriculum guide*. Hong Kong: The Education Department.
CDC (Curriculum Development Council). (2007/2014). *Liberal studies curriculum guidelines*. Hong Kong: Education Bureau.

CDC (Curriculum Development Council), and Hong Kong Examinations, and Assessment Authority. (2007). *Ethics and religious studies: Curriculum and assessment guide*. Hong Kong: Education and Manpower Bureau.
Chan, K. Y. (2013, December 9). 少數族裔開班教傳統藝術巴婦刺繡大獲好評 [Ethnic minorities open classes for traditional arts: Pakistani lady praised]. *Apple Daily*. Retrieved from http://hk.apple.nextmedia.com/
Chu, K. W., Ho, K. C., Leung, H. Y., & Cheung, K. K. (2014). *Globalization*. Hong Kong: Aristo.
Formichi, C. (2015). Religion as an overlooked category in Hong Kong legislation. *Asian Anthropology, 14*(1), 21–32.
Formichi, C., & O'Connor, P. (2015). Introduction: Overlooked religions in Hong Kong. *Asian Anthropology, 14*(1), 3–7.
[Hong Kong Human Rights Monitor] xianggang renquan jiancha. (2001). *Fandui xingjian qingzhensi shi zhongzu ji zongjiao qishi* [Resist to build mosque is racial and religious discrimination]. Retrieved November 20, 2013, from http://fungchiwood.com/mosque.htm
Hue, M. T., & Kennedy, K. J. (2014). Creating culturally response environments: Ethnic minority teachers constructs of cultural diversity in Hong Kong secondary school. *Asia Pacific Journal of Education, 34*, 273–287.
Hui, T. M. H. (2009). *Hong Kong today 2*. Hong Kong: Hong Kong Education Publishing Company.
Jackson, L. (2014). *Muslims and Islam in U.S. education: Reconsidering multiculturalism*. New York, NY: Routledge.
Jackson, L. (2015). Religion in Hong Kong education: Representation in liberal studies textbooks. *Asian Anthropology, 14*(1), 43–56.
Jackson, L. (2017a). Learning about diversity in Hong Kong: Multiculturalism in liberal studies textbooks. *The Asia-Pacific Education Researcher, 26*(1), 21–29.
Jackson, L. (2017b). Relations of blood? Racialization of civic identity in twenty-first century Hong Kong. *Discourse: Studies in the cultural politics of education* (online first). Retrieved from https://doi.org/10.1080/01596306.2017.1312283
Jackson, L., & Nesterova, Y. (2017). Multicultural Hong Kong: Alternative new media representations of ethnic minorities. *Multicultural Education Review, 9*(2), 93–104.
Jackson, L., & O'Leary, T. (2016). Education and the Hong Kong umbrella movement. *Educational Philosophy and Theory* (Online). Retrieved from https://doi.org/10.1080/00131857.2016.1268523
Kapai, P. (2015). *The status of ethnic minorities in Hong Kong, 1997 to 2014*. Hong Kong: Centre for Comparative and Public Law.
Kaviani, K. (2007). *Teachers' gatekeeping of the Middle East curriculum* (Doctoral dissertation). University of Washington, Seattle, WA.
Lagerwey, J. (2010). *China: A religious state*. Hong Kong: Hong Kong University Press.
Law, L. Y. (2015). Hong Kong citizens' understanding of Islam: The case of the Sheung Shui Mosque development project. *Asian Anthropology, 14*(1), 57–66.
Lee, W. O. (2001). Hong Kong: The quality of self in citizenship. In W. K. Cummings, M. T. Tatto, & J. Hawkins (Eds.), *Values education for dynamic societies: Individualism or collectivism* (pp. 207–225). Hong Kong: Springer/Comparative Education Research Centre.
Leung, B., & Chan, S. H. (2003). *Changing church and state relations in Hong Kong, 1950–2000*. Hong Kong: Hong Kong University Press.
Lo, K. Y. (2013, June 29). 【埋身擊】南亞仔執三萬元交阿Sir失主感動 稱對少數族裔改觀 [(Touching) South Asian boy gave 30,000 HKD back to police feeling touched and perception ethnic minorities changed]. *Apple Daily*. Retrieved from http://hk.apple.nextmedia.com/
Lui, L. S. (2013, October 27). 蘋果側奏：葵涌有個「小巴基斯坦」 [A 'little Pakistan' in Kwai Chung]. *Apple Daily*. Retrieved from http://hk.apple.nextmedia.com/
Mathews, G. (2011). *Ghetto at the center of the world: Chungking mansions*. Hong Kong: Hong Kong University Press.
McCarthy, C. (2003). After the canon: Knowledge and ideological representation in the multicultural discourse on curriculum reform. In C. McCarthy & W. Crichlow (Eds.), *Race, identity, and representation in education* (pp. 289–302). New York, NY: Routledge.

Ng, L. F., Wong, M. L., & Wong, T. C. (2010). *Hong Kong today.* Hong Kong: Aristo Publishing.
Ngai, P. K. (2010). *Globalization.* Hong Kong: Pearson Longman.
Ngai, P. K. (2013). *Hong Kong today.* Hong Kong: Pearson Longman.
O' Connor, P. (2012). *Islam in Hong Kong: Muslims and everyday life in China's world city.* Hong Kong: Hong Kong University Press.
Ravitch, D. (1990). Multiculturalism: E pluribus plures. *American Scholar, 59*(3), 337–354.
Unison Hong Kong. (2012). *Racial acceptance survey report.* Hong Kong: Unison.
Wong, K. L., Chan, E., & Ho, L. (2012, July 6). *Implementation of NSS liberal studies curriculum: A comprehensive study.* Paper presented at the Faculty of Education, University of Hong Kong, Hong Kong.
Wong, S. (2010). *Globalization II.* Hong Kong: Hong Kong Education Publishing Company.
Yang, C. K. (1961). *Religion in Chinese society: A study of contemporary social functions of religion and some of their historical factors.* Berkeley, CA: University of California Press.

Liz Jackson
Faculty of Education
University of Hong Kong
Hong Kong

LEANDRO SEPÚLVEDA AND MARÍA JOSÉ VALDEBENITO

4. EDUCATIONAL-WORK PROJECTS AND POST-GRADUATE PATHWAYS OF SECONDARY STUDENTS IN CHILE

Individual Strategies in an Unequal Education System

INTRODUCTION

Various research carried out in the field of education and its relation with the labour market has shown the increasing weakening of higher education as a tool of social mobility in Latin America (Filmus & Moragues, 2003; Jacinto & Terigui, 2007). However, despite the finding of an increasing loss of value of educational credentials, education still holds an important symbolic value, especially for the most disadvantaged groups of society. The completion of secondary education represents an instance of great importance in the subjective construction of young people´s lives, since it is associated with the chance of personal accomplishment, access to better working conditions and a fundamental and necessary step for continuing further studies at the tertiary level (Dussel, Brito, & Nuñez, 2007; Castillo & Cabezas, 2010).

In the case of Chile, the rate of completion of secondary education is currently 83%. This indicator has increased by 10 points in the last ten years, driven by the incorporation of the most vulnerable sectors into formal education, particularly to vocational education (Chilean Ministry of Education—MINEDUC, 2013). Indeed, as in other OECD (Organisation for Economic Co-operation and Development) countries, academic training[1] prevails over technical-professional alternatives. However, there are important differences when analysing its internal distribution. It should be stressed that the predominance of the technical-professional modality in sectors of lower income and higher levels of vulnerability reaches 66.4% of the first two poorest deciles. The comparable figure for the socio-economic segment pursuing academic training is only 17.3%.[2]

On the other hand, although an increase in schooling has marked the setting of Chilean society in the last decades, the main transformation of recent years is associated with an increase in access to higher education. This expansion in enrolment has been made possible to a large extent by the privatisation of the higher education system implemented three decades ago, which led to a market structure characterised by the great heterogeneity of its institutions and the weakness of mechanisms to regulate their functioning (Brunner, 2007).

Figures of effective entry into Chilean higher education institutions show that overall enrolment has quadrupled in recent years from approximately 250,000 students in 1990 to more than 1,161,200 now.[3] Currently, net rates of higher education enrolment for those aged 19 and 20 years corresponds to 40% and 45% respectively, both figures being higher than the OECD average rates of 32% and 38% (MINEDUC, 2013). This growth has particularly focused on tertiary technical education. Its enrolment has increased exponentially in the last years, accounting nowadays for 53.5% of total enrolment in the tertiary education system.[4]

Thus, the higher education system is no longer the preserve of elites, presenting higher levels of complexity and new requirements for its development. In recent years, youngsters who are the first generation to pursue further studies have entered institutions of higher education to such an extent that in 2010, 7 out of 10 new students had exceeded the level of education of their parents (Meneses, Rolando, Valenzuela, & Vega, 2010). Although there are still marked differences by socio-economic status, analyses indicate a tendency towards saturation of the representation in the system of the more privileged levels. This may require that future expansion be concentrated in medium and low-income levels of the population (Orellana, 2011).

The operating model of the higher education system is mainly based on a structure of private financing, which has led Chile to become one of the countries with the highest proportion of private spending at all levels of education provision. Most of this expenditure corresponds to the contribution by individuals and their families. Nowadays, more than 70% of enrolled students study in private universities or technical training institutes.[5] As described by the OECD and the World Bank (2009), Chileans consider education as the most important and secure path to prosperity, and thus make great efforts to access higher education beyond the effective yield this effort may bring. Despite this situation, it is not evident that such a model ensures progress towards the improvement of social equity. A major issue is the relation between the process of massification of education and increased credentialism, and the reduction of social gaps within society.

There is a great need for research to be carried out in this field, and it should be used as a basis for empirical knowledge that informs discussions of public policies and regulatory strategies needed to foster an educational system that delivers development opportunities for everyone. Research on the massification of higher education in Chile has focused on institutional analysis and proposals for changes that take account of the recent transformations. A number of studies include those related to the system of educational provision and regulatory frameworks and mechanisms for the organisation of training. One area that has received less attention and that is most relevant when analysing the transformation of the higher education system and its effects on social organisation, considers the aspirations that young people build before entrance to higher education and how these aspirations relate to possible futures. An important number of investigations on the construction of students' aspirations and the processes of choice of an educational and/or work pathway reveal the growing uncertainty that young people experience at this stage of decision-making. Similarly, the degree of freedom or structural conditioning of young people has led to deeper discussions about the effect of mass use of higher education and its eventual contribution to greater democratisation, social equality and reduction of socio-economic gaps (Lehmann, 2004; Grytnes, 2011).

Processes experienced by subjects and the strategies they develop to cope with their living conditions are issues that remain poorly addressed in educational research in Chile. From this perspective, this article provides some background to an on-going study of educational-labour pathways of young Chilean students. The material presented here originates from a 5-year longitudinal study that aims at giving an account of the aspirations and decisions of students from different socio-economic levels, rationales or social logics that define such decisions and educational-employment pathways four years after graduation. This perspective provides a base of complementary information for an informed discussion about the limits and possibilities offered by the current expansion of the education market and its capacity to attain higher levels of social equity.

CONCEPTUAL FRAMEWORK

The expansion of the offer and the demand for post-secondary studies in all sectors of society has been influenced by political rhetoric that has contributed to an increase of expectations and aspirations, emphasising that higher education is a goal to which we can all aspire (Sellar, Gale, & Parker, 2011). This has given rise to the so-called 'standardisation of aspirations' (Ball, Davies, Davis, & Reay, 2002), which values and legitimates certain educational-labour paths and life projects over others.

In tune with the emergence of this phenomenon, youth educational aspirations and expectations constitute a core theme that has taken prominence, both in the social sciences and public policy discussions. In recent decades, it is possible to observe a growing research interest in life trajectories, processes to adapt expectations to the environmental characteristics and opportunities, as well as the analysis of the interaction between structural conditions and agency in biographical experiences of people and social groups (Heinz & Kruger, 2001). Many studies have attempted to establish a significant association between aspirations and educational attainment. However, in general, these studies have adopted a descriptive approach without deepening the understanding of how and why these factors consistently affect such aspects (Jones & Schneider, 2009).

A theoretical perspective that explores this theme builds on the work of Bourdieu and his concept of cultural capital as a means of transmission and reproduction of social classes. McDonough (1997) uses this approach to demonstrate that aspirations and the type of education chosen by students at secondary level are conditioned by the social, cultural, and organisational contexts they come from, playing a fundamental role in shaping their educational experiences. Within this framework, individual aspirations respond to perceptions shared by members of a social group or class and which have an impact on possible choices. They are subjective assessments about the chances of social mobility and construction of a personal pathway, but, at the same time, they represent objective probabilities for the future for those who build them. They do not imply a rational analysis, but they represent the way in which young people of different social classes build reasonable choices based on their cultural capital. In this way, the concept of bounded rationality is used to indicate that personal decisions and the kind of choice youngsters make are tied to the degree of social constraint of their own cultural capital.

As indicated by Sellar et al. (2011), there are important differences in the way that aspirations are created amongst different social classes. For the elite, desire tends to inform possibility: what is imagined as desirable is simply made possible. For the marginalised, possibility tends to inform desire: what is possible limits the desirable to what is 'realistic'. In this sense, and in correlation with the ideas of Appadurai (2004), imagination has acquired a new power in social life as people consider a range of possible alternatives. This certainly does not mean that the ability to meet such aspirations is equal or more evenly distributed but, rather, places the field of cultural activities in a dynamic perspective, expanding beyond its merely reproductive function.

From this perspective, students from disadvantaged contexts experience more adversely the social, cultural and financial barriers embodied in higher education systems. As reported by Archer and Yamashita (2003) there are structural limits on aspirations, which apply differently according to where a person is positioned within social, cultural and economic frameworks. These are important factors. However, as agreed by several recent studies of youth transitions, there is a need to reconsider both structural influences and the sense of agency and control displayed by young people. For Wyn and Dwyer (1999), younger generations are making pragmatic choices that enable them to maintain their aspirations despite the persistence of structural influences.

Similarly, and as pointed out by Hodkinson and Sparkes (1997), educational and career decisions are bound to horizons of action, depending on the wider context and the individual's life history. "Students decision making processes are part of a life style structured by the social and cultural context as well as of an on-going biographical process in life course trajectories evolving from the interactions with the others" (Cuconato, Majdzinka, Walther, & Warth, 2016, p. 225).

Facing the same problem, studies of educational trajectories have sought to elucidate the tension between the weights that structure and agency exert[6] in the setting of paths and routes. The introduction of the concept of agency requires that we view the influence of social structure as neither direct nor deterministic. Even though some studies consider that educational trajectories are taken by individuals as a direct consequence of their choices and acts, that is, as successes and personal failures (Furlong & Cartmel, 1997), structural conditioning remains an important part of people's lives. The *epistemological fallacy of modernity* to which these authors refer would explain the discrepancy between individual reality as a social fact and individual reality as a subjective fact. Social class continues to have a strong impact on the vital opportunities of people within a framework of fragmentation of social structures that have tended to weaken collective identities. From a similar perspective, Dubet (1994) has established that autonomy of the subject is a necessary illusion with which the subject acts. Without being fully aware of doing so, the subject internalises one's own position in the social structure. Consequently, he/she intends to reproduce the situation from which the action has originated.[7]

Building on this discussion, Evans has demonstrated that agency is a socially situated and delimited process. This means that agency has limits that vary in time, confirming the hypothesis of an individualisation structured process that manifests in the experience, values and behaviour of young people:

> Our expanded concept of agency sees the actors as having a past and imagined future possibilities, both of which guide and shape actions in the present. Our actors also have subjective perceptions of the structures they have to negotiate, which affect how they act. Their agency is 'socially situated'. (Evans, 2010, p. 252)

The approach outlined here has raised the need to study processes of transition to adulthood considering both the perspective of the subject and the restrictions derived from the social structure (Evans, 2001; Casal, 1996). For these authors, the focus of interest is not the study of the events/transition in themselves (occurrence, timing and intensity), but an approach that emphasises the subject-structure dialectics, with a clear emphasis on a perspective that retrieves the individual as a core of sociological reflection (Mora & Oliveria, 2009). Their approach allows a deepening into a more complex analysis of social policies: they should be understood as being constantly redeveloped by individuals to whom they are directed. As pointed out by Sarojini (2014), policies may be conceived as cyclic systems that do not wear out at an initial legislative moment. On the contrary, they represent a dynamic process in which individuals reshape them according to their aspirations and behaviours, giving cultural determinism an important role.

RESEARCH METHODOLOGY AND SAMPLE

The data outlined here are part of a longitudinal survey conducted between 2011 and 2015 to a sample of 1,888 students attending the final year of secondary education at different types of schools in the Metropolitan Region of Santiago, Chile. The data collection was carried out with the support of FONDECYT.[8] The research is part of the tradition of research on life courses and it is organised around two fundamental phases. The first one is intended to characterise a sample of students in their last year of secondary education and includes the application of a structured instrument and a set of discussion groups. The second one is designed to follow up the sample of this cohort over 4 years, by applying a longitudinal survey and then completing it with qualitative material collected through focus groups and interviews with young people (under 21 years old) after graduation.[9]

Empirical information gathering aims at learning about young people's personal projects, their expectations regarding further studies and/or work, their assessment of the social environment and, in general, their life patterns. This includes their main habits, interests and motivations that may have an impact on their future lives. The information gathered allows us to not only understand young peoples' subjective dispositions as part of their school and work experience, but also to assess any differences arising from the variables considered by the study (socio-economic level, gender, type of school and teaching modality). Among other things, this enables us to explore how these factors influence their future trajectories, the degree of continuity or rupture existing between secondary and tertiary education and how open the labour market is for young people.

These results help us to examine some hypotheses about the relevance and modality of technical and professional secondary education. Data are represented by 8.8% of young people from the lowest socio-economic level, 34.5% in the medium-low socio-economic level,[10] 19.8% in the medium level, 19.7% in the medium-high socio-economic status, and 11.5% of students who were enrolled at institutions of high socio-economic status. In relation to the modality of studies, the sample shows a distribution of 38.3% of youngsters attending academic training (AT), 53.5% at TVET and an 8.1% by young people who finished their studies in the modality of adult education.

The data and analysis are organised around three main themes, (a) aspirations and expectations at the end of secondary education (b) the situation upon completion of studies and degree of fulfilment of expectations the following year after completion of their secondary school studies and, (c) pathways or routes four years after graduation.

EDUCATIONAL-WORK PROJECTS AND PATHWAYS OF SECONDARY STUDENTS: AN EMPIRICAL STUDY

Aspirations and Expectations at the End of Secondary Education

In order to understand their aspirations, we asked youngsters participating in this study about their educational-work projects in the medium and long term. As stated below, personal projects built by young students show a broad interest in pursuing higher education. Aspirations for the future are strongly associated with continuation of further studies prior to engagement in work activities. Only 4.7% express the desire to start working immediately and did not have an interest in continuing post-secondary studies. The vast majority in this last group correspond to youngsters from low and medium-low income levels. Approximately 45% stated that their personal project is aimed towards a university career (with 90% of cases belonging to the higher socioeconomic levels), while 21% thought that they would pursue an upper level technical career (most cases in this group belonged to the low and medium-low income levels).

Differences in options of no study and differentiation by type of post-secondary training are mostly expressed in relation to the training modality. In the case of TVET students, 11% stated that they prefer to focus on their studies and for the AT youths that percentage reaches only 2.7%. In any case, it should be clarified that in both segments there is a great number of youths that would like to pursue tertiary education, meaning that they do not see secondary education as the endpoint. The tendency of an increasing demand for higher education is so confirmed. Such demand appears in all segments. The fact that the higher education system has become less elitist is a powerful sign of the increase in aspirations of society as a whole and the TVET system is no exception (Orellana, 2011).

Distributions described here may be explained by different factors: a weakening of credentials and the reduction of opportunities for those with only secondary education, as well as the increase in aspirations and the willingness of most students' families to further invest in education. The choice of continuing studies would thus relate to a widely shared cultural disposition based on the valuing of education as the most powerful tool to achieve a better standard of living and to overcome precarious socio-economic conditions.

When asked about their projects for the future, respondents show a differentiated temporal expression in the framework of the life path. Indeed, in relation to the question: '*what are your plans for the year following graduation*'? the number of young people suggesting that they will work rises to 20% of the total number of respondents. This increase is found mainly in the medium-low and low

Table 1. *Educational project in percentage by socio-economic level*

	Socio-economic level			Modality		Total
	Low and low medium	Medium	High and medium high	AT	TVET	
Work and will not study	12.5%	5.8%	2.3%	2.7%	11.0%	7.4%
Will finish a university career	29.2%	46.1%	76.8%	73.7%	31.0%	45.2%
Will finish studies at a higher education technical institution	31.3%	22.2%	9.8%	12.2%	29.3%	21.5%
Will finish a military or police career	4.9%	4.7%	3.9%	2.7%	5.7%	4.2%
Does not know yet[11]	8.9%	7.3%	4.6%	6.0%	8.5%	7.4%
Other	13.4%	14.0%	2.7%	2.6%	14.6%	8.6%
No information						5.7%
Total	100%	100%	100%	100%	100%	100%

Table 2. *Expectations for immediate personal future in percentage by socio-economic level*

	Socio-economic level			Modality		Total
	Low and medium low	Medium	High and medium	AT	TVET	
Work	36.2%	15.8%	4.7%	4.7%	33.2%	20.0%
Study at a University	19.7%	35.5%	69.2%	65.9%	20.9%	36.5%
Study at a PI or TTC	24.1%	20.5%	8.1%	10.5%	23.4%	17.1%
Military or police career	4.5%	4.1%	2.5%	2.3%	4.5%	3.3%
Repeat last year of high school	0.4%	0.3%	0.7%	0.6%	0.4%	0.5%
Military service during the whole year	0.7%	1.8%	0.4%	0.7%	0.8%	0.7%
Preparation for Univ. Test	2.3%	4.4%	7.4%	6.6%	2.8%	4.0%
Will not do anything	0.5%	0.6%	0.5%	0.7%	0.4%	0.6%
It is not clear	6.3%	7.3%	3.9%	4.9%	6.3%	5.9%
Other	5.5%	9.7%	2.6%	3.0%	7.0%	4.9%
No information						6.6%
Total	100%	100%	100%	100%	100%	100%

socio-economic levels and principally among those studying TVET. While answers among students of AT remain somewhat constant with respect to their long-term plans, those from TVET are quite different. For example, the percentage who suggest that work will be their main activity in this period is increased by 20 percentage points. This figure decreases by the same proportion for those who express willingness to pursue higher education. The need to count on economic resources to finance their studies and to support their families may explain any temporary postponement of further studies.

Possible obstacles that might hinder the fulfilment of personal objectives were also analysed. Among factors given equal importance were the score achieved in the PSU (University selection test), the tuition and other costs of the career, and the grade average obtained at the end of secondary education. These considerations, although general, show important differences by socio-economic level. Students from low socio-economic groups gave less importance to high school grades when considering this as an obstacle (the difference with high-level students is nearly 20 points). In contrast, the tuition and other costs are a major obstacle when related to socioeconomic level, with a difference of 60 points between low and high socio-economic levels.

Table 3. Perception of obstacles that would influence choice of higher education studies; percentage of mentions by socio-economic level[12]

	Socio-economic level					Total
	Low	Medium-low	Medium	Medium-high	High	
Highs school grades	39.0%	46.2%	52.1%	62.6%	56.7%	51.0%
Scored of PSU	63.2%	59.1%	65.8%	56.3%	68.5%	58.6%
Cost or tuition of the career	77.9%	79.4%	72.2%	57.8%	20.2%	58.3%
Family opposition	2.6%	2.8%	4.6%	3.1%	3.4%	3.2%
Other	3.9%	5.6%	6.2%	3.4%	4.0%	4.4%

Table 4. Factors affecting choice of institution (university, PI or TC) in percentage terms

	Socio-economic level			Total
	Low and medium low	Medium	High and medium High	
Prestige of the institution	61.2%	61.3%	73.5%	68.2%
Rectors' Councils University (public or traditional)	19.9%	23.9%	38.0%	29.5%
Quality of training	75.5%	77.3%	75.3%	76.5%
Cost of tuition	48.0%	42.0%	22.5%	36.2%
Closeness to home	9.6%	6.3%	5.8%	7.4%
Students from different social groups enrolled	6.2%	6.7%	9.4%	7.4%
That your friends also choose it	2.4%	2.5%	1.0%	1.1%
That your family likes it	7.7%	5.5%	6.8%	6.9%
Infrastructure and space	13.4%	16.8%	23.3%	18.9%
That they develop a strong social work	16.3%	15.5%	10.0%	12.5%
Attend people similar to you	6.7%	3.8%	4.0%	4.8%
Have religious orientation	3.1%	1.7%	1.0%	1.4%
Offering the possibility of internships abroad	8.9%	10.1%	10.0%	8.6%
Offering the possibility to continue postgraduate studies	14.1%	18.5%	15.7%	15.6%
Other	2.9%	4.2%	2.0%	2.2%

On the other hand, this research shows that the quality of the training received and the prestige of the institution represent the most relevant features for young people[13] with evidence demonstrating again that there are important differences according to socio-economic levels. Indeed, although more than half of the young people of low socio-economic levels indicate the importance of the prestige of the institution, this judgement increases as the socio-economic level gets higher. In contrast, the value of tuition becomes more important for young people from the poorest households, becoming consistently less important for young people from higher income backgrounds.

Most students show a capacity to adapt their aspirations to the alternatives offered by the higher education market, choosing before high school completion a non-selective higher education alternative that requires less academic demands. Differences in the PSU regarding expectations for performance, and how they link to entry to higher education are telling, and may only be explained by an exercise of individual adaptation according to a rational reading similar to that related to choosing the TVET pathway. This situation should not represent a surprise, since the expansion of higher education has been achieved through the recognition of students' socio-economic and academic differences, thus generating specific "educational market niches" for each socio-economic reality (Torres & Zenteno, 2011, p. 74).

From the data presented here, we believe that the vast majority of young people manage information that enables them to understand how the system works and know enough to design a personal project for the future which reflects their aspirations,[14] even if those aspirations may be limited. As stated by Evans:

> Young people are social actors in a social landscape. How they perceive the horizons depends on where they stand in the landscape and where their journey takes them. Where they go depends on the pathways they perceive, choose, stumble across or clear for themselves, the terrain and the elements they

Table 5. *Main activity performed the first half of 2012 by socio-economic level and modality of studies*

What was the main activity you did the first half of this year?	Socio-economic level			Modality		Total
	Low and medium low	Medium	High and medium high	AT	TVET	
Higher Technical	18.0%	22.6%	9.7%	13.1%	18.3%	15.9%
University	10.3%	21.0%	62.3%	57.3%	12.4%	30.5%
Work	47.0%	28.4%	7.6%	9.7%	41.8%	29.0 %
Preparation for Univ. Test	5.4%	12.3%	15.8%	15.9%	6.6%	10.5%
Something different	11.7%	12.8%	4.1%	42.0%	13.5%	9.3%
Nothing	7.0%	3.7%	1.5%	14.0%	6.4%	49%
Total	100.0%	100.0%	100.0%	100.0%	100.0%	100.0%

encounter. Their progress depends on how well they are equipped, the help they can call on when they need it, whether they go alone or together and who their fellow travellers are. (Evans, 2010, p. 265)

Situation of Students after Graduation: Fulfilment of Expectations

Information regarding the situation after high school completion shows that, within months of finishing secondary education, the majority of young people were carrying out a specific activity and a high percentage of them continued directly to higher education. Indeed, when asking about the main activity carried out during the first half of the year following graduation from secondary education, 46.8 % reported having studied in a centre of higher education; 16% pursued studies at a Professional Institute or Technical Training Centre, and 30.8% at a University. One-third of respondents said that their main activity was working, while 10.5% decided to prepare and retake the test required to apply to Chilean universities (PSU). Only 4.9% of the sample did not work or study. Approximately 7.1% undertook another activity and 0.9% entered a military or police career.

Data disaggregated by socio-economic status are consistent with the above figures: the higher the socio-economic level the higher the likelihood of studying at a university or training centre. Similarly, the lower the socio-economic level, the higher the proportion of young people involved in working activities. This situation is also in line with the modality of study followed in high school: AT students tend to pursue higher education studies, while a significant percentage of TVET students decided to work.

The analysis of the comparison between expectations and achievements shows that the rate of admission to universities is considerably higher among high socio-economic levels (see Figure 1). These data confirm what has been demonstrated in several studies: while "good" students or the "elite" are welcomed by the system, "the mass of those students is left to their fate, subjected to the anguish

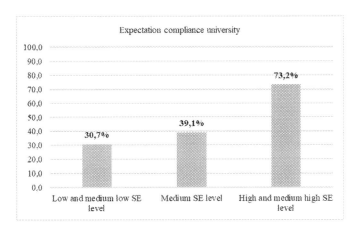

Figure 1. Rate of achievement university attendance by socio economic level

of failure" (Dubet, 2005, p. 68). Confirming the above, and as Araujo and Martuccelli express (2012), tests, since they feed the existence of a system that selects people without invalidating the weight of social positions and associated differentiated opportunities, compel the actors to be constantly fighting against transverse inconsistencies of social positions, a situation that is especially marked in Chilean society. The selection process, the University Selection Examination, forces the individual to take responsibility for his/her situation, thus reproducing the discriminatory mechanisms in the education pathway. However, as shown below, this situation is mediated by the process through which young people readjust their expectations based on the diversity of alternatives now offered by the higher education market. From this perspective, the market indeed appears as the main agent that generates alternatives for the re-elaboration of future projects.

Paths or Routes Four Years after Graduation

When taking a broader perspective of students' post-graduation pathways, the longitudinal analysis shows that most of the participants have started higher education at least once at some point during the four years after graduation from high school. As seen in the figure below, even though rates of inclusion are dissimilar between TVET and AT students, current entrance to higher education in Chile is extended and coverage reaches most socio-economic levels, excepting the low level.

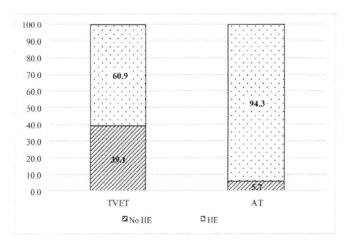

Figure 2. Percentage of students who has ever entered H.E.[15]

The analysis of educational insertion at the higher level reveals a strong correlation between educational modality studied by young people in secondary education and the type of institution they attend later. Most students from the scientific-humanist modality (AT) pursue a university career, whereas TVET students do so

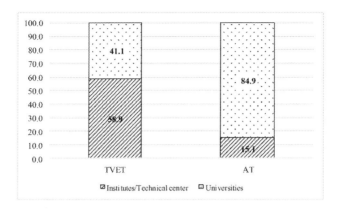

Figure 3. Type of institution

at institutions of technical education. The latter demand less academic standards for enrolment and, as compared with other institutions, their programme last less and are associated with lower costs.[16]

In this framework, it is possible to point out that young people from poorer socio-economic levels tend to adjust their initial expectations by mainly choosing a less prestigious and cheaper higher education career or by enrolling in less selective and less expensive educational institutions than traditional universities with higher reputation.

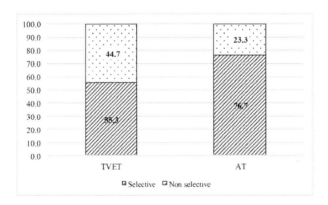

Figure 4. Type of university

From a comprehensive perspective, these data confirm that there is a significant increase of new generations of students at the higher education level. While inequalities persist when comparing the situation of young people by socio-economic strata, the extensive and diverse training offers are key features that characterise higher education in Chile. However, unequal distribution within the system reveals that social inequality is reproduced continually, a phenomenon corresponding to the findings of Furlong and Cartmel and the British case at the end of the last decade (see Furlong & Cartmel, 2009).

Main Pathways Models

Our analysis enables us to identify four types of educational-working paths. These were conceptually elaborated from previous published data (Du Bois-Reymond & López, 2004; Staff & Mortimer, 2003; Biggart, Furlong, & Cartmel, 2008) and then analysed in the light of empirical data collected through these instruments.

It is important to note that this characterisation is not associated with the definition of a stage of completion of a cycle but, rather, with the movements generated during this process. These translate into earlier or later incorporation to work, progress, or stagnation in educational paths and greater precariousness of social integration.

The first path, *exclusive continuity*, explores those pathways aimed at extended academic training, with no breaks and with an ascending transit in the education system. This is a linear path characterised by establishing staged relations of sequential events with no overlapping activities. Here, we find youngsters devoted exclusively to their studies, who do not work and maintain a high degree of dependence on their family environment. This path responds to a traditional way of understanding the processes of transition or postponement among young people, as emphasis is placed on the acquisition of skills, abilities and rights associated with adult life, a process that is mainly developed while being a student (Oyarzún & Irarrázabal, 2003). In this process, the family plays an important role through financial support to cope with the high costs of Chilean higher education.

Another path, *synchronous continuity*, corresponds to the route that, like the previous one, considers the extension of academic training, with an ascending transit in the education system. Unlike exclusive continuity paths, these may involve greater delay, since there are simultaneous working and educational activities. While there are employment detours, these may be discontinuous, precarious and informal and, therefore, may not imply that the student has left the family home. The extensive training offered within the higher education system and the high costs associated with studies means that a significant number of young people alternate between both activities without necessarily showing changes regarding their family life experience and family emancipation.

Early integration into the labour market is a third path and corresponds to a type of trajectory in which young people enter the world of work at an early stage. Even though they may have received training for work, as in the case of TVET youth, they are oriented towards poorly qualified work cultures, which, in general, are not linked to previous training. The precariousness of those jobs in terms of stability, salary, and level of qualification constrains the horizons of professional progress and renders such paths as particularly vulnerable in relation to changes in the labour

Table 6. Type of path (2012–2015). AT and TVET students

Type of path	Socio-economic level					Modality		Total
	Low	Medium-low	Medium	Medium high	High	TVET	AT	
Exclusive continuity	16.9%	16.0%	17.5%	48.4%	70.2%	22.4%	53.5%	34.3%
Synchronous Continuity	23.1%	18.9%	24.1%	30.1%	18.5%	25.0%	26.1%	22.9%
Early work	38.5%	31.4%	28.5%	3.9%	0.8%	26.9%	4.3%	19.3%
Try-error	21.5%	33.7%	29.9%	17.6%	10.5%	25.7%	14.9%	23.5%
Total	100%	100%	100%	100%	100%	100%	100%	100%

market and employment dynamics. Although some studies have established the link between this path and leaving the family home (see Casal, 1997 for the Spanish case), our study does not reveal consistent evidence to sustain this relationship.

A final pathway, *trial-error* or *greater precariousness*, corresponds to the so-called 'yo-yo' paths (López, 2002; Machado, 2002). Although they do not overlap activities of study and work, one always depends on the other. It is the kind of path followed by those who first study, then work and then study again as many times as required by their personal projects or external factors. This category represents those paths showing very sporadic or brief approaches to work activities or activities linked to professional training, and they are mainly characterised by no activity at all. It is a process in which young people (re) build their biographies following the vicissitudes of life and, as such, their choices can be confusing or difficult to categorise.

As it can be observed, even though there is a relative homogenisation of transitions—since a large group of young people reflect continuous paths, i.e., they extend their training process—these paths reveal different sequential stages and rhythms depending on socio-economic level and the modality of studies. While an important number of students begin developing work activities, in a short time they enrolled in higher education.

Here, it must be emphasised that results denote not only how the ambitions of new generations of students have increased but, also, something about the management capacity of a labour-education project beyond the limitations of the current educational model (such as inequalities in the education received for entrance and permanence in higher education and the high costs involved).

Other evidence worth highlighting refers to the segment of young people entering the world of work at an early stage. The data here shows a range of complexities. In some cases, early entry into the labour market is associated with qualified jobs and with greater job stability. In addition, correspondence between the type of education received in secondary education and the type of work to which young TVET have access demonstrates the precarious and limited nature of employment opportunities afforded to these young people. Even though these may be formal jobs, data don't show a correlation between activities carried out and training for work received in secondary education. These youngsters follow working paths similar to those of AT students and, only in exceptional situations—especially for trainings linked to the traditional industrial sector—reveal a clearer path.

The above analysis correlates with data from other studies showing that TVET graduates obtain an average salary 5% to 15% higher than AT students. This salary differential is a consequence of longer time in the work market rather than the level of secondary education received. In fact, this gap drastically decreases within a few years of work, suggesting no great comparative advantage for work opportunities between students graduated from TVET compared to those who pursued studies in the traditional education system. In relation to this point, the history of paths allows us to question the relevance of a curriculum structure and training system in secondary education that is too aligned to the requirements of the production system, an issue still being proposed and fostered by some international organisations as desirable policies for developing countries (see, for example, UNESCO, 2016). A model with greater emphasis on the development of general competencies for work would be, we believe, more appropriate to the market conditions faced by young people who engage in work activities at an early stage.

A final point concerns trial-error paths. As shown by the data, a greater proportion of young TVET and those at low-medium socioeconomic levels follow this type of path, a situation that may be linked to school dropouts in higher education. The drop-out rate of TVET youths is twice the drop-out rate in AT youths (Larrañaga, Cabezas, & Dusaillant, 2013). This problem, even though it suggests a multi-causal issue, is linked to economic difficulties and poor academic performance. This last aspect may be determined by previous training gaps and difficulties involving the alternation of educational and occupational activities.

CONCLUSION

Based on the data here reviewed, it is possible to conclude that there is a large tendency among Chilean students to privilege a continuity of studies, but that this presents important differences when analysing temporal expectations and effective options to enter higher education and eventual coordination with work activities. In this area, it is possible to distinguish a socio-economic differentiation and the emergence of various *rationales* that would account for an adjustment of future aspirations and possible paths to be reached by young students. The weight of economic requirements for continuing studies and the uncertainty in facing academic requirements for admission to higher education are two important factors affecting mostly the orientations of low-income students. It is clear that an early notion of longer temporality to fulfil personal goals becomes evident among the most vulnerable young people associated with the TVET modality.

On the other hand, the data suggest that even though there is a high level of aspiration in the group, the choice of higher education institutions is associated with social origins and available social and cultural capital. A significant number of young people from low and medium socio-economic levels adopt less demanding academic pathways (in non-selective universities) as an alternative to the fulfilment of their aspirations. Here, difficulties of academic achievement measured by the University selection test are acknowledged. Similarly, an appreciation of the positive link between training and subsequent entrance to work is causing young people with lower socio-economic capital to take actions that enhance their chances. This implies that they follow paths that combine education and work, which takes longer time and involves more changes and interrupted travels. In a period of four years, we see how structural constraints that may limit the achievement of a specific goal are avoided by the deployment of strategies aimed at identifying and financing specific educational programmes and more complex paths. As stated by other authors: "the complexity of educational trajectories in which not only do institutional factors reinforce or mitigate socio-economic factors of reproduction, but young people's subjective agency, also filters socio-economic, institutional and discursive factors" (Cuconato et al., 2016, p. 245).

Aspirations, levels of fulfilment of expectations and the analysed paths provide evidence of differentiated trajectories. In each of these analytical foci, it is possible to suggest that social reproduction is reinforced by the institutional conditions that anchor the Chilean model of education.

Regarding Latin American contexts in particular, some authors point out that the process of individuation becomes asymmetrical based on economic and social conditions provided by resources, expectations and qualifications (Jacinto, 2006). In disadvantaged situations without instances of institutional regulation and facing the pressure of finding new channels of integration, the range of choices narrows. This is indeed a particularly worrying situation, since it shows a strong imbalance between the force of an aspirational orientation as described by Appadurai—present in vast sectors of society—and the institutional responses that restrict to the rules of the market the outcome of the new demands, especially those arising from the poor sectors of society. The effect of this tension may lie in the maintenance of social segregation and differentiation, thus producing an effect of generational frustration with unpredictable consequences.

In the Chilean case, the offer of differentiated higher education—where the prestige of educational centres operates as a new sign of differentiation—seems to be a channel that, without limiting the urge to do better and the high degree of ambition in this generation, seems to meet this demand, but without modifying the differences in origin and social segmentation prevailing in the country. A labour market not linked to vocational education and training for work, which in turn shows no greater chance of upward social mobility, calls into question a model of massification of higher education as the one developed in Chile, especially its eventual effect on the reduction of social inequality that is lagging behind. Beyond the efforts of young people and their families, the data presented in this study confirms that structural conditioning in Chilean society is a *straitjacket* that makes it difficult to move in the direction of greater levels of equality.

ACKNOWLEDGEMENTS

This chapter is the result of an international collaboration with the University of Glasgow possible thanks to the financial assistance of the Chilean Commission for Scientific and Technologic Research (Comisión Nacional de Investigación Científica y Tecnológica, CONICYT).

Furthermore, the authors would like to thank Stephen Carney (Roskilde University, Denmark), Ms. Ana-Maria Concha (Universidad Alberto Hurtado, Chile) and Michele Schweisfurth (University of Glasgow, Scotland).

NOTES

[1] At the level of secondary education, the Chilean system recognises two different training modalities for the last two years of compulsory education: Academic Training (AT), which prioritizes a training model conducive to higher education studies, and Technical-Professional Education (TVET) that strictly corresponds to a modality of vocational education.
[2] Statistics from Consejo Nacional de Educación (National Council of Education). http://www.cned.cl/
[3] Statistics from Consejo Nacional de Educación (National Council of Education). http://www.cned.cl/
[4] Statistics from Consejo Nacional de Educación (National Council of Education). http://www.cned.cl/
[5] Education at a Glance, 2014. http://www.oecd.org/edu/Chile-EAG2014-Note.pdf
[6] Archer (2010 [1982]) used the concept of morphogenesis to describe a dialectic relationship between structure and agency, acknowledging that social practice is undoubtedly shaped by non-recognized actions and generates unexpected consequences which form the context for subsequent interactions.
[7] However, he believes that actors have the possibility not to limit themselves to social roles or to strategic and rational interests, but to contribute to shaping their own lives and resisting with a defensive attitude external dominating logics. Unlike autonomy, authenticity permits that an individual is able to choose and select modes of acting that do not originate from a rational strategy but from non-rational and emotional aspects.
[8] FONDECYT Project n° 1140596: "Models of trajectories and educational-labor outcome of young people; A longitudinal study in the Metropolitan Region".
[9] Despite deepening into qualitative approach, the analysis of the exposed material shows a "qualification" of the data collected and did not deploy in depth material interviews and discussion groups.
[10] This variable was constructed on the basis of characteristics established by the Ministry of Education through the application of a national instrument which measures quality of education (the SIMCE test), which differentiates educational centres in relation to the socio-economic status of the families.
[11] High percentage of TVET students who respond I DO NOT KNOW may be related to the issue that they are doing an internship practice at some company.
[12] Multiple choice question.
[13] Multiple choice question with a maximum of three alternatives.
[14] Outcome of these pathways and the effective possibilities implied by these decisions are indeed two different issues.
[15] Data correspond to a sample that is not representative of the total universe of graduates of secondary education in the country.
[16] Early entry to work is also a characteristic feature among TVET students. Four years after high school completion, 82% of TVET students have worked and only 44.1% of AT students have been involved in working activities.

REFERENCES

Appadurai, A. (2004). The capacity to aspire: Culture and the terms of recognition. In V. Rao & M. Walton (Eds.), *Culture and public action* (pp. 59–84). Palo Alto, CA: Stanford University Press.
Araujo, K., & Martuccelli, D. (2012). *Desafíos comunes*. Santiago: Lom.
Archer, L., & Yamashita, H. (2003). 'Knowing their limits'? Identities, inequalities and inner city school leavers' post-16 aspirations. *Journal of Education Policy, 18*(1), 53–69.
Archer, M. S. (2010). Morphogenesis versus structuration: On combining structure and action. *The British Journal of Sociology, 61*(1), 225–252.
Ball, S., Davies, J., David, M., & Reay, D. (2002). 'Classification' and 'judgement': Social class and the 'cognitive structures' of choice of higher education. *British Journal of Sociology of Education, 23*(1), 51–72.
Biggart, A., Furlong, A., & Cartmel, F. (2008). Biografías de elección y linealidad transicional: Nueva conceptualización de las transiciones de la juventud moderna. In R. Bendit, M. Hanh, & A. Miranda (Eds.), *Los jóvenes y el futuro: Procesos de inclusión social y patrones de vulnerabilidad en un mundo globalizado*. Buenos Aires: Prometeo Libros.
Brunner, J. (2007). *Mercados universitarios: El nuevo escenario de la educación superior*. Santiago: Universidad Diego Portales.
Casal, J. (1996). Modos emergentes de transición a la vida adulta en el umbral del siglo XXI: Aproximación sucesiva, precariedad y desestructuración. *Reis,* (75), 295–316. Retrieved from https://doi.org/10.2307/40184037
Casal, J. (1997). Modalidades de transición profesional, mercado de trabajo y condiciones de empleo. *Cuadernos de Relaciones Laborales, 11*, 19–54.
Castillo, J., & Cabezas, G. (2010). Caracterización de jóvenes primera generación en educación superior: Nuevas trayectorias hacia la equidad educativa. *Calidad en la Educación, 32*, 44–76.
Cuconato, M., Majdzinska, K., Walther, A., & Warth, A. (2016). Students decision-making strategies at transition in education. In A. Walther, M. Parreira do Amaral, M. Cuconato, & R. Dale (Eds.), *Governance of educational trajectories in Europe* (pp. 223–245). London: Bloomsbury.
Dubet, F. (1994). *Sociologie de l'expérience*. París: Éditions du Seuil.
Dubet, F. (2005). Los estudiantes. *Cpu-E, Revista de Investigación Educativa*. Retrieved July 20, 2016, from http://www.Uv.Mx/Cpue/Num1/Inves/Estudiantes.Htm#
Du Bois-Reymond, M., & López, A. (2004). Transiciones tipo yo-yo y trayectorias fallidas: Hacia las políticas integradas de transición para los jóvenes europeos. *Estudios De Juventud, 65*, 11–29.
Dussel, I., Brito, A., & Núñez, P. (2007). *Más allá de la crisis: Visión de alumnos y profesores de la escuela secundaria argentina*. Buenos Aires: Fundación Santillana.
Evans, K. (2001). Relationships between work and life. In B. Crick (Ed.), *Citizens: Towards a citizenship culture* (pp. 100–114). Oxford: Blackwell.
Evans, K. (2010). Taking control of their lives? Agency in young adult transitions in England and the new Germany. *Journal of Youth Studies, 5*(3), 245–269.
Filmus, D., & Moragues, M. (2003). ¿Para qué universalizar la educación media? In E. T. Fanfani (Comp.), *Educación media para todos: Los desafíos de la democratización del acceso*. Buenos Aires: Altamira.
Furlong, A., & Cartmel, F. (1997). *Young people and social change*. Buckingham: Open University Press and McGraw-Hill Education.
Furlong, A., & Cartmel, F. (2009). *Higher education and social justice*. Maidenhead: Open University Press.
Grytnes, R. (2011). Making the right choice: Inquiries into the reasoning behind young people's decisions about education. *Young, 19*(3), 333–351.
Heinz, W. (2009). Youth transitions in age of uncertainty. In A. Furlong (Ed.), *Handbook of youth and young adulthood: New perspectives and agendas*. London: Routledge.
Heinz, W., & Krüger, H. (2001). Life course: Innovations and challenges for social research. *Current Sociology, 49*(2), 29–45. (London: Sage Publications.)

Hodkinson, P., & Sparkes, A. C. (1997). Careership: A sociological theory of career decision making. *British Journal of Sociology of Education, 18*(1), 29–44.

Jacinto, C. (2006). *La formación profesional como estrategia para la inserción laboral de jóvenes vulnerables. Balance crítico y reflexiones sobre la experiencia los noventa* (Centro de la Juventud de la Secretaría de Promoción Social de la Municipalidad de Rosario). Santa Fe: Pcia.

Jacinto, C., & Terigi, F. (2007) *¿Qué hacer ante las desigualdades en la educación secundaria? Aportes de la experiencia latinoamericana*. Buenos Aires: UNESCO/IIPE/Santillana.

Jones, N., & Schneider, B. (2009). The influence of aspirations on educational and occupational outcomes. In A. Furlong (Ed.), *Handbook of youth and young adulthood: New perspectives and agendas* (pp. 392–398). London: Routledge.

Khattab, N. (2015). Students' aspirations, expectations and school achievement: What really matters? *British Educational Research Journal, 41*(5), 731–748.

Larrañaga, O., Cabezas, G., & Dusaillant, F. (2013). *Educación técnico profesional: Trayectoria educacional e inserción laboral de una cohorte de alumnos*. Santiago: PNUD. Retrieved from http://www.pnud.cl/areas/reduccionpobreza/2013/pdf_emtp/estudio_emtp_pnud.pdf

Lehmann, W. (2004). 'For some reason, I get a little scared': Structure, agency, and risk in school-work transitions. *Journal of Youth Studies, 7*(4), 379–396.

Lehmann, W. (2009). University as vocational education: Working-class students' expectations for university. *British Journal of Sociology of Education, 30*(2), 137–149.

López, A. (2002). *De los itinerarios lineales a las trayectorias yo-yo*. Ponencia Presentada En La Conferencia Europea Para Investigadores y Técnicos «Jóvenes y Políticas de Transición en Europa», Injuve, Madrid.

Machado, J. (2002). Laberintos de vida: Paro juvenil y rutas de salida (Jóvenes Portugueses). *Revista de Estudios de Juventud, 56*(2), 87–111.

Mcdonough, P. (1997). *Choosing colleges: How social class and schools structure opportunity*. New York, NY: State University of New York Press.

Meneses, F., Rolando, R., Valenzuela, M., & Vega, M. (2010). *Ingreso a la educación superior: La experiencia de la cohorte de egreso 2005* (Sistema Nacional de Información de la Educación Superior (Sies) y División de Educación Superior del MINEDUC). Retrieved from http://portales.mineduc.cl/usuarios/1234/File/Publicaciones/Estudios/8ingreso_a%20_la_educacin_superior.pdf

MINEDUC. (2013). Chile en el panorama internacional OCDE: Avances y desafíos. *Serie Evidencias, 2*(18), 1–8.

Mora, M., & Oliveira, O. (2009). Los jóvenes en el inicio de la vida adulta: Trayectorias, transiciones y subjetividades. *Estudios Sociológicos, XXVII*(79), 267–289.

OCDE and World Bank. (2009). *La educación superior en Chile*. Retrieved from http://www7.uc.cl/webpuc/piloto/pdf/informe_oecd.pdf

Orellana, V. (2011). Nuevos estudiantes y tendencias emergentes en la educación superior: Una mirada al Chile de mañana. In M. Jiménez & F. Lagos (Eds.), *Nueva geografía de la educación superior y de los estudiantes: Una cartografía del sistema chileno, su actual alumnado y sus principales tendencias* (pp. 80–142). Santiago: Ediciones Universidad San Sebastián.

Oyarzún, A., & Irarrázabal, R. (2003). Comportamiento de las trayectorias educacionales y laborales en jóvenes estudiantes. *Última Década, 18*, 199–227.

Reynolds, J. R., & Pemberton, J. (2001). Rising college expectations among youth in the United States: A comparison of the 1979 and 1997 NLSY. *The Journal of Human Resources, 36*(4), 703–726.

Sarojini, C. (2014). *Aspirations, education and social justice: Applying Sen and Bourdieu*. London: Bloomsbury.

Sellar, S., Gale, T., & Parker, S. (2011). Appreciating aspirations in Australian higher education. *Cambridge Journal of Education, 41*(1), 37–52.

Staff, J. Y., & Mortimer, J. (2003). Diverse transitions from school to work. *Work and Occupations, 30*, 361–369.

Torres, R., & Zenteno, M. L. (2011). El sistema de educación superior: Una mirada desde las instituciones y sus características. In M. Jiménez & F. Lagos (Eds.), *Nueva geografía de la educación superior y de los estudiantes: Una cartografía del sistema chileno, su actual alumnado y sus principales tendencias* (pp. 13–78). Santiago: Ediciones Universidad San Sebastián.

UNESCO. (2016). *Proyecto de estrategia para la Enseñanza y Formación Técnica y Professional (EFTP)*. Retrieved from http://unesdoc.unesco.org/images/0024/002438/243804s.pdf

Wynn, J., & Dwyer, P. (1999). New directions in research on youth in transition. *Journal of Youth Studies, 2*(1), 5–21.

Leandro Sepúlveda
Faculty of Education
Alberto Hurtado University
Santiago, Chile

María José Valdebenito
Faculty of Education
Alberto Hurtado University
Santiago, Chile

ELENI PROKOU

5. THE EUROPEAN QUALIFICATIONS FRAMEWORK AS AN EU POLICY INSTRUMENT FOR THE MARKETISATION OF ADULT AND LIFELONG EDUCATION

INTRODUCTION

The purpose of this chapter is to analyse accreditation policies in lifelong learning, with special reference to the introduction and promotion of the European Qualifications Framework (EQF). From the mid-1990s, the European Union (EU) stressed the aim of employability, while during the 2000s, it emphasised the validation of non-formal competences and the formation of a 'reliable accreditation system' of skills. The introduction of the European Credit Transfer System for Vocational Education and Training (ECVET) by the Copenhagen Process led to the development of the EQF, which seeks to improve transparency, comparability and portability of qualifications, as part of a discourse of promoting workers' mobility among the European member states.[1]

The chapter argues that the EQF marks a shift in responsibility from institutions (as service providers) to individuals. The economic function of lifelong learning is dominant not only in the emphasis placed on employability, but also in the shift of responsibility away from the state towards the private sector. As social welfare states decline, individuals are encouraged to utilise their skills to improve their standards of living, while minimising their cost to the state. As such, lifelong learning in the form of Vocational Education and Training (VET) can be considered part of a 'government strategy' to privatise the welfare system. Equity may still be stressed, but the role of the state to secure equitable outcomes is diminished precisely because of the crisis of the welfare state and the retreat from public education policy towards lifelong learning. In fact, it is in welfare state regimes that people have more chances to participate in VET and other forms of adult education. Furthermore, structural inequalities may persist in the labour market despite individuals' possession of highly developed skills. Stressing accredited learning means that the responsibility for learning falls on the individual, while it is the situation in the labour market that plays a crucial role with respect to entrance to employment. In a labour market with a limited demand for jobs, the government distracts citizens' attention from the necessary efforts it should make towards the direction of development and boosting the labour market. Furthermore, through the construction of a highly individualistic neo-liberal subject, notions of collective learning and wider social justice are becoming less important. Accreditation policies focus on learning outcomes and pre-determined objectives and aim at employability, which means that the aims of social inclusion, active citizenship, and personal development (aims that are more closely associated with general adult education) are undermined. Traditions of popular education in Europe, with their notions of social transformation through the development of 'critical conscientisation', are thus marginalised.

GLOBALISATION AND LIFELONG LEARNING FOR EMPLOYABILITY

Over the last three or more decades, the learning society has been emphasised by international organisations and governments. Economic globalisation stressed the aim of employability and thus, there has been a shift from adult education to lifelong learning. Since the early 1990s, the importance of lifelong learning has been stressed as a result of the growing significance of the global economy. Here, the emphasis has been on notions of competitiveness, competencies, widening participation, and the need for workers to continue learning so that countries, and their people, can maintain their economic standing in the world (Jarvis, 2000, p. 347). Interest in lifelong learning can be understood to have emerged as a consequence of the discourse of the knowledge economy and rapid changes in science and technology. In this context, lifelong learning came to be understood as learning throughout the work life. Nevertheless, the terms lifelong learning and the learning society were used rather imprecisely. Learning throughout the work life came to be known as lifelong learning, but work life and life itself are not identical. Consequently, work-life learning is different from lifelong learning. Also, society is an abstract concept and therefore, it does not and cannot learn: its members do. In the language of the learning society, 'learning' is a gerundive to describe the type of society in which we live. It is not being used to describe the process of human learning, but, rather, the type of flexible, open society that responds to the changes driven by the knowledge economy and the market. Furthermore, as learning carries with it a connotation that it is something that leads to human growth and development, discourse about the learning society has acquired a misleading value orientation—that the learning society is intrinsically a good thing. The term 'learning' in this context has not only been inappropriately used, but has also given contemporary society an appearance of goodness that is misleading (Jarvis, 2006, pp. 205–206).

What has actually happened is that as global forces have stridently demanded a more, and continually, educated workforce, adult education has been replaced by 'lifelong learning', and this is a situation reflecting the changes demanded by advanced capitalism (Jarvis, 2007, p. 63). Liberal adult education, by being a voluntary activity, could not turn into conventional policy frameworks. Under the heading of lifelong learning, 'adult' was conceptualised as 'worker' or 'citizen', and so, adult education was fully incorporated into policy (Griffin, 2009, p. 264). In fact, lifelong learning has been promoted, in the form of VET, because of the economic dimension of globalisation. The latter has generated the so-called 'learning society', a flexible and open society that meets the needs stemming from the knowledge economy and the market. Lifelong learning stresses the flexible preparation of the workforce, while the individual is expected to choose from a range of learning environments, in accordance with the emerging needs of the market (Prokou, 2009, pp. 72–75). In market terms, lifelong learning represents a global discourse for the flexible preparation of subjects: it enables the adaptability of workers in terms of their mobility within the workforce between businesses and countries. This new technology of flexible adaptation ensures that responsibility for employment tenure belongs to individuals themselves, ensures the possibility for companies to offset responsibility for social and fiscal payments, and enhances the freedom of business in a global environment. Lifelong learning substitutes the rights of workers to education with an entitlement to knowledge in an automatic system based on the ready availability of information and skills. Lifelong learning involves a restructuring of the context of education in the interests of efficiency through flexibilisation: individuals and institutions inscribe, store, process and transfer actions as learning. Learning has been redefined in terms of process and functions as information. Thus, it needs to be continuously relearned, readjusted and restructured to meet the needs of the consumer in the service information industry. In this sense, learning is understood as an ongoing permanent addition of competences and skills adapted continuously to real external needs (Olssen, 2006, pp. 221–222). In the conditions of economic globalisation, the EU promotes the EQF, as lifelong learning is stressed for employability reasons.

THE EUROPEAN UNION LIFELONG LEARNING POLICIES FOR EMPLOYABILITY AND THE PROMOTION OF THE EQF

Since the early 1990s, for the European Union (EU), employability has been the central aim of lifelong learning. Since the early 2000s, in particular, emphasis has been placed on the formation of a 'reliable accreditation system' of skills. Thus, after the Copenhagen Process for VET, the EQF gradually developed, aiming at the promotion of European workers' mobility.

Throughout the 1990s, the discourse on education and training developments at both national and European levels increasingly took into account arguments for reform. These included greater globalisation and rapid technological change requiring a permanent update of knowledge and skills, competition with other regions of the world, in particular the United States, and the EU position in the knowledge-based economy and society. At the EU level, there was a growing awareness that education and training cooperation should serve a common objective: lifelong learning (Pépin, 2007, pp. 125–126). A shift in policy discourses on lifelong learning by the EU (among other organisations, e.g. the United Nations Educational, Scientific and Cultural Organisation, and the Organisation for Economic Cooperation and Development) took place: the point and purpose of lifelong learning was understood primarily in economic terms and far less in relation to its personal and democratic function (Biesta, 2006). In 1995, the EU pronounced a policy on lifelong learning and from the outset there were two major aims to the European policy: economic competitiveness and citizenship in a new EU (Jarvis, 2009b, p. 271). However, for the European Commission (EC), the main principle of lifelong learning was understood as one of employment policies and "continuous re-skilling of the workforce" (with associated tax and other incentives) aiming at the "common economic health" of member states. As the focus had been strongly on training, it was deemed no longer *education*, but *learning* itself. This was duly incorporated into economic and employment policy (Griffin, 2006, p. 367).

The 1993 White Paper on the learning society had already led to actions of direct interest to lifelong learning and had stressed (among other issues) the work that had to be done on the validation of nonformal competences (Pépin, 2007, p. 126). According to this Paper, the 'modern route' to employability was understood in terms of integration within networks which cooperate, educate, train and learn. These networks were defined in institutional terms (education and training establishments cooperating with families or firms) or in terms of informal networks of knowledge (adult education establishments, education cooperatives, etc.) and were associated with the formation of a 'reliable accreditation system' of skills (acquired either in formal education or in a less formal way) (European Commission, 1995, pp. 15–16).

As knowledge economy objectives were adopted at EU level (from the late 1990s, in particular), the growing centrality of the education/learning area, the opacity of the space, and the need to govern it, has meant that it has emerged as a significant area of policy. Standards were considered to be essential for managing education across Europe within and between states, and in the new knowledge economy. The EQF is an example of standardisation in the way it has sought to improve the "transparency, comparability and portability" of qualifications in the EU (Lawn, 2011, pp. 262–263). To understand the general framework in which the EQF has been promoted (since the mid-2000s), it is important to trace the relevant policies from the beginning of the 2000s.

It is well known that in 2000, the aspiration of the Lisbon strategy was for Europe to become "the most competitive and dynamic knowledge-based economy in the world capable of sustainable economic growth with more and better jobs and greater social cohesion". For the fulfilment of this aim, education and training was expected to play a vital role (European Parliament, 2000). In this framework, the programme "Education and training in Europe: Diverse systems, shared goals for 2010" was approved. Its strategic goals were about facilitating the access of all to education and training systems in the EU, improving their quality and effectiveness and opening them up to the wider world (European Commission, 2002a, p. 8). With the same rationale to emphasise employability and mobility within the EU, the Copenhagen Declaration and the EC had set a number of priorities (until 2010). These priorities aimed to strengthen the *European dimension* and increasing *transparency* in VET, along with strengthening policies, systems and practices that support *information*, *guidance* and counseling at all levels of education, training and employment. Other priorities included: investigating how the transparency, comparability, transferability and recognition of competencies and/or qualifications between different countries and at different levels could be promoted; increasing support to the development of competences and qualifications; developing a set of common principles regarding validation of non-formal and informal learning for greater compatibility between approaches in different countries, and, finally, improving quality assurance in VET (European Commission, 2002b).

Given the emphasis of the Copenhagen Process in a credit transfer system for VET, the development of the ECVET began in 2002. National governments and the European Parliament gave their final approval to legislation in June 2009 (European Commission, n.d.a). The ECVET, as a European instrument to support lifelong learning, the mobility of European learners and the flexibility of learning pathways to achieve qualifications, has been in progressive implementation (European Commission, 2011, p. 1). It is based on learning outcomes (statements of what a learner knows and is able to do on completion of a learning process), which are developed in the process of designing qualifications and may be acquired through a variety of learning pathways, modes of delivery (school-based, in-company, etc.), in different learning contexts (formal, non-formal and informal) or settings (i.e. country, education and training systems). Qualifications frameworks indicate the overall level of learning outcomes in a qualification. For ECVET purposes, the EQF has been used as a reference for levels (European Commission, 2011, p. 12).

It should be noted that the EQF has been a high priority in the EU agenda since 2004: the Maastricht Communiqué noted that priority should be given to "the development of an open and flexible European qualifications framework, founded on transparency and mutual trust" (Maastricht Communiqué on the Future Priorities of Enhanced European Cooperation in Vocational Education and Training, 2004, p. 4, as cited in Cort, 2010, p. 305). Historically, the EQF has been part of a discourse of promoting worker mobility among the European member states (Cort, 2010, pp. 305–306). Agreed upon by the European institutions, the EQF was put in practice across Europe in 2008. Countries were encouraged to relate their national qualifications systems to the EQF (by means of an EQF national coordination being designated for this purpose in each country). The EQF was expected to act as a translation device to make national qualifications more readable across Europe, promote workers' and learners' mobility between countries and facilitate their lifelong learning. Individuals and employers would, thus, be able to use the EQF to better understand and compare the qualifications levels of different countries and different education and training systems (European Commission, n.d.b).

The EQF is defined as a 'meta-framework' (a framework for frameworks and/or systems) enabling qualifications systems with their implicit levels or/and national and sectoral qualifications frameworks to relate to each other. In the process of implementing the EQF, each country references its national qualifications (in terms of diplomas, certificates or awards) to the eight EQF levels via national qualifications frameworks or the implicit levels in the national qualifications systems. In the first stage, levels of national qualifications frameworks or parts of qualifications systems are referred to in terms of EQF levels, while ultimately, all qualifications awarded in Europe should have a reference to the EQF. The descriptors are written to cover the full range of learning outcomes, irrespective of the learning or institutional context (from basic education, through school and unskilled worker levels up to doctoral or senior professional levels). They cover both work and study situations, academic and vocational settings, initial and continuing education or training, i.e. all forms of learning, formal, non-formal and informal (European Commission, 2008, p. 4). Each of the eight levels of the EQF is defined by a set of descriptors (for knowledge, skills, competencies) indicating the learning outcomes relevant to qualifications at that level in any system of qualifications (Official Journal of the European Union, 2008, pp. 5–6).

The recommendations of the European Parliament and the Council (as regards the relation of national qualifications systems to the EQF) has been defined as non-binding and conforms to the principle of subsidiarity. In this sense, they support and supplement member states' activities by facilitating further cooperation between them to increase transparency and to promote mobility and lifelong learning. Implementation is in accordance with national legislation and practice (Official Journal of the European Union, 2008, p. 2).

It has become evident that policies of accreditation, as these are expressed by the promotion of the EQF, are strongly associated with the aim of employability. But what about the aim of equity/social cohesion, and the other two aims of lifelong learning (as these are also officially stated within the EU documents), namely, active citizenship and personal development? Additionally, what are the implications of the aforementioned policies for general adult education which does not have employability as its central aim?

IMPLICATIONS OF THE DOMINANCE OF THE AIM OF EMPLOYABILITY, ASSOCIATED WITH QUALIFICATIONS FRAMEWORKS, FOR ADULT AND LIFELONG EDUCATION

It will now be argued that accreditation policies (closely associated with the aim of employability) mark a shift in responsibility from institutions to the individuals, and from the state towards the private sector. Due to the decline of social welfare states, the aim of equity/social inclusion is thus difficult to achieve.

In general, the EC emphasises employability, especially when defining lifelong learning as "all learning activity undertaken throughout life, with the aim of improving knowledge, skills and competences within a personal, civic, social and/ or employment-related perspective" (EC, 2001, as cited in Jarvis, 2009a, p. 9). Thus, the EC actually offers an individualistic definition that implies an instrumental perspective. It suggests that lifelong learning must have an aim. However, learning is an existential phenomenon that is co-terminal with conscious living. Learning is lifelong because it occurs whenever we are conscious and it does not need to have an objective in itself, although it frequently does have a purpose. Lifelong learning is an intrinsic part of the process of living and it is neither incidental to living nor instrumental in itself (Jarvis, 2009a, p. 10). In this sense, the introduction of qualifications frameworks offers an instrumental interpretation of lifelong learning.

Countries introduce qualifications frameworks in order to make their education and training systems more transparent, innovative and competitive. Additional aims include the desire to improve the match between education systems and the labour market, to promote the certification of non-formal and informal learning and to encourage students to acquire competences relevant to the labour market. Qualifications frameworks enable wider access to opportunities for education and make possible more ways of acquiring qualifications (other than solely by participation in institutionalised courses) (Bohlinger, 2008, p. 96). Such systems can be understood as shifting in responsibility from institutions to individuals. Institutions do not primarily produce education but, rather, certify that learning has or has not taken place, regardless of the position in time and space that the individual occupied. The individual becomes both subject and object of his/her learning documentation, increasingly being responsible for formalising learning, especially when it occurred 'incidentally', or outside of institutional premises (Tuschling & Engemann, 2006, pp. 464–465).

Contemporary political discourses pretend to enable new and broader learning environments and a new possibility for the individual to shape and take care of his/her own learning trajectory. In the name of individual needs and desires, they offer an individual governance of learning trajectories, reducing the role of institutions to service providers. Conflicts in terms of objectives and contents do not appear and the individual is considered to be a rational subject making his/her choices in a transparent market. The ideological assumption that individuals' needs and desires can best be met by independent and separated choices in a market takes its point of departure in the disappearing habitual and automatic collective experiences of the working class, the local community, the ethnic group etc. Thus, marketability of all education and training presupposes reconstructions of their organisational formats in favour of well-defined and declared modules of fixed content and credit value (Olesen, 2006, pp. 243, 254). National qualifications frameworks (along with the establishment of accreditation institutions independently accrediting either institutions or qualifications) were aimed to counter the problem of deregulated education and training systems where independent institutions and/or private providers have facilitated a burgeoning transnational market for education. Here, the need for new mechanisms of ensuring quality (and thereby trust) in qualifications becomes urgent and the focus on outcome provides a means of regulating through quality indicators (Cort, 2010, p. 306).

However, under the imperatives of the learning economy, only the economic function of lifelong learning seems to count as 'good' or desirable learning. At the same time, there is a clear tendency to shift the responsibility for learning to the individual—or, at a larger scale, to shift this responsibility away from the state towards the private sector. Learning ceases to be a collective good and increasingly becomes an individual good. The state is less and less a provider and promoter of lifelong learning and increasingly becomes the regulator and auditor of the "learning market" (Biesta, 2006, p. 175). Lifelong learning means self-determination and self-responsibility in educational tasks, including the financial aspects, since the learner has to co-finance his/her own learning (see Commission of the European Union, 2000 as cited in Tuschling & Engemann, 2006, p. 458).

The policy discourse on lifelong learning usually projects it as an expansion of learning opportunities, but not always as an expansion of public provision. Lifelong learning is construed as a form of educational privatisation, as nation states adopt a neo-liberal and market-oriented stance towards the provision of all kinds of public services. The rhetoric of lifelong learning policy points to the failure of public education, or at least its inability to succeed in the future, either in meeting peoples' learning needs or in promoting access and equal opportunity. The responsibility of individuals and organisations for their own learning in relation to employability and competition means that public forms of education seem increasingly incapable of meeting the needs of post-industrial, post-welfare and post-modern societies (Griffin, 2000, pp. 5–8). One of the obvious elements of the changing policy context (in which lifelong learning has been conceptualised) is the increasing absence of clear distinctions between the *public* and the *private* realm when it comes to finance. Policy has ceased to be unambiguously 'public' in the face of corporate financial investment alongside public expenditure from public revenues. Instead, it has often been located in the interface between government authority and market forces (Griffin, 2009, p. 262). Associated with the marketisation of provision and the individualisation of responsibility for learning has of course been the abolition of welfare obligations of states.

Overall, lifelong learning plays a special role in implementing the outlined models of governing individuals. People are set free from the rigid frameworks of the classical social welfare states, but they are facing incentives suggesting ways of utilising individual skills and circumstances maximising their own 'life chances' while minimising their cost to the state (Tuschling & Engemann, 2006, pp. 451–452). Griffin (2000, pp. 3–12) has already described this situation in his analysis of adult education and lifelong learning policy. He notes that usually the incoherence and inconsistency of 'government policy' are addressed, although rather in isolation from other policies, such as employment, redistribution, taxation, etc. Globalisation, market forces and individualisation have thrown into ambiguity the contingency of policy analysis upon a concept of a welfare state, upon the possibilities of clearly identifying the 'social' and the 'public' spheres, and upon the perceived scope for action on the part of the state. Instead, there has been a shift from government *policy* to *strategy*, which implies that the government abandons control over the *outcomes* of policy and restricts itself to organising the *means*. Government creates the conditions in which individuals are most likely to maximise their own learning, but with the ultimate responsibility lying with them. These conditions of learning take the form of various incentives, mainly financial, but also persuasion, or even threat. Lifelong learning is part of a wider government strategy to privatise the welfare system. However, the policy discourse of lifelong learning is also a strategy on the part of the state to bring about further ends, beyond economic competitiveness, such as social cohesion, social inclusion, citizenship, and so on. Lifelong learning policies are only partly addressed to employability, human resource development, technological accreditation and global competition. They are also addressed to non-measurable outcomes: social inclusion, active citizenship, the quality of life itself.

This is because throughout its history, adult education was mainly considered to be the responsibility of national governments, and in general, although not exclusively, recognised for its compensatory and remedial functions. In the greatest part of the twentieth century, it was strongly connected with the welfare state (Milana, 2015, p. 2). Thus, there is still a view that as many as possible should have access to learning opportunities. Overall, there are tensions between ideas of education, learning and training, or human and social capital, or the construction of visions, strategies and policies in relation to social justice and so on. And the question of whether education reproduces or transforms social relations, which was associated with the 1960s' disillusion with schooling, may still be one that can be asked for lifelong learning itself (Griffin, 2009, p. 267). Nevertheless, proponents of lifelong learning have argued that since in the learning society everyone has the right to education (either the learner or the provider, or both), this society could promote economic competitiveness, personal development, life in the community and social cohesion. By promoting everyone's participation in the learning process, lifelong learning could contribute to the alleviation of inequalities in access to education and training, especially with reference to part-time workers, people with special needs or those with few qualifications. Institutions were called to create successful learning environments and the emerging learning society demanded new forms of networks, co-operation and partnership between governments, private institutions and individuals (Green, Wolf, & Leney, 1999, pp. 254–255). With respect to the qualifications frameworks, in particular, there were claims that these might attract individuals who possess the knowledge and skills required for participation, but do not participate in education and training due to a lack of resources (financial and time) or due to the organisational structure of programmes. This was attributed to the fact that qualifications frameworks focus on learning outcomes and on broadening access to education and training, while at the same time they do not threaten existing education and training routes (Bohlinger, 2012, pp. 282–283). However, the EQF was also criticised for its primary rationale of separating qualifications from educational institutions so that it can accredit non-formal or informal learning. Thus, an approach linking institutions to informal learners through supporting alternative access programmes was proposed (Young, 2008, p. 136).

In fact, the claims about citizenship, justice, equality of opportunity and social inclusion are made for lifelong learning, even though the role of the state to secure these objects of policy is diminished precisely by the globalisation forces shaping the context of lifelong learning itself. The worldwide crisis of the welfare state is a crisis of social democracy with implications for lifelong learning policy. The role of the state is crucial to the achievement of a social democratic vision of lifelong learning, since in welfare or social democratic regimes it is redistributive and interventionist in favour of those least likely to gain advantage in the market for goods or services such as educational opportunity. Furthermore, behind the argument that the learning society should be an object of social policy lies a view of education as a precondition of active citizenship (Griffin, 2000, pp. 4–10). However, the individualisation of lifelong learning has actually brought about a *reversal* of rights and duties. Whereas lifelong learning used to be the right of the individual which corresponded to the state's duty to provide resources and opportunities for lifelong learning, lifelong learning has now increasingly become a *duty* for which individuals need to take responsibility. At the same time it has become the right of the state to demand of all its citizens that they continuously engage in learning in order to keep up with the demands of the global economy (Biesta, 2006, pp. 175–176).

We are thus witnessing a *re*construction of citizenship. As the state's role shifts from intervention to facilitation (i.e. managing the contexts in which citizens make their own autonomous choices), it becomes necessary to prepare such 'empowered' citizens for their unaccustomed civic self-sufficiency. The key function of the new 'neo-liberal welfare reform' version of lifelong learning, as distinct from its older 'progressive social democratic' version, is that it becomes a crucial means by which the 'crisis in welfare' is managed and the process of institutional *de*construction and civic *re*construction is accomplished. In the reconfigured 'post-welfare' landscape, we learn to become a different kind of citizen and lifelong learning is about learning to do without welfare. If we do not learn this willingly, we are encouraged (or even coerced) to do so through various kinds of 'welfare to work' or 'workfare' programmes that teach us to learn the 'lesson' of lifelong learning. In essence, this lesson is to throw off the culture of dependency in which welfare is viewed as a substitute for work and to understand that work is the necessary precondition of welfare. Lifelong learning, often coupled in policy to 'social partnerships' between the chosen 'stakeholders' of the 'new corporatism', becomes a means of depoliticising the debate about the politics of citizenship, systematically obscuring crucial asymmetries of power and masking the managerial role of the state as orchestrator of the new consensus (Martin, 2003, pp. 575–576).

In addition, the view of learning as a cultural practice, as a lifestyle accessory of the new classes of society in a post-welfare society, removes it from the public domain of policy. The idea that learning is sited in everyday experience, and in the social relations of family, community and work, distances it from public education and removes it from the realms of both policy and strategy. Thus, lifelong learning can only be an object of policy in relation to *some* of its meanings, namely, those that reduce lifelong learning to the expansion of educational and training opportunities. Lifelong learning can remain a policy of government only if the meaning of lifelong learning is identical with an expansion of the public education and training system. The contingency of policy analysis upon a concept of social welfare focuses attention on the consequences for the professed social objectives of lifelong learning, such as social cohesion, equal opportunities and social inclusion. However, the further that public education policy retreats in favour of lifelong learning or the learning society, the less likely it becomes that such objectives can be achieved (Griffin, 2000, pp. 10–13).

It is clear then, that the nature of welfare state regimes can affect a person's capability to participate. The state can foster broad structural conditions relevant to participation and construct targeted policy measures aimed at overcoming both structural and individual barriers (Rubenson & Desjardins, 2009, p. 187). This is because the decision of a person to participate is related both to the purposeful reasoning behaviour of agents and its intersection with the constraining and enabling features of the social and material contexts of that behaviour. Dispositions and preferences depend on economic and social conditions. As such, dispositional barriers can be regarded as a form of habitus that restricts people's freedom in considering the possibility to participate. The welfare state regime can affect a person's capability to participate in lifelong learning through the way it constructs the material, social, and institutional environments and the way these result in situational and institutional, or structural, barriers as well as a person's internal state of readiness as expressed in dispositional barriers (Rubenson & Desjardins, 2009, p. 197). Furthermore, structural inequalities may persist within the labour market despite individuals' possession of highly developed skills. Individuals may remain unemployed despite being willing and able to fulfil the expectations of the employability rationale and possessing the range of desired skills. This is because a focus on the supply side shifts responsibility for skills development and labour market inclusion to the individual, whereas macroeconomic factors such as job shortages, unfavourable economic conditions or employment inequalities are ignored. The cause of unemployment is conceptualised in individualistic terms, while the employability approach has also compounded problems of social reproduction, in terms of age, gender, ethnicity and social class background (Haasler, 2013, p. 240).

Social inequalities in participation in lifelong learning should also be stressed. With reference to the educational level, as a strong determinant of the social background of participants in lifelong learning, Desjardins and Rubenson (2013, pp. 273–275) provide data from the EU Adult Education Survey (2005–2008) showing that in nearly all European countries, adults with at least some tertiary education were expected to undertake much more education beyond the age of 25. The difference was somewhat attenuated in Denmark and Finland and this was explained by data showing that the Nordic countries had the highest volume of full-time equivalent (FTE) years of education for adults over 25 with less than upper secondary qualifications, ranging from about two to three FTE years. Otherwise, in most EU countries, adults with low levels of initial formal education were expected to undertake less than 0.5 FTE years of education beyond the age of 25. In general, the authors stress that women, those who are older, from low socio-economic backgrounds, low educated, low-skilled, in low-skill jobs, unemployed, and/or immigrants were the least likely to participate in lifelong learning in both Nordic and non-Nordic countries. The distinctiveness of the Nordic countries seemed to lie in the attenuation of differences among these otherwise disadvantaged groups.

Boyadjieva and Ilieva-Trichkova (2017) refer to several studies (see OECD, 2003; Roosmaa & Saar, 2012) showing that younger adults, those with higher educational attainment, those with jobs, or those employed in high-skilled occupations, participated more frequently than older, low-educated, and unemployed people or those employed in low-skilled occupations. The authors refer also to other studies (see e.g. Kilpi-Jakonen, Vono de Vilhena, Kosyakova, Stenberg, & Blossfeld, 2012) which acknowledge that these patterns of participation led to growing inequalities, in terms of both education and labour market outcomes, over the life span. In their own research, Boyadjieva and Ilieva-Trichkova (2017) analyse data from the Adult Education Survey from 2007 and 2011 for 25 countries and show that, in most of the countries, the inclusion of people with low education in lifelong learning activities remained considerably lower in comparison with the inclusion of people with high education. This was notwithstanding signs of improvement in the fairness aspect of social justice resulting from a decrease in the overrepresentation of people with high education and in the under-representation of people with low levels of education.

Inequalities in participation could be explained by considering the case of Greece. The priorities of the Greek state as regards the field of adult/continuing education in the 2000s (and the 1990s) were given to the confrontation of social exclusion that stemmed from unemployment and, therefore, to the achievement of the aims of employability and social inclusion. These aims were in accordance with the policies of the EU, the main body funding lifelong learning, in view of an inefficient welfare state in Greece. EU funding, together with the relatively centralised character of the regulated part of adult/continuing education in Greece, were favourable factors for the expansion of training programmes for the unemployed. Empirical data, which refer to the funding of the basic adult/continuing education agencies in Greece and the aspired number of participants in the programmes that the agencies carried out, showed that in the 2000s (as in the 1990s), the state supported lifelong learning in the form of continuing vocational training—vis-à-vis general adult education—but within a framework of its privatisation. At that time, the state aimed at tackling social exclusion by offering training programmes for the inclusion of the unemployed, and of other socially vulnerable groups, in the system of employment. However, withdrawal from public education policy posed questions as to the possibility of the achievement of the aim of social inclusion/insertion, while general adult education was given less importance. The withdrawal from public education policy could be seen in the privatisation of the regulated part of adult/continuing education, i.e., the part concerning continuing vocational training, and in the individualisation of responsibility for learning, as there were no coherent policies linking training with employment (Prokou, 2011). For the same time period, the 2000s, data from the European Workforce Research showed that although the rate of participation in lifelong learning activities in Greece was doubled compared to the previous period, it remained low compared to the relevant European aim (12% until 2010). For instance, in 2006, the percentage of participation of people between the ages of 25 and 64 was 1.9% (vis-à-vis the European average of 9.6%). However, with reference to the characteristics of the population participating in lifelong learning activities, the largest gaps in participation were observed amongst aged people and those with low educational level. The level of education proved to be the most influential factor in participation (Karantinos, 2010, pp. 45–53). Finally, data from a survey during the crisis (years 2011 and 2013) showed that participation rates were increasing, mainly due to state intervention and leverage. However, the gap with other European countries continued to grow along with inequalities in participation, especially regarding the educational level and employment security, while participation costs were found to be the main barrier in participation. Overall, the stabilisation of growth trends in participation and the reduction of access inequalities in adult/continuing education in Greece were influenced by the economic crisis (Karalis, 2017).

CONCLUSION

It has been argued here that since the early 1990s, there has been a marked favouring within public policy towards the idea of the learning society. This is conceptualised as an open society that responds to the needs of the knowledge economy and the market. Under conditions of economic globalisation, there has been a shift from adult education to lifelong learning, the latter being promoted for the flexible adaptability of the workforce.

For the EU, in particular, the main focus of lifelong learning policy has been on employment strategies. In this context, emphasis has been placed on the validation of non-formal competences and the formation of a 'reliable accreditation system' of skills. The emphasis of the Copenhagen Process in a credit transfer system for VET gradually led to the development of the EQF, which sought to improve the 'transparency, comparability and portability' of qualifications in the EU, as part of a discourse of promoting workers' mobility among the European member states.

However, accreditation policies (expressed through the promotion of the EQF) mark a shift in responsibility from institutions (considered to be service providers) to individuals. The economic/employability function of lifelong learning is dominant, while there is also a shift in responsibility away from the state towards the private sector. As social welfare states decline, individuals are encouraged to utilise their skills to improve their standards of living, while minimising their cost to the state. Lifelong learning in the form of VET has thus become part of a government strategy to privatise the welfare system. Equity may still be stressed, but the role of the state to secure it is diminished precisely because of the crisis of the welfare state and the retreat from public education policy towards lifelong learning. However, the further the retreat from public education policy towards lifelong learning or the learning society, the less likely equity can be achieved. Welfare state regimes can affect a person's capability to participate, while structural inequalities may persist in the labour market despite individuals' possession of highly developed skills. Stressing accredited learning means that the responsibility for learning falls on the individual, while it is the situation in the labour market that plays a crucial role. In a labour market offering few jobs, only few individuals benefit from the EQF. Political efforts to boost the labour market are thus underestimated. Furthermore, social inequalities in participation in lifelong learning seem to be reproduced: as in most European countries, education levels predict rates of participation.

Finally, it should be stressed that as the highly individualistic neo-liberal subject has emerged from policy, notions of collective learning and wider social justice get lost. The emphasis on employability, central in the EU policies for lifelong learning (to be seen in accreditation policies, which prioritise learning outcomes and pre-determined objectives) means that the aims of social inclusion and active citizenship (but also personal development), more closely associated with general adult education, are not considered to be equally important. Traditions of popular education in Europe, with their notions of social transformation by critically interrogating established assumptions and injustices—in the way Freire (1979) has described, while explaining the pedagogical processes of the development of critical conscientisation—are thus marginalised. Economic globalisation has brought individualism and competition. Consequently, critical educators find it difficult to introduce notions of solidarity and group action. Yet, globalisation—by bringing a highly uneven development, characterised by social inequalities—requires more than ever the contributions of critical theory and transformative learning processes.

NOTE

[1] The Copenhagen Process was launched by the Copenhagen Declaration approved on 30 November 2002 by ministers responsible for vocational education and training in the Member States, candidate countries, EFTA-EEA countries, the European Social Partners and the European Commission.

REFERENCES

Biesta, G. (2006). What's the point of lifelong learning if lifelong learning has no point? On the democratic deficit of policies for lifelong learning. *European Educational Research Journal, 5*(3–4), 169–180.

Bohlinger, S. (2008). Competences as the core element of the European qualifications framework. *European Journal of Vocational Training, 42*(1), 96–112.

Bohlinger, S. (2012). Qualifications frameworks and learning outcomes: Challenges for Europe's lifelong learning area. *Journal of Education and Work, 25*(3), 279–297.

Boyadjieva, P., & Ilieva-Trichkova, P. (2017). Between inclusion and fairness: Social justice perspective to participation in adult education. *Adult Education Quarterly, 67*(2), 97–117. doi:10.1177/0741713616685398

Cort, P. (2010). Stating the obvious: The European qualifications framework is not a neutral evidence-based policy tool. *European Educational Research Journal, 9*(3), 304–316.

Desjardins, R., & Rubenson, K. (2013). Participation patterns in adult education: The role of institutions and public policy frameworks in resolving coordination problems. *European Journal of Education, 48*(2), 262–280.

European Commission. (1995). *White paper on education and training: Teaching and learning society.* Retrieved May, 2017, from http://europa.eu/documents/comm/white_papers/pdf/com95_590_en.pdf

European Commission. (2002a). *Education and training in Europe: Diverse systems, shared goals for 2010.* Belgium: European Communities.

European Commission. (2002b). *The Copenhagen declaration.* Retrieved May, 2017, from http://ec.europa.eu/education/pdf/doc125_en.pdf

European Commission. (2008). *Explaining the European qualifications framework for lifelong learning.* Luxembourg: Office for Official Publications of the European Communities.

European Commission. (2011). *The European Credit System for Vocational Education and Training ECVET: Get to know ECVET better: Questions and answers.* Retrieved November, 2013, from http://ec.europa.eu/education/lifelong-learning-policy/doc/ecvet/faq_en.pdf

European Commission. (n.d.a). *The European Credit System for Vocational Education and Training (ECVET).* Retrieved November, 2013, from http://ec.europa.eu/education/lifelong-learning-policy/ecvet_en.htm

European Commission. (n.d.b). *The European Qualifications Framework (EQF).* Retrieved November, 2013, from http://ec.europa.eu/education/lifelong-learning-policy/eqf_en.htm

European Parliament. (2000). *Lisbon European Council 23 and 24 March 2000: Presidency conclusions.* Retrieved May, 2013, from http://www.europarl.europa.eu/summits/lis1_en.htm#b

Freire, P. (1977). *Η αγωγή του καταπιεζόμενου* [The pedagogy of the oppressed]. Athens: Kedros Rappa.

Green, A., Wolf, A., & Leney, T. (1999). *Convergence and divergence in European education and training systems.* London: Institute of Education – University of London.

Griffin, C. (2000). *Lifelong learning: Policy, strategy and culture.* Working Papers of the Global Colloquium on Supporting Lifelong Learning [online]. Milton Keynes: Open University. Retrieved June, 2006, from http://www.open.ac.uk/lifelong-learning

Griffin, C. (2006). Lifelong learning and welfare reform. In P. Jarvis (Ed.), *From adult education to the learning society: 21 years from the international journal of lifelong education* (pp. 366–394). London & New York, NY: Routledge.

Griffin, C. (2009). Policy and lifelong learning. In P. Jarvis (Ed.), *The Routledge international handbook of lifelong learning* (pp. 261–270). London & New York, NY: Routledge.

Haasler, S. R. (2013). Employability skills and the notion of 'self'. *International Journal of Training and Development, 17*(3), 233–243.

Jarvis, P. (2000). Globalisation, the learning society and comparative education. *Comparative Education, 36*(3), 343–355.

Jarvis, P. (2006). Beyond the learning society: Globalisation and the moral imperative for reflective social change. *International Journal of Lifelong Education, 25*(3), 201–211.

Jarvis, P. (2007). *Globalisation, lifelong learning and the learning society: Sociological perspectives.* London & New York, NY: Routledge.

Jarvis, P. (2009a). Lifelong learning: A social ambiguity. In P. Jarvis (Ed.), *The Routledge international handbook of lifelong learning* (pp. 9–18). London & New York, NY: Routledge.

Jarvis, P. (2009b). The European Union and lifelong learning policy. In P. Jarvis (Ed.), *The Routledge international handbook of lifelong learning* (pp. 271–280). London & New York, NY: Routledge.

Karalis, T. (2017). Shooting a moving target: The Sisyphus Boulder of increasing participation in adult education during the period of economic crisis. *Journal of Adult and Continuing Education, 23*(1), 78–96.

Karantinos, D. (2010). Συμμετοχή στη διά βίου μάθηση: Τάσεις και προοπτικές [Participation in lifelong learning: Trends and prospects]. In D. Vergidis & A. Kokkos (Eds.), *Εκπαίδευση Ενηλίκων: Διεθνείς προσεγγίσεις και ελληνικές διαδρομές* [Adult education: International approaches and Greek routes] (pp. 43–62). Athens: Metaixmio.

Lawn, M. (2011). Standardizing the European education policy space. *European Educational Research Journal, 10*(2), 259–272.

Martin, I. (2003). Adult education, lifelong learning and citizenship: Some ifs and buts. *International Journal of Lifelong Education, 22*(6), 566–579.

Milana, M. (2015). A global outlook on adult education and learning policies. In M. Milana & T. Nisbet (Eds.), *Global perspectives on adult education and learning policy* (pp. 1–12). Basingstoke & New York, NY: Palgrave Macmillan.

Official Journal of the European Union. (2008). *Recommendation of the European parliament and of the council of 23 April 2008 on the establishment of the European qualifications framework for lifelong learning.* Retrieved from http://eur-lex.europa.eu/LexUriServ/LexUriServ.do?uri=oj:c:2008:111:0001:0007:en:pdf

Olesen, H. S. (2006). Beyond the abstractions! Adult education research from idealism to critical social science. *International Journal of Lifelong Education, 25*(3), 241–256.

Olssen, M. (2006). Understanding the mechanisms of neoliberal control: Lifelong learning, flexibility and knowledge capitalism. *International Journal of Lifelong Education, 25*(3), 213–230.

Pépin, L. (2007). The history of EU co-operation in the field of education and training: How lifelong learning became a strategic objective. *European Journal of Education, 42*(1), 121–132.

Prokou, E. (2011). The aims of employability and social inclusion/active citizenship in lifelong learning policies in Greece. In I. Psimmenos (Ed.), *Contemporary social inequalities, the Greek review of social research* (pp. 203–223). Athens: Panteion University.

Prokou, E. (2009). *Εκπαίδευση ενηλίκων και διά βίου μάθηση στην Ευρώπη και την Ελλάδα* [Adult education and lifelong learning in Europe and in Greece]. Athens: Dionicos.

Rubenson, K., & Desjardins, R. (2009). The impact of welfare state regimes on barriers to participation in adult education: A bounded agency model. *Adult Education Quarterly, 59*(3), 187–207.

Tuschling, A., & Engemann, C. (2006). From education to lifelong learning: The emerging regime of learning in the European Union. *Educational Philosophy and Theory, 38*(4), 451–469.

Young, M. (2008). Towards a European qualifications framework: Some cautionary observations. *Journal of European Industrial Training, 32*(2–3), 128–137.

Eleni Prokou
Department of Social Policy
Panteion University of Social and Political Sciences
Athens, Greece

NADINE BERNHARD

6. NECESSITY OR RIGHT? EUROPEANISATION AND DISCOURSES ON PERMEABILITY BETWEEN VOCATIONAL EDUCATION AND TRAINING AND HIGHER EDUCATION IN GERMANY AND FRANCE

INTRODUCTION

Introducing a lifelong learning strategy and making national educational systems more permeable are key goals, defined in national, European, and international policy declarations like the UN Sustainable Development Goals 2016. In particular, European processes such as the Bologna Process for Higher Education (since 1999) and the Copenhagen Process for Vocational Education (since 2002) emphasise the importance of lifelong learning and the provision of institutional permeability structures between general, higher, and vocational education. The signatory countries of these processes, including Germany and France, are hence asked to create flexible pathways in their education systems, in particular between vocational education and training (VET) and higher education (HE) (Bernhard, 2017).

Against this background, I compare how the question of permeability between HE and VET was discussed at the European level, in France, and in Germany from 1990 to 2012. The analysis focuses hence on one dimension of the national (and European) institutional permeability structure, namely on parts of the knowledge structure on permeability revealed in the educational policy discourses. Since knowledge structures help individuals to interpret and structure the world and also (de)legitimise political and social actions as well as institutions, changes in knowledge structures can consequently lead to changes of these institutional structures and societal and individual actions. The analysis is based on the following questions: How is permeability conceptualised in the different contexts? Is a need for permeability in postsecondary education acknowledged and how is it justified? How do the conceptualisations and justifications differ between Germany and France and the European level, and are they changing and converging over time?

Studying institutional permeability structures can reveal important insights from a social inequality perspective, as stratified skill formation systems without bridges between different education sectors impede equal opportunities in education and employment. Changes in educational systems and changes in individual life chances are intertwined across the individual life course, thereby influencing cumulative processes of educational inequalities (Hillmert, 2010; Mayer, 2004).

According to Powell and Solga (2010), reforms in national institutional structures and highly institutionalised educational pathways can result in enormous societal consequences. The question of institutional permeability is therefore closely linked to social permeability and equity. Institutional permeability of education systems can be regarded as a necessary, if not sufficient, condition of social permeability (Bernhard, 2017). Educational mobility is not possible without bridges between individual sectors of education and education levels. This is all the more important in societies like Germany and France, where the acquired educational level is a central determinant of different dimensions of social inequality (Solga et al., 2009). Increasing institutional permeability can thus lead to more equity in the education system and by enabling individuals to continue their education, it can also lead to more equity through education.

Comparing the education systems of Germany and France has a long tradition. Both systems have often been analysed as contrasting cases due to institutionalised differences in educational values, norms, and regulative structures (see Deißinger, 2001; Koch, 1998; Maurice et al., 1986, Powell et al., 2012b; Schriewer, 1986), and partly even used as contrasting models in typologies of education systems (Greinert, 2005; Goldschmidt, 1991; Bernhard et al., 2015). This kind of comparison follows the logic of difference which also holds true for the analysis in this chapter since the institutionalisation of the organisational fields VET and HE and their relationship in both countries differ considerably.

The German education system is characterised by a historically evolved strong institutional division between VET and general education including HE (Baethge & Wolter, 2015), which Baethge (2006) calls 'German educational schism'. Germany is renowned for its extensive system of collective vocational skill formation. The VET system has, however, evolved mostly separate from higher education, leading to different institutional logics and forms of governance (Baethge, 2006). This strict institutional segmentation of VET and HE results in a lack of direct pathways for the individuals, meaning that transitions from VET to HE are rarely possible. The "underlying general institutional logic of segregated learning" (Powell & Solga, 2011, p. 54) in Germany, beginning in the highly tracked German school system, has solidified this divide, as each track with the respective secondary school leaving certificate leads to different options of further education. Those tracks, which end after lower secondary schooling (after nine or ten years of schooling), are traditionally designed to lead into vocational education, whereas the *Gymnasium* track, where the pupils receive the general higher education entry certificate, the *Abitur* (after twelve or thirteen years of schooling) traditionally leads into higher education.[1] In contrast to higher education, there is no specific formal certificate to access vocational education. Accessing the HE system via the vocational track has long been difficult. VET graduates usually have to re-enter the general education system and pass their Abitur. The tracking within the school system as well as afterwards into the vocational and the higher education track simultaneously leads to social segregation (Shavit & Müller, 2000). In Germany, access to HE is very socially selective (Müller et al., 2007). Thus the question of permeability is particularly crucial in education systems which can be described as highly tracked like the German one (Kerckhoff, 2001). Furthermore, qualifications or competences earned in VET or HE are often not mutually recognised. In sum, permeability throughout the German education system has been limited. European demands to increase permeability therefore present a major challenge for the German system.

The French skill formation system, which is known to be less stratified (Kerckhoff, 2001), has no strict division between HE and VET. The French system is highly differentiated and it is possible to enter HE via the vocational track of secondary schooling with the vocational baccalaureate, which was introduced in 1985, or via the recognition and validation of prior learning. Moreover, in contrast to Germany, no elaborated system of further postsecondary vocational education outside HE exists. Nonetheless, a permeability problem between HE and VET exists because students with a vocational baccalaureate may have the right to access higher education but also have systematically lower chances of graduating in HE compared to students with a technological and general baccalaureate (MESR, 2012, p. 4).[2] This problem is aggravated by the stigmatisation of secondary vocational education in France and a performance-based negative selection into the vocational track of secondary education after the *collège* (Brauns, 1998, p. 65; Brucy, 2005), where the first four years of secondary education take place. The French case thus shows that permeability is not only a question of formal access but also of providing structures that enable educational success.

However, the case selection of France and Germany cannot be explained by the different education systems alone. Both countries are also influential member states of the European Union and of the European education processes of Bologna and Copenhagen. These processes as well as the supranational European education policy are said to result in an increasing normative pressure affecting the nation states (Powell & Solga, 2010; Lawn, 2011), since they are based on an "ideational impetus" that has led and is still leading to the cross-national transfer and internationalisation of norms (Balzer & Rusconi, 2007, p. 59). This chapter will analyse to what extent this also holds true for the permeability discourse. Although it is not possible to trace direct effects of the European processes into the nation states in this analysis, it will be shown to what extent the analysed parts of the national educational policy discourses on permeability[3] resemble each other and to what extent the discourses of the main actors in the organisational fields of HE and VET in both countries have changed since the beginning of the Bologna and Copenhagen processes.

The tracing of changes in the perception of the permeability problem in France and Germany reveals the discursive construction of symbolic orders and the possibly competing politics of knowledge (Keller, 2011) regarding the permeability between HE and VET. Since permeability structures influence to what extent social groups are excluded or gain access to different education levels and fields, and thus possibly lead to social closure (Weber, 1922 [1980], p. 577), competing politics of knowledge can be expected. The question of institutional permeability can therefore be understood as a question of societal redistribution of (cultural capital) resources, which can also be put as a question on equity in and through education. In discourses, the Europeanisation processes can then be interpreted as an affirmation of existing symbolic orders or as a catalyst for change. However, comparison of the national and European discourse elements can only give a hint on the role of Europeanisation processes in this matter, since converging (discursive) structures do not automatically need to be a result of exogenous pressures like international or European processes[4] (Bernhard, 2017).

The first part of the chapter describes to what extent the topics of lifelong learning and permeability have been on the political agenda in European education policy in general and in the processes of Bologna and Copenhagen in particular. Building on sociological neo-institutionalist theories, it then discusses to what extent these might have isomorphic effects. It shows what a discourse analysis of the political educational debates based on the Sociology of Knowledge Approach to Discourse (SKAD) (Keller, 2008, 2011) can contribute to the understanding of changing permeability structures. Next, the data and methods used will be briefly described. Finally, the general understanding of what permeability means in the different contexts and the comparison of the justifications of why permeability is needed, is presented.

EUROPEANISATION PROCESSES AND LIFELONG LEARNING

In this part of the chapter, I show that the topics of further education, lifelong learning and permeability have not only been on the political agenda of the different nation states. The increasing demand for national and European policies, which favour and enhance these principles, has, in fact, also been articulated at the European level.

Beginning with the Treaties of Rome in 1957, the necessity to strengthen continuing education in the member states was emphasised in Article 118. In the Resolution on Cooperation in Education,[4] drafted in 1974, the European ministers emphasised the need for transparent educational systems and the aim to create equal opportunities in order to provide each citizen with full access to all forms of education. In the Maastricht Treaty, drafted in 1992, which was the founding treaty of the European Union, the urgent need to increase continuous education in each member state was stressed in article 127. However, the fact that the European Union has hardly any competences regarding educational policy was stipulated as well (Maastricht Treaty, Art. 126/127). Nevertheless, the topic of education has become increasingly important on the European agenda. Accordingly, 1996 was named the 'European Year of Lifelong Learning'. The objective of this year was first and foremost to foster the awareness of the importance of lifelong learning amongst the European public, to advance better cooperation between education and training structures and the business community, to enhance the academic and vocational recognition of qualifications within the European Union, and, finally, to stress the contribution made by education and training to the equality of opportunities (European Parliament & European Council, 1995).

European cooperation in educational policy was intensified with the following two intergovernmental processes: the Bologna Process for HE and the Copenhagen Process for VET. During the Bologna and Copenhagen processes the member states have met repeatedly, discussed further goals and evaluated with the help of stocktaking reports what has been achieved within the member states.

The Bologna Declaration, originally signed in 1999 by 29 European ministers, aims to establish a Europe-wide higher education area to facilitate individual mobility, qualification transparency and recognition. Many of the goals declared during the Bologna process aim directly at the fostering of a permeable educational system (Bernhard, 2017). Furthermore, one explicit aim of the process is the promotion of lifelong learning in the higher educational system. Over time the topic of lifelong learning and permeability has become more and more salient.

The Copenhagen Declaration—aiming to enhance European cooperation in vocational education and training—was signed by 31 ministers in 2002. Its goals include a unitary framework of qualifications and competencies, a system of VET credit transfer, common quality criteria and principles, as well as the improvements in citizens' access to lifelong learning. Here, permeability and lifelong learning have been on the agenda right from the beginning. In contrast to the Bologna process which developed as a consequence of the declared cooperation of four main EU-member states (Germany, Great Britain, France, Italy) in the Sorbonne Declaration 1998, the Copenhagen process was stirred by the European Commission and can be seen as a result of the Lisbon strategy that aims to make Europe the most competitive and dynamic knowledge-based economy in the world capable of sustainable economic growth with more and better jobs and greater social cohesion (Lisbon European Council, 2000).

Education in particular is seen to play a key role in achieving this goal. In order to ensure the required further qualification of European citizens, lifelong learning is declared indispensable. The Lisbon process integrates all actions in the fields of education and training at European level, including vocational education and training ('Copenhagen') as well as higher education ('Bologna'), both of which contribute actively to the achievement of the Lisbon objectives.

In May 2009, the European ministers of education adopted (with the strategic framework education and training ET 2020) the overall basis for EU-wide co-operation in education and training for the following ten years. Here, the promotion of lifelong learning was given top priority (strategic objective 1). The ministers additionally defined a goal (strategic objective 3) that aims at the establishment of a permeable educational system which especially enables citizens from disadvantaged backgrounds to complete their education and to also take part in lifelong learning (Council of the European Union, 2009).

A series of meetings of the Bologna and Copenhagen processes has advanced ideas, standards, and policies in education. Furthermore, the above review could demonstrate that Europeanisation has been gaining strength incrementally with increasing communication and programmes and processes to foster lifelong learning and permeability. Notably, nations voluntarily gave their support for the goals declared in those European declarations of the Bologna (and Copenhagen) processes without the need of direct, coercive intervention by European Union supranational governance (Witte, 2006). Nevertheless, these processes result in an increasing normative pressure affecting the nation states (Powell & Solga, 2010). As Ravinet (2008) and Musselin (2009) argue, countries seem to misinterpret their own voluntary commitment to processes such as Bologna, seeing as binding and imposed European policy, especially when they are used to legitimise national reform programmes. However, the European Union still has no direct say in the educational policy of its member states. Furthermore, the processes of Bologna and Copenhagen are based on methods like the Open Method of Coordination (OMC) which has no legally binding effect on the member states. The OMC works through self-commitment by the members and is based on processes of mutual learning as well as the regular planning and examination of shared goals, so-called benchmarks (see Ravinet, 2008; Sabel & Seitlin, 2007). Benchmarks as a form of performance measure of education systems often occur in form of certain numbers, percentages or thresholds which should be met. One important part of this method is thus using data as a new technology of governance—a 'governing by numbers' (Grek, 2009).

ISOMORPHISM, DIFFUSION AND THE ROLE OF DISCOURSES

Theoretically the governance methods like the OMC can stir processes of diffusion leading to isomorphism or convergence of structures between national systems. DiMaggio and Powell (1983) originally define isomorphism as a structural equivalence of organisations within an organisational field. The concept of the organisational field refers to the totality of the actors in an institutional arena. It emphasises the relationships between the organisations, and the multitude of networks in which the organisations are located and operating. Organisational fields are:

> those organisations that, in the aggregate, constitute a recognized area of institutional life. (DiMaggio & Powell, 1983, p. 64f.)

Moreover, organisational fields are the main arenas in which new ideas, practices, procedures, and rules diffuse (DiMaggio & Powell, 1983). In this analysis, the national organisational fields of VET and HE are the focus of the analysis that aims to investigate to what extent the discourses on permeability are changing. The analysis remains at the level of the policy actors of the organisational fields and does not examine the changed practices within the organisations. Diffusion can refer to the diffusion of ideas, values, and norms, but also rules. Following this understanding, not only regulative structures or organisational standards or norms can become more similar, but also the ideas and conceptualisation of problems might converge.

Different mechanisms that lead to diffusion can be distinguished: Dobbin et al. (2007), but also Maggetti and Gilardi (2014), define quite similar mechanisms. Firstly, there may be diffusion through coercion by powerful actors or law. Having no binding consequences for the nation states, this form of diffusion is unlikely in the case of the analysed European education processes. Competition is also acknowledged as a mechanism. Successful policies are adopted in order to enable organisations or countries to compete in certain areas. In the environment of the Bologna and Copenhagen processes, competition amongst the member states is likely since the different countries are compared regarding their development and the achievement of the benchmarks. Furthermore, learning is recognised as an important mechanism of diffusion. Possible approaches to changing their own structures are derived from the experiences of other organisations and countries. As one important feature of the OMC method, best practice examples are also used in both intergovernmental processes. Finally, there is the mechanism that Dobbin et al. (2007) call social construction and which can be found, in particular, in works that follow the world-polity approach (see Ramirez, 2012). In contrast to the mechanism of learning, the symbolic level is the significant one here. Institutional changes that are to be adopted have more legitimacy if they also correspond to the cultural guiding principles of the world society and therefore fulfil environmental expectations. Lifelong learning can be seen as an example of such a cultural guiding principle.

In their study, Jakobi and Martens (2007) show how international organisations like the OECD act as agents of diffusion by expanding the relevant organisational field, which is situated in the national sphere, in particular with regard to education policy, to the international level. International organisations create structures "in order to constitute a field and thus to initiate long-term alignment processes between the states" (Jakobi & Martens, 2007, p. 250). The development of shared goals, an "increase in the amount of information on a specific topic" and the "intensification of interaction" (Jakobi & Martens, 2007, p. 250) are a prerequisite for the constitution of the extended organisational field. If these assumptions made by Jakobi and Martens with regard to the OECD are applied to the European processes of Bologna and Copenhagen, these structural characteristics can also be identified. Firstly, common objectives and the ways to achieve them are set within the European processes in the declarations and communiqués. Secondly, these conferences, as well as the established working groups on various topics and their regular meetings, result in increased interaction of various actors. Not only the governments of the member states but also the national stakeholders in the fields of vocational and higher education have been integrated into the process (Walter, 2006). Finally, various forms of information exchange are institutionalised in the Bologna and Copenhagen processes. On the one hand, this is done through the national reports, in which the countries represent their progress with regard to the jointly adopted benchmarks. Best practice examples from the countries are also presented and, in the end, the institutionalised working meetings are themselves places where ideas and information about, for example, the possibilities for credit transfer are exchanged. The education processes of Bologna and Copenhagen thus fulfil the theoretical prerequisites so that a diffusion of ideas, norms, and policies within the 'extended' organisational field of the national education systems can take place.

However, to what extent influences such as the European education processes or singular events lead to change, depends on how they are discussed or whether they are discussed at all. At this point, the role of the discursive production of reality becomes obvious because only if factors are used discursively or interpreted to create new ideas and models, do they have an effect (Schmidt & Radaelli, 2004).

Foucault defines discourses as "practices which systematically form the objects of which they speak" (Foucault, 1981, p. 74). These collective practices of knowledge production are situated in the respective historical and societal context, producing, reproducing and transforming world and reality orders. Or as Keller (2011, p. 46) puts it: "Discourses are considered as historically situated 'real' social practices, not representing external objects but constituting them". They provide knowledge in the long term and also contribute to the transformation and dissolution of institutionalised interpretations (Keller, 2006, p. 131). Discourses are thus "regulated practices of interpretive production and construction of reality" (Keller, 2006, p. 125).

This construction is always connected to a historically situated power constellation. The social stock of knowledge must be conceived as being in constant motion. There is not only one interpretation of reality. The distribution of power and the interests of social groups are decisive in establishing which competing interpretation becomes hegemonic and crystallised in institutions. In discourses, therefore, institutional actors determine the essential elements of the symbolic order of a society and thus their understanding of reality. This production and mediation of interpretive offerings is always subject to conflict (see Schwap-Trapp, 2001) because the interpretations produce guidelines for political and social action and decide how they are perceived and evaluated. They legitimise social and political action, but also institutions.

Following this outlined understanding of discourse put forward by Keller's 'Sociology of Knowledge Approach to Discourse (SKAD)' (Keller, 2011, 2008), I analyse in this chapter the discourse about permeability between HE and VET. The aim is to trace possible changes of the knowledge structure, but also understand to what extent the national discourses and the European one, that are put forward in the declarations and communiqués of the Bologna and Copenhagen processes, are similar or differ.

DATA AND METHODS

In this part of the chapter I will briefly describe how the national and European discourses were analysed and which materials I used.[5] To adequately portray the discursive developments, I analysed two different time periods. One period was before the initiation of the processes of Bologna and Copenhagen, starting in France in 1985 with the creation of the vocational baccalaureate and in Germany in 1990 with the reunification, and one starts in 1999 with the beginning of the Bologna process. The analysis ends in 2012.

At the centre of the empirical analysis is the discourse analysis according to SKAD (see Keller, 2006, 2008) which is based on 256 key documents with references to the permeability problematic at the national level.[6] These documents are the position papers of the main actors of the two organisational fields of HE and VET in Germany and France. My analysis focuses on the coordinated discourse space according to the differentiation of Schmidt (2008). The coordinative discourse space is supported by actors who are at the centre of policy formulation and who are involved in the further development of programmes and policies (Schmidt, 2008). In this study, the position papers of the ministries of education, employer associations, trade unions, and associations of higher education institutions were analysed. Since in Germany HE policy is mostly governed by the federal states, I also selected position papers of the Standing Conference of the Ministers of Education and Cultural Affairs of the Länder.[7]

According to Keller (2011) the analysis of discourses can focus on different elements; in this chapter the focus is on parts of the so-called phenomenal structure, which consists of those components that are necessary for a topic to be constructed as a problem in the public agenda (Keller, 2011). These elements give answers, for example, to the following questions: What is the problem? Why is it a problem? What should be done to solve it? Who should do it? Who should benefit? In this chapter, emphasis lies on the first two questions: the conceptualisation of the problem of permeability and the reasons for dealing with it. The analysis is based on a "mosaic" of analysed documents that only together allow the reconstruction of the structures of knowledge and meaning (Keller, 2011). The concrete textual analysis as well as the selection of documents to be analysed was informed by Grounded Theory Methodology (Strauss & Corbin, 1996).[8]

To analyse the political discourse on permeability between HE and VET at the European level, I used a theory-guided qualitative content analysis (Gläser & Laudel, 2009) of the English-language versions of the Bologna and Copenhagen declarations and conference communiqués.[9] This form of qualitative content analysis (Gläser & Laudel, 2009) specifies categories beforehand but at the same time also permits an inductive extension of categories in the step-by-step process of the analysis. In this case, the leading categories and linked questions were: which problems with regard to the different permeability dimensions (Bernhard, 2017) are addressed and what are the justifications for a supposed need of permeability?

Representing the results of the deliberative negotiation of the involved stakeholders rather than the position of a specific actor, the European documents embody a compromise of joint goals, problem perceptions, and ideas of how to develop the European space of education. It is assumed that due to this deliberative origin, the agreed upon standards and ideals serve as a model of diffusion and can be more easily legitimised at the national level (Powell et al., 2012a). In a final step, I compare the European understanding with the national conceptualisations.

DISCOURSES ON PERMEABILITY BETWEEN HE AND VET IN EUROPEAN AND NATIONAL POLITICAL EDUCATION DEBATES

Relevance of the Permeability Discourse

Before the conceptualisations of permeability and the justification patterns are presented[10] and compared, this section gives an overview of the overall relevance of the topic in the national education debates.

The analysed documents show that the question of permeability between HE and VET is much more prominent in the German education policy debates than in the French ones. In the first period, before the beginning of the European processes, there was hardly any debate about it in France. The only topic which came up was that higher education institutions (HEI) should be more open for work-experienced vocationally qualified individuals (Bernhard, 2017). Further education should thus be supported. Graduates with a vocational baccalaureate, who already had the right to enter HE, were not mentioned as a group which should be dealt with in HE.

In Germany, however, the topic of permeability between HE and VET was increasingly discussed in the years between 1990–1998. I identified two discourse strands (Bernhard, 2017). One strand, which I call structural-critical, favours more permeability between HE and VET and emphasises the need for reform. The other strand, which I call structural-conservative, emphasises the risk of changing the education structures to a more permeable system: The access to HE for vocationally qualified non-traditional students might endanger the quality of HE teaching and research and squander the resources on students who are presented as not capable of or not sufficiently prepared for studying. Interestingly, the argumentation of the structural-conservative discourse strand remains about the same over the two analysed periods but it gets weaker in comparison to the structural-critical one in the second analytical period (Bernhard, 2017). So in contrast to the rare French debates on permeability, the debates in Germany were strongly contested between the two discourse strands.

Looking at the period from 1999 till 2012, when the Europeanisation processes set in, the topic of permeability between HE and VET became even more salient in Germany. This also holds true for the French educational policy debates. Here, especially the decrease in HE drop-outs of vocational baccalaureate graduates has become the main focus. Still, the question of permeability in general was much less discussed in France than in Germany. Looking at the European documents, the question of permeability between HE and VET also became more prominent over time, especially with the start of the Copenhagen process, where permeability became an explicit goal (Bernhard, 2017).

Conceptualisation of Permeability

What is understood by the term permeability in the different national discourses?

Analytically, the concept of permeability[11] can be differentiated along four dimensions (Bernhard, 2017): The *first* dimension is access to educational sectors/organisations. The *second* dimension is the question of recognition and validation of learning from other educational sectors. Here it is assumed that equivalent competencies can be gained via different learning pathways, e.g. learning in VET or HE. The *third* dimension includes the organisational linkage between educational sectors, e.g. the integration of (vocational and academic) curricula in one programme or a double qualification. Permeability is then promoted by a deliberate breaking of the separation of education sectors through the institutionalisation of typical logics, norms, and rules for both education sectors in one organisation or education course (Graf, 2013). The *fourth* dimension of permeability includes institutional structures which aim to meet the diverse needs of learners. This is to show that permeability should not only enable transitions between educational sectors, but also allow for a successful completion of the course. Examples of these structures might be information and guidance structures, financial aid, differentiated pedagogics and the culture of an organisation that can be either more closed or open towards new groups of learners.

In Germany, before 1999, permeability was mainly discussed as a question of access to HE and to some degree the discourse was about the development of organisational linkages in the form of dual study programmes.[12] In France, permeability was only conceptualised as getting access to HE by recognising vocational competencies of vocationally qualified individuals with work experience (Bernhard, 2017).

In the period after 1999, the narrowly used understanding of permeability in Germany changed to a multidimensional conceptualisation (Bernhard, 2017): whether access should be provided at all was discussed less, but rather who or which group of the vocationally qualified individuals should be entitled to enter HE and who gets to decide on access regulations. In the discourse on permeability now also the question of recognition and validation of vocational competences in HEI was discussed. This is a major shift in discourse since the critics of permeability have been traditionally questioning the VET graduates' overall ability to study. Now learning in VET programmes or work experience is acknowledged to even lead to equivalent competences to the ones gained in HE. With this new element of the permeability conceptualisation the equal value, the parity of esteem of competences gained in VET and HE gets discursively and thus socially constructed.

Organisational linkages, especially dual study programmes, are also discussed as a way to increase permeability. Finally, the existing study structures, which only focus on the needs of traditional students, are questioned. Changes to the structures, e.g. increase in part-time study possibilities or guidance and information offers in order to better fit the diverse needs of the student body are increasingly discussed.

After 1999, also in France all four dimensions are tackled when discussing the permeability between HE and VET (Bernhard, 2017). In the French discourse the support of heterogeneous needs of the students is especially important. More support, information and guidance structures for (vocationally qualified) students at risk are demanded. One aim is that school graduates with a vocational baccalaureate who enter higher education (even though this type of baccalaureate is still regarded more a labour market entry certificate) get help to find the appropriate study programme and to finish their studies. Moreover it is argued that vocationally qualified students should be able to enter the selective vocational HE programmes (like in the IUT and the BTS)[13] linking VET and HE instead of going to the non-selective purely academic university programmes for which they are not prepared. In the French HE system, it is only access to university that is non-selective. The consequence was that graduates with a technological or general baccalaureate (which are more highly regarded in comparison to the vocational one) are preferred in the selective programmes even though they are vocationally oriented (Beaud, 2008). Finally, it can be said that in France, even though graduates with a vocational baccalaureate formally have already had the right to enter higher education since 1985, in the discourse they only got recognised as a legitimate student group after 1999 (Bernhard, 2017).

In the European documents all four dimensions of permeability were also discussed. However, the propositions on how to implement these structures have been rather unspecific. Access to HE should be provided especially for those who are described as capable (Berlin Communiqué, 2003). The question of recognising and validating learning in VET and HE which is formally, non-formally, or informally gained has been a major issue in both processes (Bergen Communiqué, 2005; Maastricht Communiqué, 2004). Integrating more work-based experiences in HE was also discussed and also more guidance and information structures to help learners were continuously demanded (Bergen Communiqué, 2005; Bruges Communiqué, 2010). Likewise a shift of pedagogy to a learner-centred approach is seen as important to help the learners to graduate (Maastricht Communiqué, 2004).

When comparing the conceptualisations of permeability at the national and European level, the main finding is that, increasingly, all four dimensions of permeability are discussed during the second time period. In France and in Germany the conceptualisation gets more similar, but still different foci of the discourses persist.

Permeability Perceived as Necessity or Right

In analysing the discourses, it became clear that the need for more permeability was justified either by functionalist or by universalistic arguments. Improving the permeability between HE and VET is thus perceived in the national pro-permeability discourses and the European documents as a question either of necessity or a question of individual (human) rights.

It is not insignificant to look at how reforms are justified because functionalist and universalistic argumentations reveal different logics and implications for reforms. When arguing for a reform process like introducing permeability between HE and VET from a functionalist point of view, the reform is presented as a functional necessity, for example on the basis of certain societal developments. When this context changes the reform might be reversed or stopped because the necessity is no longer given. Reforms, however, which are justified mainly by universalistic rights-based arguments are less likely to be reversed as easily due to the high legitimacy and stability of universal human rights (in western democracies). But it is not only a question of how sustainable educational reforms are, but also of the actual measures which are taken to implement the reforms. These possible measures, however, are not disconnected from the justifications (Bernhard, 2017). In Germany for example, there were several occasions in the last century when, due to perceived labour market needs (a functional argument), access to HE was partly opened for so-called non-traditional students. This opening took always place via exceptional pathways like introduction of an extra examination (Schwabe-Ruck, 2010). A general entitlement for the access to HE for vocational certificates as an equivalent of a rights-based implementation was not introduced before 2009.

In the German structural conservative discourse only functionalist arguments are used to emphasise the possible risks of permeability: the reduction of the quality of higher education or a waste of resources for the vocationally qualified students who are expected to drop out. In the following, the analysis for the German case only will focus on the structural critical discourse favouring permeability.

In table 1 the main functionalist arguments in favour of more permeability can be seen. These were relatively similar in France and Germany before 1999 (Bernhard, 2017). In both countries, permeability between HE and VET aims at satisfying the labour market needs, which are said to have changed due to a structural change of the economy. However, in Germany, reforms should lead to more vocationally qualified workers whereas in France more academically qualified workers were said to be needed. The rationale behind an increase of permeability in Germany was thus mainly to increase the attractiveness of the German VET system by signalling that a VET certificate can enable further education and is not an impasse. In both national debates permeable education structures should reduce the unemployment risk of individuals and offer the chance to continue learning and enable educational and career mobility (Bernhard, 2017).

Looking at the period 1999 to 2012, the argumentation is very similar in Germany and the European documents and to a great extent also in France (Bernhard, 2017). A structural change of the economy and a demographic change are perceived to lead to changed labour market needs. In the national and European discourses, more permeability should lead to more academic qualified workers. In France permeability should also increase the attractiveness of VET and increase the number of students interested in secondary vocational education. Compared to the period before 1999 in Germany this argumentation was less important. In the German discourse in contrast to the French one, the European processes of Bologna and Copenhagen are used to justify the need for educational reforms. In both countries, permeable structures are understood as helpful for individuals to continue learning in order to increase their employability, reduce their risk of unemployment, and develop their careers (see Table 1).

Table 1. Functionalist arguments in the national and European discourse favouring permeability

Functionalist arguments (pro permeability)	1990–1998		1999–2012		
	DE	FR	DE	FR	BoCo
Labour market needs (more vocationally skilled workers)	x			x	
Labour market needs (more academically skilled workers)		x	x	x	x
Structural change of economy	x	x	x	x	x
Economic Competition (EU/Global)	(x)		x	x	x
Demographic change			x		x
External/European requirements			x		
Reduction of unemployment risk	x	x	x	x	
Individual Career development	x		x	x	
Employability			x		x

x relevant argumentation; (x) argumentation hardly occurred

Compared to the functionalist arguments, the ones which I call universalistic were much less important in the German discourse, extremely rare in the European documents, but very important in the French case (Bernhard, 2017). Before 1999, the main universalistic arguments (see also Table 2) in both countries supporting permeability reforms were to increase equality of opportunity in the education system (Bernhard, 2017). Moreover it was argued that a permeable education system is essential to implement the right to education and that education is a public good and everybody needs to have the opportunity to continue learning. In France, permeability between HE and VET was also discussed as a way to allow for a second chance of getting an academic degree and thus decreasing social inequality in society. In Germany, a permeable education system should lead to more parity of esteem between VET and HE.

After 1999, the arguments generally stayed the same but were extended. Permeability between HE and VET was primarily discussed as a means to ensure equality of opportunity and to increase social cohesion in society and simultaneously decrease social inequality. Increasingly, the parity of esteem between VET and HE via permeability reforms is now also demanded in France and to some extent

Table 2. Universalistic arguments in the national and European discourse favouring permeability

Universalistic arguments (pro permeability)	1990–1998 DE	1990–1998 FR	1999–2012 DE	1999–2012 FR	1999–2012 BoCo
Equality of opportunity	x	x	x	x	x
Parity of esteem btw. VET and HE	x		x	x	(x)
(Further) education as a right	x	x	x	x	
Social cohesion			x	x	x
Decrease social inequality		x	x	x	(x)
Education as a public good	x	x	x	x	
Implementation of republican ideals				x	
Education of democratic citizen				x	(x)
Democratisation of HE				x	
Meritocracy				x	

x relevant argumentation; (x) argumentation hardly occurred

also in the European documents, pre-eminently in the Copenhagen process. Permeability is not discussed as being a pre-condition of education as a right in the European documents—in the French and German debate this is an important argument. Finally, especially in the French discourse the arguments in favour of permeability point to the role of education in socialising democratic citizens who should incorporate republican ideals. Moreover, in the French discourse a permeable system is seen as a precondition to democratise the HE system and to ensure that the ideal of meritocracy can be implemented (Bernhard, 2017).

CONCLUSION

In this chapter I compared how the question of permeability between HE and VET was discussed at the European level, in France, and in Germany from 1985/1990 to 2012 focusing hence on stability and change of the knowledge structure on permeability revealed in the educational policy discourses.

When comparing discourses of permeability between HE and VET the following main similarities can be identified. Firstly, the question of permeability has become more and more important in Germany, France, and the European documents. This rising awareness of barriers within the education system, that prevent educational mobility and can result in inequalities of individual life chances, is a necessary step for reforms increasing permeability which can lead to greater equity in and through education. As stated above, it is assumed that the changes in discourses which are "regulated practices of interpretive production and construction of reality" (Keller, 2006, p. 125) can lead also to the (de)legitimisation of existing institutions, in this case of educational structures and hence to perceived reform needs. The discursive change is, moreover, not only significant for the perceptions and acting of the political actors, but also for the individuals of society in general. With the increasing relevance of permeability issues in the discourse, for these, for example, studying after VET can become an actual option for action.

Secondly, a multidimensional understanding of permeability based on all four dimensions is used increasingly in all discourses. The expansion of the permeability conceptualisation is important insofar as it also offers multi-dimensional approaches to the improvement of the permeability structures. This can lead ultimately to an increased chance not only to get access to HE, but also with sufficient guidance structures and with recognition of previously learned competences successfully completing the studies without time loss.

Third the functionalist and universalistic argumentations have been to a great extent similar, even though the functionalist ones dominated the German and European debates and the universalistic ones are central in France. To what extent the growing similarities between the national discourse structure and the European documents are a direct result of the diffusion of the European processes cannot be answered here. However, the converging discourse structures may be a first hint to it, since the major changes occurred in the second period of analysis.[14]

Not only similarities but also differences were identified in the discourses. The main difference is that in Germany a structural conservative discourse could be identified which has aimed at conserving the existing separation and hierarchies between HE and VET. Secondly, in the European and German discourses the need for permeability is much more justified from a functionalistic point of view whereas in the French discourse, the universalistic argumentation is at least as important as the functionalistic one. The dominance of functionalist argumentation reveals that equity and equality of opportunities are not the main concerns of the reform demands but foremost economic needs. In consequence the main focus of possible reforms is on achieving these functionalist goals and less on achieving equity through educational reforms. Third, the universalistic arguments in France go beyond the arguments of the German and European discourse.

The differences, especially between the German and French discourse structures, are only comprehensible against the background of the national historical development of education systems (Bernhard, 2017). In Germany, for example, the traditional division between HE and VET, which is interlinked with a hierarchical symbolic order between VET and HE, is mirrored in the division between structural-critical and structural-conservative discourse. So it is not surprising that in particular the political actors representing the organisational field of general and higher education in Germany have been warning about the risks of opening the access to HE (Bernhard, 2017). Also in France, a long tradition of referring to the role of education as a democratising device and as the means to achieve social mobility and equality exists (Brauns, 1998; Dobbins, 2011). That is a reason why this universalistic argumentation has been important in the discourses.

However, a universalistic framing alone is not sufficient for achieving the goal of equality of opportunity and equity (Bernhard, 2017). An example is the "myth" of the baccalaureate (Duru-Bellat, 2007). In France, any certificate called baccalaureate "must" give access to HE and strongly symbolises the chance of educational mobility by entering higher education (Duru-Bellat, 2007). The creation of the vocational baccalaureate in 1985 originally only aimed at signalling parity of esteem between technological, general, and vocational education and to stop the trend of stigmatisation of VET (Brucy, 2005). In contrast to the symbolic name of the certificate, the programme was foremost created as a labour market entry certificate and was not supposed to prepare the students to enter HE. Hence, the curriculum of the vocational baccalaureate was not created for this task and also the HE organisations were not prepared to deal adequately with the new group of students. In the students' perceptions, however, the societal myth of the baccalaureate and the associated expectations have been transferred to the vocational baccalaureate which has led to an increasing number of graduates entering HE with a high risk of drop out. This example shows, on the one hand, the efficacy of social myths. However, it also shows that reforms must not be allowed to remain on the discourse level, but also that one-dimensional regulatory changes alone can lead to unintended effects. In order for institutional permeability to take effect, adaptation is needed in educational organisations as well, which includes the institutional structures of the organisations and the practices of the actors therein. Discursive changes are hence necessary but not sufficient conditions for institutional changes towards more permeability in the education system and towards more equity in and through education.

ACKNOWLEDGEMENTS

This chapter draws to a large extend on the empirical analysis of my dissertation (Bernhard, 2017) which was supported by the Deutsche Forschungsgemeinschaft [SO 430/5-1]. The author also would like to thank Camilla Addey (Humboldt-Universität, Germany), Stephen Carney (Roskilde University, Denmark) and Michele Schweisfurth (University of Glasgow, Scotland).

NOTES

[1] With the increasing academisation of VET some VET courses in Germany are now also only accessible with the Abitur.
[2] 56% of students with a vocational baccalaureate dropped out of higher education compared to only 29% with a technological and 9% with a general baccalaureate (MESR, 2012: 4)
[3] A much more differentiated analysis of the national permeability discourses looking not only at justifications but the whole phenomenal structures, interpretative schemes and subject positions can be read in Bernhard (2017).
[4] The European processes like Bologna and Copenhagen cannot be simply characterized as exogenous since the different stakeholders of the member states are involved in the shaping process.
[5] This chapter draws on a larger dissertation project in which the research design and the concrete proceedings of the analysis are described in detail (Bernhard, 2017).

6. The list of the analysed documents can be found in Bernhard (2017).
7. Analyzed stakeholders in Germany were the following: Bundesministerium für Bildung und Forschung (BMBF), Kultusministerkonferenz (KMK), Hochschulrektorenkonferenz (HRK), Deuscher Gewerkschaftsbund (DGB), Deutscher Industrie- und Handelskammertag. The French stakeholders were: Assemblée des Directeurs d'Instituts Universitaires de Technologie (ADIUT), Confédération générale du travail (CGT), Conférence des présidents d'université (CPU), Fédération syndicale unitaire, Ministère de l'éducation nationale (MEN), Ministère chargé de la recherche et de l'enseignement supérieur (MESR), Ministère délégué à l'enseignement professionnel (MDEP), Mouvement des entreprises de France (MEDEF).
8. For a more detailed description of the analyses see Bernhard (2017).
9. The analyzed Bologna process documents are the following: Sorbonne Declaration (1998), Bologna Declaration (1999), Prague Communique´ (2001), Berlin Communique´ (2003), Bergen Communique´ (2005), London Communique´ (2007), Leuven/Louvain-la-Neuve Communique´ (2009), Budapest/Vienna Declaration (2010) and Bucharest Communiqué (2012). The Copenhagen process documents are the following: Copenhagen Declaration (2002), Maastricht Communique´ (2004), Helsinki Communique´ (2006), and Bordeaux Communique´(2008) and Bruges Communiqué (2010).
10. The presentation of the empirical results in this chapter draws on the in-depth discourse analysis of the German and French Case study as well as on the analysis of the European documents in my dissertation (Bernhard, 2017). So the results should be understood as a summary of these analyses.
11. This concept was developed on the basis of the analysis of existing German (mainly) literature on permeability between HE and VET.
12. Dual study programmes combine elements of VET and HE like curricula, teaching staff and funding, and systematically connect and coordinate the learning environments of HEI and the firm. In Germany these programmes began to develop in the 1970s and have been increasingly expanding since 2000 (Graf, 2013).
13. Both organisations the sections de technician supérieur (STS) and the instituts universitaire de technologie (IUT) offer vocationally oriented, two-year short courses in HE.
14. Due to the circular nature of the governance structure of the Bologna and Copenhagen processes, the influence of Europeanisation cannot to be regarded as purely exogenous. Before all, the national actors themselves are the ones, who influence the progress of the processes.

REFERENCES

Baethge, M. (2006). *Das deutsche Bildungs-Schisma: Welche Probleme ein vorindustrielles Bildungssystem in einer nachindustriellen Gesellschaft hat (SOFI-Mitteilungen No. 34)* (pp. 13–27). Retrieved from http://www.sofi-goettingen.de/fileadmin/SOFI-Mitteilungen/Nr._34/Baethge.pdf

Baethge, M., & Wolter, A. (2015). The German skill formation model in transition: From dual system of VET to higher education? *Journal for Labour Market Research, 48*(2), 97–112.

Balzer, C., & Rusconi, A. (2007). From the European commission to the member states and back: A comparison of the Bologna and the Copenhagen process. In K. Martens, A. Rusconi, & K. Leuze (Eds.), *New arenas of education governance: The impact of international organizations and markets on educational policy making* (pp. 57–75). Basingstoke: Palgrave.

Beaud, S. (2008). Enseignement supérieur: La "démocratisation scolaire" en panne. *Formation Emploi, 101*, 149–165. Retrieved from http://formationemploi.revues.org/index1146.html

Bergen Communiqué. (2005, May 19–20). *The European higher education area.* Achieving the Goals Communiqué of the Conference of European Ministers Responsible for Higher Education, Bergen.

Berlin Communiqué. (2003, September 19). *Realising the European higher education area.* Communiqué of the Conference of Ministers responsible for Higher Education, Berlin.

Bernhard, N. (2017). *Durch Europäisierung zu mehr Durchlässigkeit? Veränderungsdynamiken des Verhältnisses von Berufs- und Hochschulbildung in Deutschland und Frankreich.* Opladen: Budrich UniPress Ltd.

Bernhard, N., Graf, L., & Powell, J. J. W. (2015). Stratifizierung von Berufs- und Hochschulbildung in Europa: Deutschland und Frankreich im Spiegel klassischer Vergleichsstudien. In A. Dietzen, J. J. W. Powell, A. Bahl, & L. Lassnigg (Eds.), *Soziale Inwertsetzung von Wissen, Erfahrung und Kompetenz in der Berufsbildung* (pp. 144–159). Weinheim: Beltz Juventa.

Brauns, H. (1998). *Bildung in Frankreich. Eine Studie zum Wandel herkunfts- und geschlechtsspezifischen Bildungsverhaltens.* Opladen: Leske & Budrich.

Brucy, G. (2005). L'enseignement technique et professionnel français. *Cahiers de la Recherche Sur l'Éducation et les Savoirs*, (4), 13–34. Retrieved from http://journals.openedition.org/cres/1226

Bruges Communiqué. (2010). *The Bruges communiqué on enhanced European co-operation in vocational education and training for the period 2011–2020.* Retrieved from http://ec.europa.eu/education/lifelong-learning-policy/doc/vocational/bruges_en.pdf

Council of the European Union. (2009). *Council conclusions on a strategic framework for European co-operation in education and training ("ET 2020").* Retrieved from http://www.consilium.europa.eu/uedocs/cms_data/docs/pressdata/en/educ/107622.pdf

Deißinger, T. (2001). Zur Frage nach der Bedeutung des Berufsprinzips als "organisierendes Prinzip" der deutschen Berufsausbildung im europäischen Kontext: Eine deutsch-französische Vergleichsskizze. *Tertium Comparationis, 7*(1), 1–18.

DiMaggio, P. J., & Powell, W. W. (1983). The iron cage revisited: Institutional isomorphism and collective rationality in organizational fields. In P. J. DiMaggio & W. W. Powell (Eds.), *The new institutionalism in organizational analysis* (pp. 63–83). Chicago, IL: University of Chicago Press.

Dobbin, F., Simmons, B., & Garrett, G. (2007). The global diffusion of public policies: Social construction, coercion, competition, or learning? *Annual Review of Sociology, 33*, 449–472.

Dobbins, M. (2011). *Französische Hochschulpolitik: Wandel durch Internationalisierung?* (TranState Working Papers No. 152). Bremen: Universität Bremen.

Duru-Bellat, M. (2007). *L'orientation dans le système éducatif français, au collège et au lycée.* Retrieved from http://www.hce.education.fr/gallery_files/site/21/52.pdf

European Parliament & European Council. (1995). European Parliament and council decision n° 95/2493/EC of 23 October 1995 establishing 1996 as the European Year of Lifelong Learning.

Foucault, M. (1981). *Archäologie des wissens.* Frankfurt am Main: Suhrkamp.

Gläser, J., & Laudel, G. (2009). *Experteninterviews und qualitative Inhaltsanalyse als Instrumente rekonstruierender Untersuchungen* (3., überarb. Aufl. ed.). Wiesbaden: VS Verlag für Sozialwissenschaften.

Goldschmidt, D. (1991). Idealtypische Charakerisierung sieben westlicher Hochschulsyteme. *Zeitschrift für Sozialforschung und Erziehungssoziologie, 11*(1), 3–17.

Graf, L. (2013). *The hybridization of vocational training and higher education in Austria, Germany and Switzerland.* Opladen: Budrich UniPress.

Greinert, W.-D. (2005). *Mass vocational education and training in Europe.* Luxembourg: Office for Official Publications of the European Communities. Retrieved from http://languageforwork.ecml.at/Portals/48/ICT_REV_LFW/CEDEFOP_History-of-VET.pdf

Grek, S. (2009). Governing by numbers: The Pisa "Effect" in Europe. *Journal of Education Policy, 24*(1), 23–37.

Hillmert, S. (2010). *Cumulative inequality along the life course: Long-term trends on the German labour market* (ESOC Working Paper 1/2010). Tübingen: University of Tübingen.

Jakobi, A. P., & Martens, K. (2007). Diffusion durch internationale Organisationen: Die Bildungspolitik der OECD. In K. Holzinger, H. Jörgens, & C. Knill (Eds.), *Transfer, diffusion und konvergenz von politiken* (pp. 247–270). Wiesbaden: VS Verlag für Sozialwissenschaften.

Keller, R. (2006). Wissenssoziologische Diskursanalyse. In R. Keller, A. Hirseland, W. Schneider, & W. Viehöver (Eds.), *Handbuch Sozialwissenschaftliche Diskursanalyse. Band 1: Theorien und Methoden* (pp. 115–146). Opladen: Leske+Budrich.

Keller, R. (2008). *Wissenssoziologische Diskursanalyse. Grundlegung eines Forschungsprogramms.* Wiesbaden: VS-Verlag für Sozialwissenschaften.

Keller, R. (2011). The Sociology of Knowledge Approach to Discourse (SKAD). *Human Studies, 34*(1), 43–65.

Kerckhoff, A. C. (2001). Education and social stratification processes in comparative perspective. *Sociology of Education, 74*(Extra Issue), 3–18.

Koch, R. (1998). *Duale und schulische Berufsbildung zwischen Bildungsnachfrage und Qualifiokationsbedarf. Ein deutsch-französischer Vergleich.* Bielefeld:

Lawn, M. (2011). Standardizing the European education policy space. *European Educational Research Journal, 10*(2), 259–272.

Lisbon European Council. (2000, March 23–24). *Presidency conclusions.* Brussels: Lisbon European Council.

Maastricht Communiqué. (2004). *Maastricht communiqué on the future priorities of enhanced European co-operation in Vocational Education and Training (VET): Review of the copenhagen declaration of 30 November 2002.* Retrieved from https://www.google.co.in/url?sa=t&rct=j&q=&esrc=s&source=web&cd=3&ved=0ahUKEwjzrdXzucDYAhUQw2MKHRFDAmkQFggvMAI&url=http%3A%2F%2Fwww.cedefop.europa.eu%2Ffiles%2Fcommunique_maastricht_priorities_vet.pdf&usg=AOvVaw0fNFjZL7SdT-QbIqgm_xJg

Maggetti, M., & Gilardi, F. (2014). *How policies spread: A meta-analysis of diffusion mechanisms.* Retrieved from http://citeseerx.ist.psu.edu/viewdoc/download?doi=10.1.1.397.3637&rep=rep1&type=pdf

Maurice, M., Sellier, F., & Silvestre, J.-J. (1986). *The social foundations of industrial power: A comparison of France and Germany.* Cambridge, MA: The MIT Press.

Mayer, K. U. (2004). Whose lives? How history, societies and institutions define and shape life courses. *Research in Human Development, 1*(3), 161–187.

Mayer, K. U., Müller, W., & Pollak, R. (2007). Germany: Institutional change and inequalities of access in higher education. In Y. Shavit, R. Arum, & A. Gamoran (Eds.), *Stratification in higher education: A comparative study* (pp. 240–265). Stanford, CA: Stanford University Press.

MESR. (2012). *Les bacheliers professionnels dans l'enseignement supérieur* (Note d'information n°12.04, juin 2012).

Musselin, C. (2009). The side effects of the Bologna process on national institutional settings: The case of France. In A. Amaral, G. Neave, C. Musselin, & P. Maasen (Eds.), *European integration and the governance of higher education and research* (pp. 181–205). Dordrecht: Springer.

Powell, J. J. W., Bernhard, N., & Graf, L. (2012a). The emerging European model in skill formation: Comparing higher education and vocational training in the Bologna and Copenhagen processes. *Sociology of Education, 85*(3), 240–258.

Powell, J. J. W., Graf, L., Bernhard, N., Coutrot, L., & Kieffer, A. (2012b). The shifting relationship between vocational and higher education in France and Germany: Towards convergence? *European Journal of Education, 47*(3), 405–423.

Powell, J. J. W., & Solga, H. (2010). Analyzing the nexus of higher education and vocational training in Europe: A comparative-institutional framework. *Studies in Higher Education, 35*(6), 705–721.

Powell, J. J. W., & Solga, H. (2011). Why are participation rates in higher education in Germany so low? Institutional barriers to higher education expansion. *Journal of Education and Work, 24*(1–2), 49–68.

Ramirez, F. O. (2012). The world society perspective: Concepts, assumptions, and strategies. *Comparative Education, 48*(4), 423–439.

Ravinet, P. (2008). From voluntary participation to monitored co-ordination: Why European countries feel increasingly bound by their commitment to the Bologna process. *European Journal of Education, 43*(3), 353–367.

Rogers, E. M. (1995). *Diffusion of innovation.* New York, NY: The Free Press.

Sabel, C. F., & Zeitlin, J. (2007). Learning from difference: The new architecture of experimentalist governance in the EU. *European Law Journal, 14*(3), 271–327.

Schmidt, V. A. (2008). Discursive institutionalism: The explanatory power of ideas and discourse. *Annual Review of Political Science, 11*(1), 303–326.

Schmidt, V. A., & Radaelli, C. M. (2004). Policy change and discourse in Europe: Conceptual and methodological issues. *West European Politics, 27*(2), 183–210.

Schriewer, J. (1986). Intermediäre Instanzen, Selbstverwaltung und berufliche Ausbildungsstrukturen im historischen Vergleich. *Zeitschrift für Pädagogik, 32*(1), 69–90.

Schwabe-Ruck, E. (2010). *"Zweite Chance" des Hochschulzugangs*. Düsseldorf: Hans-Böckler-Stiftung.
Schwap-Trapp, M. (2001). Diskurs als soziologisches konzept: Bausteine für eine soziologisch orientierte diskursanalyse. In R. Keller, A. Hirseland, W. Schneider, & W. Viehöver (Eds.), *Handbuch sozialwissenschaftliche diskursanalyse. Band 1: Theorien und methoden* (pp. 263–286). Opladen: Leske+Budrich.
Shavit, Y., & Müller, W. (2000). Vocational secondary education: Where diversion and where savety net? *European Societies, 2*(1), 29–50.
Solga, H., Berger, P. A., & Powell, J. J. W. (2009). Soziale Ungleichheit – Kein Schnee von gestern! Eine Einführung. In H. Solga, P. A. Berger, & J. J. W. Powell (Eds.), *Soziale Ungleichheit – Klassische Texte zur Sozialstrukturanalyse* (pp. 11–45). Frankfurt: Campus.
Strauss, A., & Corbin, J. (1996). *Grounded Theory: Grundlagen Qualitativer Sozialforschung* (Original: Basics of qualitative research: Grounded theory procedures and technique [1990]). Weinheim: Beltz, Psychologie Verlags Union.
Walter, T. (2006). *Der Bologna-Prozess. Ein Wendepunkt europäischer Hochschulpolitik*. Wiesbaden: VS Verlag für Sozialwissenschaften.
Weber, M. (1922 [1980]). *Wirtschaft und Gesellschaft: Grundriß der verstehenden Soziologie*. Tübingen: Mohr.
Witte, J. (2006). *Change of degrees and degrees of change: Comparing adaptations of European higher education systems in the context of the Bologna process* (Doctoral thesis). Center for Higher Education Policy Studies (CHEPS), University of Twente, Enschede.

Nadine Bernhard
Institute for Comparative and International Education
Humboldt-Universität
Berlin, Germany

JAN MCGHIE

7. MENTORING IN WIDENING ACCESS TO HIGHER EDUCATION

INTRODUCTION

Widening access to higher education for young people from areas of social and economic disadvantage has become a prominent policy issue in Scotland. Researchers have investigated the efficacy of interventions aimed at addressing the under-representation of this group, but few have focused on the use of student mentors as role models to these young people. 'Mentoring' is seen as a quick and cost-effective solution to redress the inequality gap, but little is understood about different models of mentoring and how they could be used to their full potential within inclusion initiatives.

The primary focus of this research is on student mentoring programmes as part of 'widening access'[1] intervention strategies, which address the under-representation of young people from areas of social and economic disadvantage in higher education. The study aims to explore the impact of using student mentors as facilitators within a subject-specific summer programme and to investigate if engagement with mentors influences a young person's decision to apply to and enter higher education. Furthermore, the research aims to examine the nature of the mentor-pupil relationship created and establish the mentors' perception of their impact on the young people they work with.

Rationale

Despite encouraging progress in recent years, current statistics indicate that progression to higher education of young people from the most deprived areas in Scotland[2] still requires attention:

Table 1. Young Scottish-domiciled entrants to full-time undergraduate courses at the Scottish HEIs, 2013–14 to 2015–16 (Scottish Funding Council, 2017)

	2013–2014	2014–2015	2015–2016
Percentage of entrants from the 20% most deprived areas	10.4%	10.8%	10.4%
Percentage of entrants from the 40% most deprived areas	24.5%	25.2%	24.8%

The statistics highlight the need for greater equity in accessing higher education and the associated benefits that young people from more disadvantaged backgrounds are likely to miss out on, such as, "better employment and healthier lifestyle prospects resulting in greater contributions to public budgets and investment" (OECD, 2012, p. 9).

An area emerging as a popular strategy for sharing information and knowledge is by using current University students as 'mentors' to engage young people about the benefits and expectations of higher education. Little examination into the use of mentors as role models has been conducted and this is linked to concerns regarding a lack of rigorous research, which is holding back progression in widening access and similarly, mentoring. With higher education policy currently under scrutiny and funding bodies seeking best value for money from widening access interventions, it is now highly appropriate to consider the potential value and influence of mentors and the unique mentor-pupil relationships.

Four key questions led the research conducted:

- What does research in the field of widening access inform us about the potential for student mentoring?
- What is the perceived value to participants of using mentors on the Accelerate summer programme?
- What is the perceived impact of engagement with mentors on the decision to apply to and enter higher education?
- What are the implications for future interventions and research in this field?

Background to the Study

'Accelerate' has been running since 2010 and is a week-long programme for secondary school pupils aged 15–18 interested in studying a specific subject area at University. Based at the University of Strathclyde in Glasgow during June and July each summer, challenges are offered in disciplines such as Business, Chemistry and Law. Participants primarily engage with student mentors studying in their selected subject of interest. The majority of mentors are paid for their employment; however some individuals can also gain academic credit towards their degree.

By working through challenge-based activities with the mentors, together with University staff and industry professionals, the aim is for participants to gain a full picture of their potential higher education experience and opportunities beyond graduation. Accelerate is a universal provision, open to all school pupils; however recruitment and funding efforts are targeted towards those from widening access backgrounds.

Each challenge progresses with mentors providing theory and information to support participants to enable them to complete their main challenge project, culminating in a group presentation of results/proposals. A number of challenges also have accreditation on the Scottish Credit and Qualifications Framework; therefore if pupils pass their submitted coursework, they can gain credits that display their ability to work at an academic level of first year at University.

Higher Education in Scotland

As a devolved power from Westminster, the structure, funding and legislation of the education system comes under the responsibility of the Scottish Government. Education Scotland is the government agency responsible for driving educational change, including implementation of the school curriculum and policy priorities. The main legislation relevant to this study is the Post-16 Education (Scotland Act 2013), which marked a significant milestone in higher education. The introduction of 'widening access agreements' as part of this legislation have a key purpose, "...enabling, encouraging or increasing participation...by persons belonging to socio-economic groups which are under-represented in fundable higher education" (Post-16 Education (Scotland) Act 2013, s. 3).

To supplement this, the Government announced the creation of the Commission on Widening Access in 2014, to investigate the issues faced within the sector and to inform recommendations in addressing them. 'A Blueprint for Fairness' was the final report published by the Commission in 2016, which set out 34 recommendations for shaping the future of access in Scotland and to facilitate the target that, "by 2030, students from the 20% most deprived backgrounds should represent 20% of entrants to higher education"[3] (Scottish Government, 2015). The Commissioner for Fair Access was appointed in late 2016 and is currently working through the recommendations to inform how this target could be achieved. For example, in relation to table 1 above, there is an interim target of achieving a 16% representation of students from the 20% most deprived backgrounds (Commission on Widening Access, 2016, p. 18). Furthermore, the use of contextualised admissions in higher education is seen as a move towards a more equitable policy, taking into account other factors surrounding performance, not only academic achievement. Each institution is responsible for setting its own thresholds; however it is acknowledged as a complex system which requires simplification to allow greater accessibility for those whom the admissions policy would be applied (Minty, 2016, p. 52).

The role of the Scottish Funding Council should also be highlighted, supporting not only the funding of University and college places, but embedding widening access as a strategic priority and providing support and funding to access initiatives such as the Schools for Higher Education Programme (SHEP). This is a collaborative programme, involving Universities and colleges across four regions in Scotland, working with a target group of pupils in schools with a higher education progression rate of less than 22% across a 5-year period. It is also important to emphasise the significant role of colleges in Scotland, as the uptake of higher education at college[4] plays a significant role in widening access (Gallacher, 2009) and therefore ensures that Scotland has the highest rate of HE participation in the UK.

Equity and Social Mobility

Current research highlights that the gap between those from the poorest and richest backgrounds can already be 10–13 months by the time a child is aged 5 (Sosu & Ellis, 2014). The gap widens as children progress through different phases of school, to the critical stage when pupils are undertaking exams for their qualifications. It is at this point that attainment challenges are likely to have a greater detrimental impact on young people from more disadvantaged backgrounds. Most recently, the National Improvement Framework and Improvement Plan 2017 has a particular focus on "achieving excellence and equity" in Scottish education. With specific targets for raising attainment in literacy and numeracy and closing the aforementioned attainment gap, this plan indicates six "drivers of improvement"[5] and how these will impact on a number of levels including, "child, parents, school, local, national" (Scottish Government, 2017, p. 3).

Attainment is currently in the spotlight, following the release of the most recent PISA results in 2016, seen as providing a common benchmark for education systems across the world. The performance of the UK as a whole has declined, but standards also appear to have reduced in Scotland, with previously above average results in key areas such as maths and reading in 2012 now credited as average. This has prompted criticism of the Scottish Government in relation to the implementation of the new national curriculum in 2010, which brought changes to assessment arrangements and the qualifications awarded to pupils. As a result, the Government is considering the reintroduction of standardised testing in literacy and numeracy at key school stages which would allow for any issues to be identified and addressed far earlier.

One policy perceived as particularly equitable in higher education, is that Scottish students studying at Scottish institutions have their tuition fees paid by the Student Award Agency Scotland, a Scottish Government agency. Scottish students studying at institutions in the rest of the UK however, would be responsible for their fees, although this is not an upfront payment and students become liable for repayment on graduation and on receipt of a particular salary threshold.

Organisations such as the Social Mobility Foundation and the Social Mobility Commission are also using research in an effort to encourage a professional dialogue across different sectors in how we can engage in better practice. A recent report evidenced for example, that individuals employed in the 'top' jobs in Scotland, with the most influence and pay, were mostly educated at independent schools and highly selective universities (Social Mobility & Child Poverty Commission, 2015).

MENTORING

Establishing strong theory is problematic as researchers appear to have difficulty in agreeing on a distinct definition[6] of the mentoring concept (Colley, 2003; Paczuska, 2004; Terrion & Leonard, 2007). This leads to a common misconception that any interaction with adults must equate to some form of mentoring (Rhodes & DuBois, 2008). The consequence of such lack of conceptual clarity is that:

...it remains the case that mentoring in both the USA and the UK remains poorly theorised, with little consensus about the precise definition and nature of the concept. Similarly, little is understood about the underlying processes and the different stages of mentoring relationships. (Phillip, 2003, p. 102)

With a narrow focus on the nature and outcomes of the relationship created and the structure within which mentoring occurs, this excludes the "complexity of mentoring relationships" (Spencer, 2007, p. 348) and how mentoring impacts upon individuals being mentored. Researchers should therefore be examining the nature, quality and length of the mentor-pupil relationship created (Randolph & Johnson, 2008; Sipe, 2002) and approach mentoring as "...a set of processes"[7] (Phillip, 2003, p. 110).

In offering a solution to balance these two suggestions, one proposal is based on a model of group mentoring, "...based on its emphasis on relationship building and group processes as a primary means of targeting developmental achievements among group participants' (Kuperminc & Thomason, 2013, p. 274). Although originating from group psychotherapy, this model is useful in understanding the interaction and overlay of the potential relationships created within the group mentoring environment, highlighted in Figure 1.

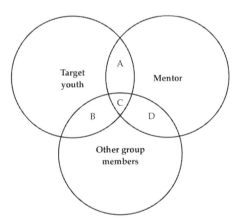

Figure 1. *"Opportunities for interaction within group mentoring"*
(Kuperminc & Thomason, 2013, p. 275)

Crucially therefore, the focus of the mentor is upon the interaction of the group as a whole, not singling individual pupils out for attention (the relationship between sections A and B in Figure 1). The benefits are still experienced by all group members, even if not directly involved in the interaction between sections C and D. These direct and indirect relationships are particularly beneficial for those who may feel intimidated by a one-by-one experience (Kuperminc & Thomason, 2013) and for school pupils, more likely to enjoy an entirely different learning experience from the classroom at school (Gorard & See, 2013).

Structure and Impact of Mentoring Programmes

Sipe (2002) acknowledges that with the rise of mentoring, there is clear variance between programme structures, depending on the age and stage of the young people participating. Research suggests that mentoring programmes need to be well implemented and the relationships created need to be effective to produce results, integrated into a strong, structured programme (Rhodes & DuBois, 2008). In attempting to determine how to achieve this, the inclusion and quality of mentor recruitment, training programmes and support mechanisms are identified as key indicators (Randolph & Johnson, 2008; Spencer, 2007). It is also necessary to consider the impact of these processes on the creation of positive mentor—pupil relationships.

One major barrier to establishing the effectiveness of mentoring arises from the quality of evaluative models used. Varied programme aims, outcomes and evaluative methods (Sipe, 2002) also affect the ability to make appropriate comparisons between programmes. With this in mind, caution is urged when considering transferability of successful initiatives based on evaluative evidence showing positive results from mentoring programmes as, "…we do not really know why some mentoring relationships work and others do not" (Rhodes, 2002, as cited by Dappen & Isernhagen, 2006, p. 162). It can also be problematic to effectively assess "…psychological constructs such as attitudes, aspirations, motivation and self-concept" (Gorard & See, 2013, p. 9), which are complicated to measure and can change over time. Concerns are raised about the tendency to stereotype pupils from disadvantaged backgrounds, excluding the interplay of potential barriers of the social world to higher education:

> Future research must deploy an inclusive definition of the social processes shaping higher learning ranging from those that promote (bridges) to those that inhibit (barriers) differential participation in, progression through and outcomes from HE for certain individuals and social groups.[8] (Kettley, 2007, p. 343)

Why Use Student Mentoring in Widening Access?

With the consideration that young people from non-traditional backgrounds contemplating higher education are, "…making very different kinds of choices within very different circumstances and constraints" (Reay, Davies, David, & Ball, 2001, p. 860), how do these young people navigate the decision making process to seek appropriate and high quality information?

The potential influence of parents and peers is vital (Archer, Hollingworth, & Mendick, 2010; Connor, 2001) and research suggests that, overall, parents are supportive, but disparity exists in the level of information they can provide. Young people are highly selective when asking individuals about higher education and there appears to be a distinction between individuals they are familiar with who are,

"...'hot' rather than 'cold'—meaning they deliver information potential students might listen to and rely on" (Paczuska, 2004, p. 64), linking into the perception that 'official' sources are in some way untrustworthy (Ball & Vincent, 1998).

This subsequently creates a powerful opportunity to use students as "...mentors or champions for higher education" (Connor, 2001, p. 222) or as role models (Terrion, 2012). Mentors who are current/recent students can provide valuable advice and support to help young people negotiate their way through the information overload regarding higher education, having been through the application process and entered the system themselves. Student mentors are also able to engage and enthuse young people for higher education through sharing their own first hand experiences. Mentors would therefore be perceived as having 'hot' knowledge and in an ideal position to help young people fill the gaps in their knowledge.

In an examination of why young people make their decisions surrounding higher education, one study showed that concerns were mainly financial and that application and entry to higher education was perceived as "risky" in terms of "...time, money and effort" (Archer & Hutchings, 2000, p. 560). Non-participants often indicate that they prefer to enter employment to begin earning money (Connor, 2001), but would consider higher education if financial assistance and good quality information were made accessible. It is appreciated that the decision to enter higher education requires a level of financial commitment and it can be difficult for young people from disadvantaged backgrounds to engage on the subject, particularly if they feel that their family is not in a position to help financially. While mentors would not be encouraged to divulge personal financial details, they can talk about their own experience of budgeting or part-time work while studying, for example.

Aspiration is a key word often associated with widening participation interventions and research evidence counters the widespread impression that young people from widening access backgrounds have low aspirations (Archer et al., 2010; Archer, DeWitt, & Wong, 2014). Many non-participants, however, genuinely wanted to pursue higher education as a mechanism for getting a 'better job' and in their eyes, 'bettering themselves' (Connor, 2001), but the perceived high level of risk outweighed the potential benefits.

The risk of failure and a lack of confidence are, unfortunately, the primary barriers identified in realising these aspirations (Bowers-Brown, 2006; Connor, 2001; Terrion, 2012). Policy is therefore questioned as to whether it drives towards a focus on raising aspirations (Archer et al., 2014; Gorard & See, 2013) or if it simply "...re-enforces a deficit model of young people and their families in which they are viewed as having intrinsically low aspirations for their future careers" (Wilson, Hunter, Spohrer, Brunner, & Beasley, 2014, p. 4).

Social and Cultural Capital

Prior studies have discussed that by using student mentors as role models (Cummings, Laing, Law, McLaughlin, Papps, Todd, & Woolder, 2012), widening access programmes aim to raise a young person's social and cultural capital (Connor, 2001; Haggis & Pouget, 2002). Archer (2014) provides a succinct definition of these concepts:

> Cultural capital can encompass qualifications, knowledge (dominant forms of knowledge and understanding useful for e.g. navigating the education system)... Social capital, from a Bourdieusian perspective, refers to the ability to gain value from social relations and networks of contacts. (Archer et al., 2014, p. 60)

Some authors do question the level of influence attributed to capital and would argue that the structure of the higher education sector and perceived institutional hierarchies (Baker & Brown, 2007; Brooks, 2008) are seen to emphasise structural inequalities of society, causing further detriment to those from disadvantaged backgrounds (Howieson & Iannelli, 2008). Subsequently, it is recommended that institutional change must be made, as "...unless Universities begin to recognise and address such inequalities, such cycles of exclusion will not be broken" (Archer & Hutchings, 2000, p. 571). One of the problems however, is that studies frequently identify such problems, but rarely provide firm recommendations as to how these issues can be addressed.

The perception of higher education is also an issue, with many young people from disadvantaged backgrounds thinking they are not good or clever enough to go to University, particularly where institutions are seen as 'elite' (Archer & Hutchings, 2000). This links into Bourdieu's concept of "habitus", where young people have preconceived ideas of "...what is normal for 'people like me'" (Archer et al., 2010, p. 93). This encourages young people to exclude themselves from participation on this basis (Reay et al., 2001) or to apply only to institutions where they feel they are more likely to meet the entry requirements, rather than those they would genuinely like to attend (Raffe & Croxford, 2013).

The key messages of the literature focus on young people learning from mentors as role models, in the hope that they gain new knowledge about the structure of higher education, different ways of learning (Reay, Crozier, & Clayton, 2010) and what a university would expect from them (Haggis & Pouget, 2002). Caution is raised however, as although there is clearly a demand for such programmes, any strategy involving mentors must be carefully considered in terms of structure and evaluation before implementation, to ensure the best possible results are achieved for the young people involved.

RESEARCH APPROACH

This interpretivist study looks to examine the perceived impact in two key areas: firstly, the mentor-pupil relationship on the higher education decision making process and secondly, the use of mentors as facilitators on the Accelerate programme. Consideration of the 'guiding principles' of the Scottish Educational Research Association Ethical Guidelines for Educational Research were applied to ensure the research was conducted to a high ethical standard.

Data collection was structured into three phases:

- Key Informants
- Student mentors working on Accelerate 2014
- Previous participants of Accelerate, now current students at the University of Strathclyde

Phase One: Key Informant Interviews

In establishing the current landscape of widening access, interviews with senior figures in this field were considered vital to establish the "…theoretical or conceptual basis" of existing initiatives (Randolph & Johnson, 2008, p. 179). Crucially, these interviews explored the significance of using student mentors as facilitators from a managerial perspective and also the potential impact of policy on the content and structure of interventions.

Phase Two: Mentors

A non-probability and purposive sample (Bryman, 2012) of six mentors working on Accelerate were identified, firstly by gender and then as to whether they were 'new' mentors, working for the first time on the programme, or 'experienced' mentors, who had worked on at least two occasions. There is an uneven male/female split of staff on the programme, therefore two male and four female mentors were selected to reflect this.

Mentors were asked to write their reflections each day for the duration of the programme and submit their journals at the end of the working week. To ensure mentors were not influenced by any predetermined questions, they were provided with suggested topics they could cover, for example, the group dynamic, how the pupils were coping with the activities set and the nature of any questions they may be asking. One of the benefits of using a journal is that they were able to inform additional questions for the semi-structured interviews with mentors, to gain an insight into their perceptions of their role and gauge their thoughts as to their potential influence on the young people they mentor.

Phase Three: Previous Participants

Secondary data from the University of Strathclyde allowed identification of previous participants of Accelerate from 2011, 2012 and 2013, who are now current students at the University.

Participants were selected from a purposive sample across schools in two selected local authorities in the West of Scotland. This enabled the researcher to gain an insight into the decision making of young people from local authorities with both low and high progression rates. Furthermore, this reduced possible identification of participants on

Table 2. Characteristics of local authorities selected by HEPR (Scottish government, 2015) and SIMD local authority datazones

	Glasgow	East Dunbartonshire
Number of secondary schools	37	8
2012/13 Higher Education Progression Rate (HEPR) (%)	30.8%	57.4%
Percentage of the 15% most deprived areas in Scotland	29.6%	0.3%

the basis of their individual school, but allows the researcher to compare and contrast findings based on the above characteristics of each authority.

The sample focused on a total of six students, one male and two females from each local authority. Attendance on Accelerate does not encounter an even balance of gender, therefore it was problematic to guarantee an even male/female split. These interviews were also semi-structured and aimed to assess the potential impact of working with mentors on Accelerate and to investigate the reasoning behind their own higher education decisions. Problems did arise in accessing students and as a result, only three interviews were conducted, with two male students (Glasgow and East Dunbartonshire) and one female student (Glasgow).

Analysis

Due to the qualitative nature of the research, a thematic analysis was selected as the most effective method of illustrating the underlying and potentially complex issues presented (King & Horrocks, 2010). A variation of a "thematic map" was created, to provide an illustration of where the overarching themes sit within answering the research questions (Braun & Clarke, 2013).

FINDINGS

On completion of the data analysis of the mentor journals and interviews, six key themes emerged:

Programme-Based Findings:

- Recruitment and training
- Widening Access agenda

Participant Experience Findings:

- Relationships
- Insight into university life

- Impact on decision making
- The role of the mentor

Programme-Based Findings

Recruitment and training. In relation to 'best practice' for mentoring programmes (DuBois, Holloway, Valentine, & Cooper, 2002), both key informants explained that undertaking a process of mentor recruitment was vital, particularly when offering an initiative with subject specificity that requires a level of expertise and knowledge during the programme delivery. They also emphasised the importance and need for appropriate training of mentors to ensure staff convey the nature and quality of the mentor-pupil relationship to be established. Mentors should also understand and be sensitive to potential issues or vulnerabilities of young people from widening access backgrounds (Wilson et al., 2014) and training should therefore provide sufficient advice for mentors to be proactive in addressing any issues, should they arise.

The widening access agenda. One of the key areas of concern raised by the key informants surrounded the commitment and duration of funding to widening access. As discussed previously, the Commission on Widening Access has a significant role in implementing its recommendations for the sector and assisting the Scottish Government in taking its access goals forward. The first report from the Commissioner for Fair Access is due for publication in 2018.

A further critical issue addresses the perceived contrasting measurements used as performance indicators to assess the achievement of programme aims and outcomes. A number of initiatives, for example, aim to increase participation in schools identified as having an HEPR below a certain threshold. Conversely, due their institution-specific nature, University Outcome Agreements tend to adopt the MD40 postcode measure (the two SIMD quintiles of highest deprivation). One key informant said this disparity was "unhelpful".

Participant Experience Findings

This section documents the four main themes identified relating to the overall experience of participants on the Accelerate programme.

The importance of relationships. In attempting to unpick the "complexity of mentoring relationships" (Spencer, 2007, p. 348), this study identifies relationships as key in the perceived value of the use of student mentors. This is primarily because young people recognise that a different relationship is created from their familiar teacher-pupil relationship. One of the fundamental aspects to nurturing strong and successful relationships is that the young people appeared to be aware of their position and role in the two-way mentor-pupil relationship (as in Paczuska, 2004). In examining the perceived differences between mentors and teachers, both participants and mentors focused on a contrast in the delivery of learning, in that mentors have more freedom to encourage independent learning, autonomy and ownership of the Accelerate group project.

Through the nature of group work and also the nurture of the mentor-pupil relationship over the week, the mentors recognised an enhancement in the confidence of the young people. This was echoed by previous participants who felt that the mentors are able to not only nurture confidence and ability in the subject area, but also boost their general confidence overall. This helped them to be confident about their own abilities to succeed at school and see university as a genuine and realistic option. Both the mentors and former participants spoke of the advantages of the smaller age gap between them and it was highlighted that young people often share interests or hobbies with mentors, which is beneficial in striking up an effective relationship with someone with a 4–6 year age gap. This would be seen as rare in a teacher-pupil relationship.

Models of mentoring. Although Accelerate is acknowledged as unconventional in comparison to the traditional model of mentoring (Eby et al., 2008; Terrion & Leonard, 2007), this study is able to confirm that the programme is using a model of 'group mentoring',[9] as identified by Kuperminc and Thomason (2013).

The focus of Accelerate is on the benefits obtained from the mentor-pupil relationship and the mentors are mindful of how this relationship is created. The nurturing of the relationship over the week, illustrated in the development of the confidence of young people, highlights the 'emphasis of relationship building' within the Kuperminc and Thomason model. Mentors become aware of individual needs within a group as the week progresses, therefore they are able to provide support and guidance without drawing attention to individuals within the group.

This also links into pupils' 'developmental achievements', highlighted by the nature of independent group work and it instils a sense of achievement for pupils at the end of the Accelerate week. Supplementing this with an examination of how effective relationships can be achieved, this study shows that the nature of the mentor-pupil relationship is a crucial element contributing to the impact of the Accelerate programme. It provides a strong functioning example to illustrate the effectiveness of the group-mentoring model, during the school and university summer holidays.

Insight into university. The findings revealed that a further perceived benefit of using student mentors is sharing their experience of applying to and studying a particular subject or course at University (Terrion, 2012). All three previous participants said that they took part in Accelerate as it was a good way to see what university would be like. The mentors played a key role in providing them with this insight, as the mentors have the potential to explain and reassure young people that in their experience, university is "not scary". While participants are not undertaking a full "test drive" (Moogan, Baron, & Harris, 1999, p. 213), they are certainly experiencing a taster and insight of its potential, enhanced by working on a university campus. This insight included an appreciation by participants that university is not only about lectures and studying in the library but that it also offers a wider circle of extra-curricular activities.

While parents and family members support and encourage entry to higher education, there can be difficulties for young people in accessing appropriate and up to date information from them. It was strongly acknowledged that mentors are able to fill this gap in knowledge, particularly in relation to entry requirements and student finance. A further important contribution of the mentors was the discussion of practical aspects of University life, such as taking lecture notes, the use of tutorials for learning and using time management skills in practice. For young people who are concerned about the transition from school to University in terms of workload and difficulty, the perspective of the mentors can reassure them.

With each individual Accelerate challenge centred around a specialist group project and presentation at a realistic higher education level, the pupils are not only absorbing the university experience; they undertake a deeper level of learning, by participating in a project which reflects a university learning experience as far as practicably possible. The pupils are therefore not only being told about lectures and the lab facilities that the students use; they are actively participating in lectures and using the specialist equipment the University has to offer. The mentors guide pupils through this process and are able to show them how this facilitates their studies. Furthermore, it displays how the university experience is different from school, but this must be conducted positively, not simply to be negative towards the school experience. Throughout the process of completing this task, pupils can enhance their subject-specific skills, as the mentors are able to push their knowledge of the subject. Previous participants conveyed they had also gained and enhanced university-appropriate skills, such as teamwork and presentation skills.

> It's a good way of learning about the nature of what you want to study by talking to people who have done what you're going to do and are at various stages and making yourself a little bit more comfortable. (Interview, Previous participant, Glasgow)

By working with different mentors during the week, it allows young people to appreciate the varying experiences, subjects and backgrounds of a university population. Consequently, young people can access tailored advice and have the opportunity to understand different perspectives of University, particularly for those who are concerned about moving away from home or working part-time while they study.

The findings suggest therefore, that if Accelerate can provide an enhanced insight into University, combined with increased knowledge such as entry requirements and articulation routes from college to University, the programme has the potential to break down some of the barriers to higher education for young people from widening access backgrounds. This could contribute to these pupils realising their existing aspirations for higher education, addressing the common misconception of low aspirations being held (Archer et al., 2014; Connor, 2001).

Phillip (2003) proposed that researchers should investigate the processes undertaken to establish how mentoring creates an impact, rather than simply looking at mentoring on its own within an overall picture. The primary question arising from this study is whether or not the benefits and impact on the young people could have been achieved if mentors did not facilitate the Accelerate programme. It is argued therefore that mentors are integral as the facilitators in achieving the programme aims and outcomes.

Impact on the higher education decision-making process. Within the three parties interviewed, there was consensus that mentors also contribute to the reported increase in objective knowledge of higher education. This was achieved, in part, by sharing their experience and knowledge of the current application system, particularly the different routes to university entry, such as articulation from college.

All three participants said that attending the Accelerate programme had a positive impact on their decision to attend university. Furthermore, all of them had attended events or programmes at other institutions, which impacted upon their impression of Strathclyde and other institutions.

> If university presents itself as being quite an ancient, quite formal… I think that's automatically going to put off people who come from a background where that kind of thing isn't seen as prestige. (Interview, Previous Participant, Glasgow)

By displaying passion and enthusiasm for their subject, combined with enhanced objective knowledge, such as degree entry requirements, the mentors felt they were able to provide young people with the drive to aim for University and motivate them to see the benefits of working hard at school. The mentors explained that they felt it was important to show the young people their achievements over the week, to reinforce their potential for the future.

All previous participants indicated that they had attended events or programmes at other institutions and consequently gained respective positive and negative impressions (Moogan et al., 1999). With some young people doubting their ability to attend university or unsure if they would "fit in" due to their background (see Gorard & See, 2013), the mentors can contribute to addressing this uncertainty. Previous participants of the Accelerate programme identified making new friends, for example, as a significant benefit. This is facilitated by young people integrating with pupils from other schools and backgrounds on their challenges and the previous participants from Glasgow observed that the people they met were different to their school friends. Furthermore, they said that meeting like-minded people on the programme was beneficial as they raised similar concerns in their groups and therefore did not feel like they were on their own in having these worries. This opportunity can break down many of the barriers about higher education, particularly for those who worry that they might not fit in because of their background or that everyone else will be more intelligent than them, cementing the link between social and cultural capital and habitus (Archer et al., 2014). This situation reflects the reality for many first year students entering university who worry about not fitting in to their new environment, but it is an experience that the mentors are able to discuss and in turn, provide reassurance to the young people.

The role of the mentor. The level of engagement established by the mentors was seen as a key aspect of developing relationships within the participant experience. By talking to young people in a casual and honest manner, they have the potential to engage groups much more effectively. If mentors are perceived as friendly and approachable, this subsequently allows the young people to open up and feel confident to ask questions and to perhaps push themselves further than they normally would.

> I think it helps create the kind of environment where young people are able to take on challenges, to be outside their comfort zone but without fear of failure.
> (Interview, Key Informant 1)

Both key informants agreed that using mentors as part of interventions in the future will expand and could not have been clearer about the value that they perceive mentors to bring to widening access programmes.

This research did not intend to provide evidence of raising social and cultural capital of young people, but it does show that mentors make a contribution to an enhanced perception of higher education (Baker & Brown, 2007; Brooks, 2008). Subsequently, two further sub-themes emerged from the findings that provide a basis for further research in how to establish mentors as effective facilitators. They highlight the key role of the mentor in showing young people from widening access backgrounds who may perceive attending university as unachievable, that the transition from school to higher education concerns ability and capability, not background. With mentors enabling access to information that family members may be unable to provide from first hand knowledge of higher education, the risk of failure (Archer & Hutchings, 2000) and lack of confidence is hopefully reduced (Bowers-Brown, 2006; Connor, 2001; Terrion, 2012).

Mentor characteristics. In asking all interviewees what they thought made a good or effective mentor, a number of characteristics perceived as desirable for a mentor emerged. All three groups said that a good mentor should be friendly, approachable, caring, a role model and genuine. The mentors in particular emphasised the latter and the need to have an interest in the young people and to know how to interact with them. It was also important for the mentors to portray that they actually wanted to be there to help the young people, not just for payment or academic credits.

The key informants leaned towards the qualities of a good mentor and emphasised the importance of having the ability to distinguish between a level of authority and friendship when trying to relate to the young people. The responses from the mentors and previous participants created a blend of their perception of what makes a good mentor, identifying the following desirable mentor characteristics: leadership, confidence, and being relaxed, motivational, good communicator and a good listener and to have the ability to encourage young people.

Impact on mentors. An unexpected finding from this study highlighted that there are significant benefits to the mentors from working on the programme. In addition to the academic course credits or payment that mentors receive, Table 3 indicates the differences in responses between the key informants, and their ideas as to the perceived benefits to mentors, and the responses from the mentors, as to the actual benefits they gained.

Table 3. Perceived benefits to mentors

Both key informants and mentors	Key informants only	Mentors only
Enhances and develops knowledge of the subject area	Employability skills	Meeting new people
(Good) general work experience	Enhances CV	Organisation skills
Leadership skills	Communication skills	IT skills
Being able to help young people	Team working skills	Creativity
	Formal course accreditation	Work experience for teaching
	Learning from peers "shared community of practice"	
	Deepens understanding of society	

Furthermore, from the perspective of the mentors, they felt that providing a positive experience for participants was an important responsibility and they saw this as a crucial element of their role: to have the ability to shape, influence and inspire a young person's future based on the advice and experience they provide on the programme. This appeared to confirm the comments from the key informants regarding the high level of responsibility that being a good role model to young people can bring.

SUMMARY AND CONCLUSIONS

Conclusions

With a focus on subject specificity, the Accelerate programme is well positioned within the provision of widening access initiatives and the overall findings of this study would support its continuation in the future. Although establishing the true benefits of a mentoring programme can be problematic (Cummings et al., 2012; Spencer, 2007), this study was able to identify clear positive benefits from using mentors as facilitators, not only to the participants, but the mentors themselves.

Investigation of the role of mentoring within Accelerate suggests that by sharing their experience of applying to and entering higher education, mentors have the potential to show a holistic view of what studying at university can offer, both in terms of academic and social life. The mentors are also able to contribute to enhancing participants' objective knowledge, in areas such as student finance and entry requirements, in addition to input from Admissions Officers, for example.

The integration of a strong programme structure is identified as one of the key elements in the success of a mentoring programme (Rhodes & DuBois, 2008). It is argued that the model of group mentoring used within Accelerate enables positive mentor-pupil relationships to be created. Although unconventional in the traditional sense of mentoring, it is the most effective mechanism for participants to experience the full programme benefits. The study also found a depth of information regarding desirable characteristics of mentors, underpinning why numerous successful mentoring relationships are reported from both mentors and former participants.

The findings suggest that the most effective way of achieving the programme aims is the combination of engaging student mentors within a strong overall structure. Although it is acknowledged that young people may be influenced in their decision making by other interventions or University visits (Cummings et al., 2012), for the previous participants interviewed, the Accelerate programme and working with the mentors certainly made a substantial contribution to their final decision. This is one of the advantages of pursuing a study that examines the impact of an intervention a few years after it has occurred (Dappen & Isernhagen, 2006; Randolph & Johnson, 2008). Whether it was the sole reason for their decision making however, cannot be established.

Limitations of the Study

While the findings of this study are promising, the author acknowledges that certain aspects are limited, particularly the scope of the study. The sample of previous participants could have been expanded to include those who selected higher education institutions other than the University of Strathclyde, those who decided not to apply to higher education and those who applied, but were unsuccessful, to see if they pursued the goal of higher education or followed another path. This may have illuminated the potential differences between the backgrounds of the previous participants and their perception of higher education, with a particular focus on those from widening access backgrounds.

The Future

Mentoring holds a strong position in supporting interventions such as Accelerate in the goal to widen access to higher education. There does however, need to be an acceptance that there are different types of mentoring for practitioners to draw on, but there should be some attempt to categorise these models. Subsequently, this would assist in evaluation and research, allowing for direct comparisons to be made between interventions using similar models of mentoring. Furthermore, there needs to be a push for more and better quality evaluation and research in this field and in

Scotland, this is likely to be led by a renewed Government policy focus. This does need to be sustained however, by long-term funding, to support staff in producing their own research or by employing researchers to undertake this process. This also applies to programme staff having the skills to interpret findings of research and acting on their results.

The Accelerate programme not only demonstrates an effective model of mentoring in practice, but also how to create positive mentor-pupil relationships. Engaging with the programme and Accelerate staff could assist practitioners proposing a new widening access initiative involving student mentors. Furthermore, the findings propose that a thorough process of recruitment is undertaken and that a strong training programme is put in place. This provides programme managers with the opportunity to impart the programme aims and expectations of staff, but also gives mentors the opportunity to understand and appreciate more about the young people they will be working with.

In conclusion, and in the drive to widen access to higher education for young people from areas of social and economic disadvantage, student mentoring provides an exciting opportunity for young people to gain an honest and realistic perspective on university life and to feel confident about their ability to pursue higher education. By tightening up evaluative and research processes, is it hoped that in future, staff involved in widening access will be able to gain a stronger understanding of how to implement effective models of mentoring within their own programmes. By doing so, practitioners will be able to strengthen educational equity to ensure that all young people, no matter their background, are able to realise their aspiration for higher education.

NOTES

[1] The terms 'widening access' and 'widening participation' are used interchangeably in this study. It is acknowledged however, that 'access' tends to be used in Scottish publications, whereas 'participation' is frequently found in publications from the rest of the UK.
[2] Relative levels of deprivation according to the Scottish Index of Multiple Deprivation (SIMD) is the primary measure used.
[3] Across both University and college sectors.
[4] HN level study (Higher National Certificate (HNC) or Higher National Diploma (HND)).
[5] "School leadership, teacher professionalism, parental engagement, assessment of children's progress, school improvement, performance information" (Scottish Government, 2017, p. 3).
[6] There is however, agreement and support of the definition of the traditional mentoring model: "…an older, more experienced person serves one of two main functions: a task-related or career-related function (providing advice, support, and information related to task accomplishment, professional development, and career success); or a psychosocial function (providing emotional and psychological support)" (Kram & Isabella, 1985, as cited in Terrion & Leonard, 2007, p. 150), although Terrion would later argue whether the support provided is limited to having only these two functions (Terrion, 2012).
[7] Emphasis in original.
[8] Emphasis in original.
[9] Defined with, "…its emphasis on relationship building and group processes as a primary means of targeting developmental achievements among group participants" (Kuperminc & Thomason, 2013, p. 274).

REFERENCES

Archer, L., & Hutchings, M. (2000). 'Bettering yourself'? Discourses of risk, cost and benefit in ethnically diverse, young working-class non-participants' constructions of higher education. *British Journal of Sociology of Education, 21*(4), 555–574.
Archer, L., DeWitt, L., & Wong, B. (2014). Spheres of influence: What shapes young people's aspirations at age 12/13 and what are the implications for education policy? *Journal of Education Policy, 29*(1), 58–85.
Archer, L., Hollingworth, S., & Mendick, H. (2010). *Urban youth and schooling*. Maidenhead: McGraw-Hill and Open University Press.
Baker, S., & Brown, B. (2007). Images of excellence: Constructions of institutional prestige and reflections in the university choice process. *British Journal of Sociology of Education, 28*(3), 377–391.
Ball, S. J., & Vincent, C. (1998). 'I heard it on the grapevine': 'Hot' knowledge and school choice. *British Journal of Sociology of Education, 19*(3), 377–400.
Bowers-Brown, T. (2006). Widening participation in higher education amongst students from disadvantaged socio-economic groups. *Tertiary Education and Management, 12*(1), 59–74.
Braun, V., & Clarke, V. (2013). *Successful qualitative research: A practical guide for beginners*. London: Sage Publications.
Brooks, R. (2008). Accessing higher education: The influence of cultural and social capital on university choice. *Sociology Compass, 2*(4), 1355–1371.
Bryman, A. (2012). *Social research methods* (4th ed.). Oxford: Oxford University Press.
Colley, H. (2003). *Mentoring for social inclusion: A critical approach to nurturing mentor relationships*. London: Routledge Falmer.
Connor, H. (2001). Deciding for or against participation in higher education: The views of young people from lower class backgrounds. *Higher Education Quarterly, 55*(2), 204–224.
Cummings, C., Laing, K., Law, J., McLaughlin, J., Papps, I., Todd, L., & Woolder, P. (2012). *Can changing aspirations and attitudes impact on educational attainment? A review of the interventions*. York: Joseph Rowntree Foundation.
Dappen, L., & Isernhagen, J. C. (2006). Urban and nonurban schools: Examination of a statewide student mentoring program. *Urban Education, 41*(2), 151–168.
DuBois, D. L., Holloway, B. E., Valentine, J. C., & Cooper, H. (2002). Effectiveness of mentoring programs for youth: A meta-analytic review. *American Journal of Community Psychology, 30*(2), 158–197.
Eby, L. T., Allen, T. D., Evans, S. C., Ng, T., & DuBois, D. L. (2008). Does mentoring matter? A multidisciplinary meta-analysis comparing mentored and non-mentored individuals. *Journal of Vocational Behavior, 72*(2), 254–267.
Gallacher, J. (2009). Higher education in Scotland's colleges: A distinctive tradition? *Higher Education, 63*(4), 384–401.
Gorard, S., & See, B. H. (2013). *Overcoming disadvantage in education*. Abingdon: Routledge.
Haggis, T., & Pouget, M. (2002). Trying to be motivated: Perspectives on learning from younger students accessing higher education. *Teaching in Higher Education, 7*(3), 323–336.
Howieson, C., & Iannelli, C. (2008). The effects of low attainment on young people's outcomes at age 22–23 in Scotland. *British Educational Research Journal, 34*(2), 269–290.
Kettley, N. (2007). The past, present and future of widening participation research. *British Journal of Sociology of Education, 28*(3), 333–347.
King, N., & Horrocks, C. (2010). *Interviews in qualitative research*. London: Sage Publications.
Kuperminc, G. P., & Thomason, J. D. (2013). Group mentoring. In D. L. DuBois & M. J. Karcher (Eds.), *Handbook of youth mentoring* (pp. 273–290). Thousand Oaks, CA: Sage Publications.
Minty, S. (2016). Getting into higher education: Young people's views of fairness. *Scottish Educational Review, 48*(1), 48–62.
Moogan, Y., Baron, S., & Harris, K. (1999). Decision-making behaviour of potential higher education students. *Higher Education Quarterly, 53*(3), 211–228.
OECD. (2012), *Equity and quality in education: Supporting disadvantaged students and schools*. Paris: OECD Publishing.

Paczuska, A. (2004). Learning communities: Student mentoring as a 'site' for learning about higher education. *Journal of Access Policy & Practice, 2*(1), 59–70.

Phillip, K. (2003). Youth mentoring: The American dream comes to the UK? *British Journal of Guidance & Counselling, 31*(1), 101–112.

Post-16 Education (Scotland) *Act 2013*, s.3.

Raffe, D., & Croxford, L. (2013). How stable is the stratification of higher education in England and Scotland? *British Journal of Sociology of Education, 36*(2), 1–23.

Randolph, K. A., & Johnson, J. L. (2008). School-based mentoring programs: A review of the research. *Children & Schools, 30*(3), 177–185.

Reay, D., Crozier, G., & Clayton, J. (2010). 'Fitting in' or 'standing out': Working-class students in UK higher education. *British Educational Research Journal, 36*(1), 107–124.

Reay, D., Davies, J., David, M., & Ball, S. J. (2001). Choices of degree or degrees of choice? Class, 'race' and the higher education choice process. *Sociology, 35*(4), 855–874.

Rhodes, J. E., & DuBois, D. L. (2008). Mentoring relationships and programs for youth: Current directions in psychological science. *Association for Psychological Science, 17*(4), 254–258.

Scottish Educational Research Association. (2005, March). *Ethical guidelines for educational research*. Retrieved from http://www.sera.ac.uk/

Scottish Executive. (2006). *A curriculum for excellence: Building the curriculum 1*. Retrieved from https://www.education.gov.scot/Documents/btc1.pdf

Scottish Funding Council. (2017). *Participation indicators for HEIs*. Retrieved from http://www.sfc.ac.uk/statistics/higher_education_statistics/HE_performance_indicators/Participation_indicator_for_Scottish_HEIs.aspx

Scottish Government. (2015). *SIMD 2012 key findings report*. Retrieved from http://simd.scotland.gov.uk/publication-2012/simd-2012-results/overall-simd-results/most-deprived-datazones/

Scottish Government. (2016). *A blueprint for fairness: The final report of the commission on widening access*. Retrieved from http://www.gov.scot/Resource/0049/00496619.pdf

Scottish Government. (2017). *2017 national improvement framework and improvement plan for Scottish education*. Retrieved from http://www.gov.scot/Resource/0051/00511513.pdf

Sipe, C. L. (2002). Mentoring programs for adolescents: A research summary. *Journal of Adolescent Health, 31*(6), 251–260.

Social Mobility & Child Poverty Commission. (2015). *Elitist Scotland?* London: David Hume Institute.

Sosu, E., & Ellis, S. (2014). *Closing the attainment gap in Scottish education*. York: Joseph Rowntree Foundation.

Spencer, R. (2007). "It's not what I expected": A qualitative study of youth mentoring relationship failures. *Journal of Adolescent Research, 22*(4), 331–354.

Terrion, J. L. (2012). Student peer mentors as a navigational resource in higher education. In S. J. Fletcher & C. A. Mullen (Eds.), *The Sage handbook of mentoring and coaching in education* (pp. 383–396). London: Sage Publications.

Terrion, J. L., & Leonard, D. (2007). A taxonomy of the characteristics of student peer mentors in higher education: Findings from a literature review. *Mentoring & Tutoring, 15*(2), 149–164.

Weedon, E., Boeren, E., Edward, S., & Riddell, S. (2014). *Widening access to higher education: Does anyone know what works?* (Report for Universities Scotland). Edinburgh: Centre for Research in Education Inclusion and Diversity and University of Edinburgh.

Wilson, A., Hunter, K., Spohrer, K., Brunner, R., & Beasley, A. (2014). Mentoring into HE-A useful addition to the landscape of widening access to HE? *Scottish Educational Review, 46*(2), 18–35. Retrieved from http://www.intergenerationalmentoring.com/files/2015/02/Mentoring-into-higher-education2.docx

Jan McGhie
University of Strathclyde
Glasgow, Scotland

JOANNA NAIR

8. DISCOURSE AND DESIRE

Wellbeing as Escape from Nepali Village Life

INTRODUCTION

This exploration of locally held understandings of personal wellbeing as escape from Nepali village life, and the discourses affecting these, was conducted in Mallagaon, a rural village of Far West Nepal. I consider specifically understandings relating to: the community's increasing geographical and social mobility; the local school's curriculum; and the hostel-based education afforded to many by Children's Education World (CEW), a non-profit, UK-based children's education trust which provides scholarships for economically poor but academically bright secondary level students.

My chapter illustrates that both institutionalised discourses and nascent discourses derived from the direct experience of individuals contribute to understandings of wellbeing as escape from Nepali village life. However, I also found nascent discourses which seem to have the potential to contribute to community regeneration.

The data I use in this chapter was collected during my PhD research into understandings of development and wellbeing in Mallagaon, which involved my living in the community for eight months. My role was that of 'participant-as-observer', in that I was involved and my real identity was known to the community (Gold, 1958, in Bryman, 2008). I conducted semi-structured interviews with 95 community members and had innumerable informal conversations. I also took extensive field notes. For ethical reasons, I use pseudonyms to refer to the community, the organisations connected to it, and the individuals I quote.

I began my fieldwork with deliberately broad definitions of development and of wellbeing, taking an explorative, discourse-oriented approach which enabled me to explore my research participants' understandings rather than impose mine upon them. Allowing only broadly defined theories to shape my initially general interpretations and to sensitise me to data, I chose the more detailed theory, best suited to my exploration (Ezzy, 2002).

This process enabled me, after my fieldwork, to choose the two main theories on which I base this chapter's analysis, those best suited to a multiple level exploration. One is Perri 6's (2012) 'institutional form[s] of social organisation' and their effect on sense-making. The other is Zittoun et al.'s (2003) 'symbolic resources' in constructing new meanings in periods of change by reinforcing or challenging 'social representations'. The former enables me to explore understandings of wellbeing as institutionalised discourses, structured by forces external to individuals. The latter enables me to consider them as more subjectively held, internal processes, affected by individuals' desire for status both in relation to others and to their self-image.

Willis (2005) noted that development interventions [such as CEW's] tend to be based only on the understandings of those in power. Wishing to help redress this inequality, I explore the understandings of wellbeing of different social groups found in Mallagaon, including those differentiated by caste, gender, income and social and geographical mobility. Meanwhile, recognising that my former identities in the community as, for example, teacher and CEW staff member, may affect my findings, I take a self-reflexive approach which acknowledges that "talk among speakers is interactively (dialogically) produced and performed..." (Riessman, 2008, p. 105), and brings out the importance of identity and its effect on relationships.

CONTEXTUALISATION

A Hindu Kingdom until 2006 when monarchy was abolished, Nepal officially became a secular state in 2008 (UNDP, 2016). The 'Federal Democratic Republic of Nepal', with a population of approximately 26, 500,000, is landlocked by China and India (ibid.). It has three geographical areas: the Himalayan area to the north, the Terai (plain) to the south and a hilly area in between (ibid.). The capital city Kathmandu, though located in the so-called 'central' region, is in Nepal's eastern half. Mallagaon, a pseudonym for the rural village upon which this chapter is based, is in the hills of the Far West Region. Furthest from the 'centre' Kathmandu, the Far West is officially referred to as 'backward' and 'underdeveloped' (e.g. Upreti, 2006).

As a mixed-caste Hindu community, Mallagaon is strongly hierarchical due to the caste structure. Brahmans, traditionally the dominant, are at the 'top'; Chhetrias are also upper caste but 'beneath' the Brahmans; Dalits, (the 'untouchables'), are discriminated against and at the 'bottom'. Women also face discrimination irrespective of caste.

Apart from a few shopkeepers, all householders farm either their own land or that of Mallagaon's wealthier members, growing staple crops and a limited number of vegetables. The local economy relies increasingly on cash, although a barter system still exists, usually when the Dalit tailor caste is paid. All householders supplement their income, either by teaching or shop-keeping, or with money sent home by emigrated family members. Most emigrants live in Dhangadhi, a town in the more fertile Terai. Others live in Kathmandu.

First arriving in Mallagaon in 1993, I stayed in the village for two and a half years as paying guest of a Brahman family while working for Voluntary Service Overseas (VSO) as an English teacher and teacher trainer at the local school.

Established in 1958 by an upper caste clan member, who was also a renowned social reformer, the school was at that time one of only three in Far West Nepal. It quickly gained a reputation for excellence, which was further enhanced in 1993 by another member of the clan ensuring its status as one of the first schools to offer a sixth form level teacher training course, then new to Nepal. This course was badly needed at the time and the school not only formally trained most of the region's unqualified teachers but also went on to produce most of the area's trained teachers. In 2009, the school expanded to include a college offering the Bachelor of Education.

From 1996, I began working for CEW, whose scholarships fund hostel accommodation and extra hostel-based tuition. I secured funding, from the British Embassy in 1996 and from CEW in 2000, for the construction of two girls' hostels. In 1997, I arranged for CEW sponsorship for students at the school, especially focusing on girls and Dalits. The programme is ongoing and has in the past necessitated my visiting the school for several one-week trips, most recently in 2009. Then, from October 2011 to May 2012, I spent eight months there for my PhD fieldwork.

Through my work as a staff member with CEW, I know that the expectation amongst its trustees—perhaps based on an inadequate grasp of local circumstances—was that scholarship recipients would contribute, as adults, to the wellbeing of their communities by living and working in them. This they hoped would in turn decrease emigration from the community. However, Mallagaon's permanently resident population (not including hostel students and staff, who are there only during term-time) has decreased further—from 468 to 258—over the past two decades.

Most of Mallagaon's powerful Brahman upper caste has migrated for better opportunities (the 210 people who have emigrated over the last 20 years are from 39 households, 32 of them Brahman), meaning that Brahmans no longer form the majority, which is now Dalit. In recent years, this trend has increased, partly due to Nepal's civil war (1996–2006) during which Brahmans perceived their lives to be threatened by the insurgent Maoists. Meanwhile, the male members of the impoverished Dalit castes have for long been temporarily migrating to India for work.

CEW's scholarship programme also appears to have contributed to migration over the past two decades, albeit indirectly, by helping more individuals to become better qualified for jobs in urban areas in Nepal and abroad. This is of interest to me since I set up the programme, the original intention of which—mentioned earlier—was the opposite.

WELLBEING AS A CYCLE AFFECTED BY SOCIAL STRUCTURES AND HUMAN AGENCY

Analysing my data in terms of how and why individuals understand wellbeing to reside in escape from Nepali village life, I recognise that understandings of wellbeing are constructed through the interplay of social structures and human agency, and that:

> …the meanings of wellbeing will differ… according to the cultural context, purposes, agency, and social identities of the people concerned. (White & Ellison, 2007, p. 174)

I therefore consider wellbeing to be a social construct (White, 2010), taking as my model White's (2014) 'Wellbeing Cycle'.

I see wellbeing as does White (ibid.), not as a static condition that people experience but as part of a cycle of cause and effect, in which structures, policies and relationships affect the experience of every individual. These experiences can therefore be better understood as part of this cycle, rather than in isolation. There are the structures and institutions which form the environment which shapes the interactions and behaviour of individuals. But at the same time there is a degree of autonomy or agency, meaning that every individual responds differently to the same situation. These individuals' responses and actions also form part of the cycle, affecting people's interactions and the wider environment, and ultimately leading to the reproduction or re-shaping of the original structures and institutions.

In mixed-caste communities such as Mallagaon, the upper castes and the institutions they traditionally operate through have social power—through their privileged access to scarce resources—over the actions and ideas of the lower castes. However, the lower castes are increasingly able to exercise agency and take some control. Similarly, women are gaining more power in the male-dominated community. Hence, in the struggle to maintain or gain power, the perceived value of these resources (reflected in understandings of wellbeing) are likely to be in flux.

In considering how the cyclical processes of institutionalised structures and human agency contribute to the construction of understandings of wellbeing, I draw on the two main theories referred to in the introduction. Unlike White (2014) who recognises that every individual has agency and can affect as well as be affected by institutions, 6 (2012) takes a neo-Durkheimian approach. He argues that commitments to differing notions of wellbeing depend entirely upon the 'institutional form of social organisation' individuals consider valid, with wellbeing dependent upon the ways people, under the different institutions, "*make sense...* of their lives and their social world" through the "guiding tropes" these institutions provide (ibid., pp. 131–132) (emphasis in original). Hence, the potential for wellbeing is considered to lie not in individuals, who lack agency, nor in their resources but 'in social relations and social organisation' (ibid.).

Amongst 6's (ibid.) four institutions—'Isolate', 'Enclave', 'Hierarchy' and 'Individualism'—the latter three are relevant to this chapter. 'Hierarchy' considers wellbeing as satisfaction gained

> ...through appropriate and skilled performance of [one's] ascribed or achieved place in [the] social order. (Ibid., p. 134)

'Community order' is the core value of 'Hierarchy' (ibid., p. 139). This is the form of social organisation predominant in traditionally hierarchical, caste-based Mallagaon. 'Individualism' considers wellbeing as the "successful pursuit and achievement of personal objectives over the course of life" (ibid., p. 135). 'Liberty' is its core value (ibid., p. 139). In Mallagaon, it is likely to have come about in recent years through modernisation processes. 'Enclave' takes wellbeing as the "committed enactment of shared principles in [the] community" (ibid., p. 135), with 'Equality' its core value (ibid, p. 139). Having always been treated as inferior by the upper castes, with discriminatory rules applied to them, the Dalits are most likely to derive wellbeing from a commitment to this form of social organisation, made available to them through the social changes brought by the Maoist civil war.

The introduction of the 'Individualism' and 'Enclave' institutional forms of social organisation to rural Nepal's Hindu communities, traditionally structured by 'Hierarchy', is thus relatively recent. This is likely to mean that those who have been making sense by subscribing to 'Hierarchy' may react to the real or perceived threat from, for example, 'Individualism (which emphasises personal success) to their sense-making (2012, p. 6). This reaction may take the form of seeking wellbeing with stronger "affirmation, of the sanctioned social order" (ibid., p. 136).

Recognising the powerful influence of institutions in creating people's worlds (Escobar, 1995, p. 107), my approach is informed by Critical Discourse Analysis and its concern with "the *social power* of groups or institutions" to "control the acts and minds of (members of) other groups" through having a "*power base* of privileged access to scarce social resources" (van Dijk, 2006, pp. 354–355) (emphasis in original).

The second main theory I draw upon is Zittoun et al.'s (2003) exploration of the agency people show in using "symbolic resources" to disrupt "social representations" and construct new meanings in periods of change, thus enabling transition to a new stability. Their theory is pertinent because increasing modernisation and political changes are likely to mean that Mallagaon community members are experiencing social disruption and change.

'[S]ocial representations' are:

social facts that exceed the symbolic activity of any one individual ... [being] ... structure[s] emerging from patterns and programmes of communications and practices that take place within a given social space. (Ibid., p. 420)

They are constituted by the discourses and actions of the local group to which they apply (Wagner et al., 1999) and are 'horizontally distributed system[s] of meaning' (Zittoun et al., 2003, pp. 420–421).

'Symbolic elements', which are "shared concrete things, or some socially stabilized patterns of interaction or customs that encapsulate meanings or experience for people", become "symbolic resources" when used (ibid., p. 417) either to challenge "social representations" in the transition to a new socio-cultural formation or to reinforce extant "social representations" (ibid.). 'Symbolic resources' may be used for: 'external' effect to enable individuals to achieve new identities, repositioning themselves in "the webs of social relations;" and/or for 'internal' effect to "regulate emotional experiences [and] change... understandings of things", reshaping how they represent their own worlds (ibid., p. 419). A 'symbolic resource' is thus a 'punctual element that makes a vertical connection' between the individual and the social (ibid., p. 421).

How 'symbolic resources' are used and valued is especially relevant in a community which contains distinct groups; extremely privileged and extremely under-privileged individuals. The means used to attain or retain cultural and symbolic capital may, I contend, be best understood in terms of 'symbolic resources'. Bourdieu (1991, p. 230) argued that, because of its autonomous nature, cultural capital in the form of educational qualifications can become symbolic capital ("prestige, reputation, fame"), which is the form capital takes when "perceived and recognized as legitimate". In contexts such as Mallagaon, where access to schooling and academic qualifications have recently increased massively amongst traditionally excluded groups, the traditionally advantaged:

> ...step up their investments... [in education] to maintain the relative scarcity of their qualifications.... (Bourdieu, 2010 [1984])

Although the qualification is a form of 'symbolic capital' (Bourdieu, 1991), I argue that the actual efforts taken by the privileged to keep their position in the caste structure are better understood in terms of Zittoun et al.'s (2003) 'symbolic resources', which consist of 'symbolic elements' which the privileged deliberately use to reinforce the threatened 'social representation' in which they are powerful, and to ensure their prerogative to 'symbolic capital'.

WELLBEING AS MIGRATION FOR A BETTER EDUCATION

I will now present voices from the community in the light of the theories I have just outlined, beginning with an understanding of personal wellbeing as migration for a better education further and further afield from Mallagaon.

Devi, a Brahman in her early forties, lived in Mallagaon until she was twenty-five, studying at the local school until Class 10, at a time when only 6% of girls in the area secured the School Leaving Certificate. When I first met her in 1993 she was at home, awaiting an arranged marriage, and usually helping in the fields, fetching water, washing clothes or cooking. Subsequently, however, her brothers enabled her to leave the village and study midwifery in a nearby town. When I met her in 2012 she told me, with pride and gratitude in her voice:

> My brothers said okay, our sister is old but we will educate her, my brothers educated me... My brothers did very good by me.

After training, Devi married, moved to the district headquarters and began work in the hospital as a midwife. Despite the wellbeing Devi told me she experiences through the status she now has in the hospital as a health counsellor, she described the issue she now has:

> My daughter has grown up. I am very worried about her... about her study.
> ... For my daughter, there is nothing here. Therefore, I must either go to Dhangadhi or Kathmandu.

Devi wants her daughter to study sixth form level Science, making her eligible to train as a staff nurse or pharmacist, but these courses are unavailable locally. Hence, in two years, when her daughter reaches that level, Devi "will have a big problem".

Devi's mother was uneducated and has lived in Mallagaon since marriage. Devi is proud to have left such a life behind. However, despite her positive experience directly resulting from her training and work in the nearby town, she has higher aspirations for her daughter; the locally available midwifery course would be insufficient for the future she has planned for her.

Devi reveals wellbeing to be a relational process of interaction with others, in which she values her control of resources which were formerly controlled by men. Her understanding is affected by 6's (2012, pp. 134–135) 'Individualism' and 'Hierarchy' 'institutional forms of social organisation'.

Increasing opportunities outside the community have led to Devi's valuing the 'Individualism' form; as the first woman in her immediate family to have her own income and a job which affords her status, she derives wellbeing from the liberty this gives her. Even though couched in negative terms, Devi seemed proud to be in a position to be able to play a part in choosing whether to move to the capital city for her daughter's further education. Both the "material prospering" and the "successful pursuit and achievement of personal objectives" (ibid., p. 135) of the 'Individualism' form of social organisation contribute to her plans to migrate further afield for her daughter's education.

Mallagaon's lower castes are increasingly gaining access to hostel-based education and are hence also able to realise their desire to move from Mallagaon to nearby towns and cities for better opportunities, as explored later in the chapter. Possibly in response, Mallagaon's wealthy upper castes like Devi now send their children even further afield for education. Devi intends to step up her investments in education by migrating increasingly far from her natal village, thus maintaining her family's "ascribed... place in [the] social order" (ibid., p. 134) of Mallagaon, at the top of the caste hierarchy and maintaining the symbolic capital of her family's superior educational qualifications relative to those of most Mallagaon families.

I consider her proud talk of her plans to be a 'symbolic resource', through use of which she derives wellbeing through the external effect it has on her social position of increasing power, and which she also uses to reinforce the threatened 'Hierarchy' form of social organisation which favours her. Increasing social and geographical mobility of all Mallagaon's social groups has resulted in shifting aspirations. Because of the increasing opportunities for the disadvantaged, the advantaged find means to maintain their social advantage and their 'top' position relative to other current or former community members, leading to a continuation of social reproduction.

Some upper caste members of Mallagaon who have emigrated for better educational opportunities recognise that their emigration may be detrimental to the wellbeing of their community. One such, Gyana, stated regretfully:

> People used to contribute in school and society but now people... [are] not taking that sort of responsibilities. Could be due to the lack of a good leader... he or she can unify the voice and make all the things into transformation. We educated people are not in the community.

This understanding also undermines the personal wellbeing Gyana may derive from the better education he has accessed by emigrating. Identifying himself as one of Mallagaon's educated, he voices his regret that their migration from the community has led to the loss of 'community order', the core value of the 'Hierarchy' form of social organisation (6, p. 139) favoured by Gyana's Brahman caste. In doing so, he re-affirms this now threatened form of social organisation.

WELLBEING THROUGH 'OUT-KNOWLEDGE'

In part owing to the example set by the upper castes such as those described above, many Dalits also yearn to escape the community and move to a town or city. Vikram, the first of his Dalit clan to become literate, wished to migrate (and has done so since I carried out my research), despite the niche he had made for himself locally as a successful businessman, no longer dependent on Mallagaon's upper castes for his survival. This is also because he believes that the local school provides an education that is "not useful for life", and that he and his son would gain greater knowledge (unavailable locally) in a city.

Vikram described '*out-knowledge*', as he and other in Mallagaon term it, thus:

> Knowledge of outside, after going out your good and bad people, good and bad trends, all can be understood. The children there [in Dhangadhi] who have completed Class 2 or 3 have more experience than those who have done Intermediate Education and Bachelor of Education here. They know about everything.

Although he prefers Mallagaon, his birthplace, Vikram explained that:

> ...there is not that much [opportunity here] ... If you live outside good knowledge comes.

If he could afford it, Vikram dreams of sending his son to a private, English-medium day school in Dhangadhi in order that he may benefit from '*out-knowledge*' and so escape village life since:

> Until one gets out of here one is like a frog in a well. A frog in a well cannot go anywhere... does not know anything about things outside.

The newly forming discourse of '*out-knowledge*' appears to include formal education outside the village, informal learning derived from wider experience (both good and bad) and opportunities which people living in rural areas like Mallagaon are often unaware of, or cannot access.

Vikram's thirst for '*out-knowledge*' probably led him to dismiss Mallagaon as "your village area" believing that children who stay will be "ruined"; his decisions seem greatly influenced by how much '*out-knowledge*' he can access, or dream of accessing, for himself and his family. The value Vikram attaches to '*out-knowledge*' comes from personal experience; it is from skills training in Kathmandu, not from the local school, that he believes he learnt what he required to be a successful businessman.

Shivapriya, a young Chhetria upper caste woman who emigrated after studying a sixth form level teaching course at the local school, similarly appreciates life in the city for the new things that can be learnt, including skills such as knitting and knowledge outside textbooks, especially about coping in the outside world. She will educate her son anywhere except in the villages because there "they don't have knowledge of outside things".

The ways in which Vikram, marginalised by caste, and Shivapriya, disadvantaged by gender, talk about their plans for their children's education outside the village can also be understood as symbolic elements made, through their verbalisation, into symbolic resources. Their capacity to imagine different futures improves their self-image and helps them to reposition themselves in the social hierarchy, experiencing wellbeing through the different interactions they are now able to have with others more privileged than themselves, even if their aspirations come to nothing.

The understanding that urban life and education lead to personal wellbeing through '*out-knowledge*' may derive from the familiarisation of the outside world through radio, television and increased geographical mobility. It is also derived from a discourse of development as modernisation still prevalent in Nepal and explored by Pigg in the early 1990s. She found that many Nepalis saw '*bikas*' (development) as either something external to Nepal or city-based, the city representing the economically rich future to be strived for and the village the poverty-ensnared past to be left behind. This leads to polarisation of village and city and to villagers' understanding that '*bikas*' involves external agency and goods, and that, as 'villagers', community members are ignorant and left behind (Pigg, 1992, 1993).

Thus far, I have shown how the dominant understanding of wellbeing as escape from rural village life is relational, dependent upon the actions and opportunities open to other community members and structured by institutional forms of social organisation and the discourses associated with them. I have also demonstrated how these understandings and discourses develop through human agency and personal experience. Women and Dalits value symbolic resources as means to attain wellbeing through either talk of escape, which gives them a sense of greater equity and freedom as well as improving their self-image, or through actual escape from the village for better opportunities and for liberty from the gender or caste restrictions experienced in Mallagaon. This process leads to the formation of new discourses and thus helps to change institutionalised discourses and practice, as I will explore, having first illustrated how the school and CEW's hostel-based programme contribute to the desire to leave the community.

THE SCHOOL AND HOSTELS' CONTRIBUTION TO THE DESIRE TO ESCAPE

Naming two Dalit men who have gone on to become teachers in local towns and one Dalit woman studying for a master's degree in Kathmandu, another Dalit noted that, due to their CEW-funded hostel-based education, 'discriminated against people have been able to become teachers'. While this illustrates CEW's contribution to social equity, it also illustrates that the education provided prepares people for jobs which usually necessitate their leaving the community, hence increasing their understanding that economic and social wellbeing lies outside the village.

In commenting on the benefits to the personal wellbeing of CEW scholarship recipients, several school teachers showed the understanding that the scholarship is useful in enabling people to leave the community, as indicated in the emboldened text below. A senior teacher said:

> ...bright children *have gone abroad.* Another good thing, just as CEW is giving help—likewise people who get a salaried job once they have become successful, they can do the same thing *in other places*—giving help. (emphasis added)

Another senior teacher said:

> The main advantage of the CEW funding is that people can get higher level education; only a few are able to study beyond School Leaving Certificate unless they live here in the hostel. However, the education provided here is not relevant because book learning is not enough. People who are not rich and do ploughing sell all, including their fields, so that their children can study from Class 11 upwards. But only a few of these children are able to get jobs, despite their qualifications. The problem is that the education provided is not a practical education. Sewing, carpentry and how to build would be useful as part of a practical education. There are jobs available for people who are interested in these things. For example, there are only two carpenters in the whole of this VDC [Village Development Committee]. Agriculture and horticulture would be especially useful since villagers *cannot go immediately to the city* (emphasis added).

The final sentence of this quote reveals an understanding, shared by most of the staff, that emigration from the village is the long-term goal of all its members. Both quotes indicate that the school's hidden curriculum is that education should contribute to community members' ability to move elsewhere. This is compounded by the example set by the teachers and descendants of the school's founder. Almost all of those who work in both the school and hostels educate their children elsewhere having in effect emigrated from the community; their families live elsewhere and they reside in Mallagaon only to work during term time.

The rest of the statement quoted above illustrates the teacher's recognition of the school's and its hostels' failure to provide the vocational education relevant to the needs of the local community that CEW attempted to provide in the latter. The same teacher also noted that the hostels undermine the basic skills of every villager:

...the CEW programme also means that the children will probably be unable to do the work of the home.

For example, the girls' hostel warden noted that the girls, not getting opportunities to cook when living in the hostel, never learn this skill.

As these examples illustrate, despite my identities as a former teacher in the school and CEW staff member, many felt able to criticise both the school and CEW's scholarship programme. Even lower caste members of the community who until recently felt unable to speak out against any of its institutions, spoke of the school's failure to prepare them with the practical skills they needed for their businesses. One Dalit, advocating practical training in tailoring instead of the theory currently offered by the school, noted that "nothing" about his school education had helped in his tailoring business. The local goldsmith, also a Dalit, said school had not helped him, while Vikram, from the most marginalised of Mallagaon's Dalit castes, stressed that "until now there has been no benefit at all from school education".

Vikram also argued that CEW benefits only those who have greater wealth and some education before they start school, indicating his belief that only those with cultural capital can secure CEW scholarships. Others felt similarly; the Dalit tailor Dinakar claimed that he used to argue with CEW that the children of the poor rather than those of school staff should be supported. Even successful graduates of CEW's scholarship programme felt able to criticise it. One young Dalit man told me that at times he wished he had never received the CEW scholarship because, as a student, he had felt so miserable and discriminated against by the school staff, since he and other Dalits were made to live in separate rooms from the upper caste boys. Another Dalit told me that they had to eat separately and that at times he was frightened. Both young men are now well qualified: one is a teacher outside the community and another is a junior vet. They consider the negative experience they had as scholarship boys in the school hostels as worth it in the overall process of attaining wellbeing through better jobs and hence greater equality with the upper castes and escape from the caste discrimination they experience in the community. One of them understood his wellbeing to lie in being secretary of a local NGO and on having recently chaired its meeting, especially since the post and opportunity had until then been the reserve of the upper castes. At the same time, their experiences illustrate that even educational programmes designed to address casteism may inadvertently contribute to it, and hence to the desire of the lower castes to leave the community to live and work in Nepali towns or cities where casteism is less.

NEW DISCOURSES AGAINST THE LOCAL SCHOOL AND THE HOSTEL-BASED CEW PROGRAMME

In the early 1990s I found, as did Parajuli during research he conducted in Mallagaon between 1999 and 2004, an apparently "unconditional faith towards education or schooling" (2008, p. 32). Parajuli's finding reassured me that it was not simply due to my identities as former teacher and CEW staff member that I had made this finding. Discourses around the value of the theory-led education offered by the school, especially relating to the sixth form level teaching course offered since 1993, prevented any questioning of its relevance even when it later, with local saturation of the teachers' job market, became clearly irrelevant. Constructed and shaped predominantly by its powerful upper caste males who were until recently the only ones able to benefit from the education offered, these discourses had remained unquestioned until the last decade. However, the 'Hierarchy' form of social organisation, with which the school as an institution is associated, is being increasingly challenged by the 'Enclave' form of social organisation with its emphasis on equality.

The increasingly open criticism of the school and CEW by the Dalit castes, explored in the previous section, can be in part explained by Maoist discourse which questioned the existing system of formal education (Bhattarai, 2000, in Thapa, 2003), opposing formal schooling because of its elitism and its failure to bring about equality. Such discourse, associated with the 'Enclave' form of social organisation, came to Mallagaon during the civil war (between 1996 and 2006) and enabled the marginalised to challenge Mallagaon's dominant discourse of schooling as entirely positive. The ability to question the worth of the school appears to contribute to the wellbeing of the marginalised members of the Mallagaon community, the act of questioning itself being a symbolic resource valued as a means of demonstrating their changing relationship with the upper castes, their increased awareness, voice and independence. It is also valued as a means of representing their own social world differently, even where no actual change occurs.

Meanwhile, modernisation may also play a part in changing attitudes to the local school. An upper caste migrant from the community explained that Mallagaon, once virtually self-sufficient, has now become dependent on cash and goods from outside, with the cost of living rising due to improved transportation and communication. Consequently, whereas in the past local people prioritised education and literacy, they now ask, "what to do?" once literate, and question whether this education can "contribute to their happiness and income to run their daily needs". He added that nowadays, therefore, people are thinking in terms of income generation. This way of thinking, relatively new to Mallagaon's lower castes, belongs to the 'Individualism' form of social organisation which favours material prosperity and the pursuit of personal success. Since salaried jobs are scarce in the Mallagaon area, it also contributes to the desire to leave the community.

All these factors have led to new discourses in which two of the community's institutions are now openly criticised; the education offered by the school is portrayed as irrelevant to community members' wellbeing, while CEW is seen as unfairly favouring the better off and excluding the poor. As a result, in a relational wellbeing cycle of cause and effect, it actually undermines the wellbeing of the marginalised. These perceptions, along with those explored earlier showing the school's hidden curriculum favouring migration, contribute to the desire amongst

Mallagaon community members to migrate for a more relevant education and for better job opportunities, and amongst the Dalits to escape Mallagaon's casteism and to avail of the same opportunities enjoyed by the community's upper castes.

Although the hostels continue to provide extra tuition only for theory-based education, the school has recently added (in April 2016) an agricultural course which runs through the final four years of school. This is being offered alongside the traditional, theory-oriented education for the School Leaving Certificate and the sixth form level teacher training courses currently on offer. This decision may well have been made in response to the new discourses anti the systems of local education and in favour of '*out-knowledge*'.

A NASCENT DISCOURSE AS POTENTIAL CHANGE AGENT

I have already discussed '*out-knowledge*' as a local discourse which encourages migration. Although only a nascent discourse, it may also play a part in bringing community members back and contribute to an understanding of education as wellbeing *for* life within the village, as I will now explore.

Dinakar, a tailor caste Dalit in his thirties, left the community with very little formal education which he had after all found useless. He became an apprentice under a cruel tailor master in Mumbai. On returning to Mallagaon, he used his '*out-knowledge*' as a way of gaining entry, denied to his caste, into a Brahman home to measure a sofa for a cover. Dinakar explained to the householder, who initially tried to stop him from entering by offering to take the measurements himself, that making a sofa cover is complicated and he would rather lose the order than take the responsibility for the work using the Brahman's measurements. The Brahman finally gave in. Later, while stitching the cover, Dinakar realised that it was his skill, modernised by his experience in Mumbai, not he, that was victorious over the Brahman's casteism and that without his skill he has no value. Dinakar derives wellbeing from his tailoring experience in India, despite having had difficulties there. This is because the skill it provided him with has not only contributed to his pursuit of economic success but also to greater social equity for him within Mallagaon, by enabling him to fight the caste hierarchy.

Meanwhile, Dinakar wants his son to go elsewhere for a high quality formal education, train to become a doctor, and then return to Mallagaon or a similarly rural place to practise medicine and improve people's health. More important to Dinakar than his son's potential earning power was the possibility that his son, as a doctor, might be able to change mind-sets. He explained that people could not show discrimination towards his son if he were a doctor; he would be allowed to go inside an upper caste home, even to the woman of the family who, if ill, would be unable to come outside.

Dinakar's narration of his story and of his aspirations for his son can be understood as a symbolic resource, narratives in which the 'Hierarchy' form of social organisation manifested locally in the caste system is punctured by events

151

which achieve greater social justice for Dalits. Committed to the 'Enclave' form of social organisation, Dinakar gains wellbeing through freeing himself from the restrictions of casteism, by dreaming of even greater freedom and equality for his son, and by contributing towards a community which is fairer, being based on shared rather than exclusionary principles.

Vikram (whose understandings I explored earlier) and Dinakar understand temporary migration for work or training as positive because of the '*out-knowledge*' thus gained. Both men value such learning for the social mobility, status and opportunities it affords them and their families to break through the village caste hierarchy. Although ultimately Vikram's aspirations for himself and his son involve emigration from Mallagaon, Dinakar's involve temporarily leaving in order to return with the '*out-knowledge*' needed to build a better, more equitable future in his community.

This discourse around '*out-knowledge*', developed out of the grounded experience of marginalised community members, is becoming increasingly powerful locally. It is valued by the marginalised members of the community for its potential to bring material prosperity, freedom, independence, status and greater equity (and hence the opportunity to utilise symbolic resources to disrupt the hierarchy of the village). It may also have contributed to the local school's recent recognition that it needs to change its curriculum to provide a more practical vocational and technical education.

CONCLUSION

The value placed on geographical and social mobility by the upper caste women Devi and Shivapriya, the upper caste man Gyana, and the two male Dalits Vikram and Dinakar, illustrates White's (2014) 'Wellbeing Cycle'. Their understandings of wellbeing affect, and are affected by, the social structures and institutions of Mallagaon. These understandings, shifting according to what resources others in the community can access, show wellbeing as relational.

As opportunities for others in the community improve, both Devi and Shivapriya consider wellbeing to lie in migration for better educational opportunities for their children, and derive wellbeing through talk of their plans. This illustrates how much they understand wellbeing to lie in their ability to access resources scarcely available to women of their background: the power to make decisions relating to their families' migration for better education for their children. In this process, both women show agency. They make sense of their social worlds not only through 6's 'Hierarchy' 'institutional form of social organisation' (2012) whereby they strive to maintain their castes' superior access to symbolic capital, but also by actively liberating themselves from the restrictions on women and pursuing or planning to pursue their own personal objectives. Valuing their ability to do so, they also begin to make sense of their social worlds through 6's 'Individualism' (ibid.).

Devi, Shivapriya, Vikram and Dinakar use talk of education and/or of vocational training as a symbolic resource. This enables them to reposition themselves in the local social setting both to internal effect by enhancing their self-image and to external effect by bringing about actual change (Zittoun et al., 2003).

Vikram's and Dinakar's understanding of wellbeing lies in the extent to which they can access or imagine accessing, '*out-knowledge*'. This is because they understand such knowledge and their new-found power to talk about it, as best enabling them to break the stronghold of the discriminatory 'Hierarchy' in Mallagaon. '*Out-knowledge*' also enables them to make sense of their social worlds through forms of social organisation which bring greater power to them and which are relatively new to the community. Vikram, as the first of his caste to run a successful business in the local bazaar and thus to be no longer dependent on the upper castes for his livelihood, understands wellbeing to lie in 6's (2012) 'Individualism' form, which emphasises liberty, personal success and material prosperity. Dinakar, with his pride in breaking through the discriminatory taboos placed on his caste, is less concerned by material prosperity. He understands wellbeing to lie in the 'Enclave' form, which guides his plans and actions, with its emphasis on equality and on having principles shared by all in the community.

6 notes that, when under threat from other forms of social organisation, individuals who subscribe to 'the sanctioned social order' may react by ever stronger affirmation of it (2012, p. 136). Gyana, in common with Devi and many of his Brahman caste, has already left the community for better educational and employment opportunities. However, he re-affirms the 'Hierarchy' form by making a point of rueing Mallagaon's loss of community order—Hierarchy's core value (ibid.)—stating this to be the result of his educated caste's emigration.

The school's and hostel's hidden curriculum appears to be that wellbeing lies in emigration for enhanced education and employment opportunities. Teachers, most of whom have emigrated from the community, talk positively of the CEW scholarship programme because of the opportunities it gives individuals to leave. At the same time, CEW has failed to contribute to a more locally relevant vocational education, with the hostels it supports continuing to offer only extra tuition in support of the theory-based school curriculum. CEW and the school thus contribute to the locally dominant discourses and hence dominant understandings that wellbeing lies in education that enables escape from village life, as well as in the ability to access '*out-knowledge*'.

Despite having provided for decades an education largely irrelevant to local needs and despite the increasingly dominant discourse of '*out-knowledge*' the local school and CEW remained uncriticised until recently. This illustrates the power of the dominant upper castes, who founded the school and who continue to run it, to control the minds of others in the community through powerful institutions and the discourses associated with them. However, the increasing strength of the 'Individualism' and 'Enclave' forms in Mallagaon, and the resultant greater social equity and independence for Dalits and women, have recently enabled criticism of both the school and CEW's programme in the hostels. Zittoun et al. (2003) note that individuals show agency in using symbolic resources to disrupt 'social representations' and bring about new meanings in times of transition; Mallagaon's Dalits especially derive wellbeing from their relatively recent power to openly question the worth of these institutions and so break through the 'social representation' of the school and CEW as being beyond criticism. It is possibly in response to this that the school recently modified its curriculum to include a more vocationally oriented course.

As 6 (2012) points out, wellbeing depends upon the forms of social organisation being in balance. There is potential for the individuals in Mallagaon, its school and hostels to experience greater wellbeing with 'Enclave' and 'Individualism' co-existing with 'Hierarchy'. This could happen once the de-stabilising period of transition is over and when the marginalised lower castes have gained sufficiently powerful agency.

As for CEW, the contribution I believe it should now make is to help the school provide a curriculum to equip students with Gee's (1996) 'liberating literacy'. This is 'a meta-Discourse (a set of meta-words, meta-values, meta-beliefs)' which enables the critique of other discourses and how they shape us and 'situate us in society' (ibid., p. 144). The aim should be to 'draw attention to the processes that underpin the dominance of some stories and the marginalisation of others' (White, 2013, p. 198) with the goal of empowering people to choose whether to subscribe to them or not, and to resist them where necessary (Gee, 1996). This could contribute to a more equitable, inclusive and empowering education that helps ensure community and personal wellbeing, enabling people of all backgrounds to work in and for Mallagaon, as well as beyond it should they so choose.

REFERENCES

6, P. (2012). Sense and solidarities: Politics and human well-being. In J. Haworth & G. Hart (Eds.), *Well-being: Individual, community and social perspectives* (pp. 131–149). Basingstoke: Palgrave Macmillan.
Bourdieu, P. (1991). *Language and symbolic power*. Cambridge: Polity Press.
Bourdieu, P. (2010). *Distinction*. Oxon: Routledge Classics. (First published 1984.)
Bryman, A. (2008). *Social research methods* (3rd ed.). Oxford: OUP.
Escobar, A. (1995). *Encountering development: The making and unmaking of the third world*. New Jersey, NJ: Princeton University Press.
Ezzy, D. (2002). *Qualitative analysis practice and innovation*. London: Routledge.
Gee, J. (1996). *Social linguistics and literacies: Ideology in discourses* (2nd ed.). London: Routledge Falmer.
Parajuli, M. (2008). Schooling: The way people see it. *Journal of Education and Research, 1*(1), 31–40.
Pigg, S. (1992). Inventing social categories through place: Social representations and development in Nepal. *Comparative Studies in Society and History, 34*(3), 491–513.
Pigg, S. (1993). Unintended consequences: The ideological impact of development in Nepal. *South Asia Bulletin, XIII*(1–2), 45–58.
Riessman, C. (2008). *Narrative methods for the human sciences*. London: Sage Publications.
Thapa, D. (Ed.). (2003). *Understanding the Maoist movement of Nepal*. Kathmandu: Martin Chautari and Centre for Social Research and Development.
UNDP. (2016). *UNDP in Nepal*. Retrieved November 11, 2016, from http://www.np.undp.org/content/nepal/en/home/countryinfo/
Upreti, B. (2006). *Nepal: Dilemmas of development and change in far Western Hills*. New Delhi: Indus.

van Dijk, T. (2006). Critical discourse analysis. In D. Schiffrin, D. Tannen, & H. Hamilton (Eds.), *The handbook of discourse analysis* (pp. 352–371). Oxford: Blackwell Publishing Ltd.

Wagner, W., Duveen, G., Farr, R., Jovchelovitch, S., Lorenzi-Cioldi, F., Marková, I., & Rose, D. (1999). Theory and method of social representations. *Asian Journal of Social Psychology, 2*(1), 95–125.

Walker, R. (1995). *Rationale for the case study from the Centre for Applied Research in Education (CARE)*. Norwich: University of East Anglia Collection.

White, S. (2010). Analysing wellbeing: A framework for development practice. *Development in Practice, 20*(2), 158–172.

White, S. (2013). Making international development personal. In M. Butcher & T. Papaioannou (Eds.), *New perspectives in international development* (pp. 191–214). London: Open University and Bloomsbury Academic.

White, S. (2014). Introduction: Why wellbeing? In S. White & A. Abeyasekera (Eds.), *Wellbeing and quality of life assessment*. Rugby: Practical Action Publishing Ltd.

White, S., & Ellison, M. (2007). Wellbeing, livelihoods and resources in social practice. In I. Gough & J. McGregor (Eds.), *Wellbeing in developing countries: From theory to research* (pp. 157–175). Cambridge: Cambridge University Press.

Willis, K. (2005). *Theories and practices of development*. London & New York, NY: Routledge and Taylor & Francis Group.

Zittoun, T., Duveen, G., Gillespie, A., Ivinson, G., & Psaltis, C. (2003). The use of symbolic resources in developmental transitions. *Culture and Psychology, 9*(4), 415–448.

Joanna Nair
University of East Anglia
Norwich, England

NELLI PIATTOEVA

9. DOING EQUALITY THROUGH GREATER TRANSPARENCY?

Troubling Surveillance Expansion in the Russian School System

INTRODUCTION

In this chapter, I examine the politics of surveillance of the administration of national standardised exams by the Russian Federation authorities. National standardised exams serve one of the key societal tasks of compulsory schooling to certify and sort students into different life paths and roles, while supporting and legitimising this stratification practice with the rhetoric of meritocracy, impartiality and equality. Broadly speaking, equality in this context refers to 'equality of educational opportunity', meaning opportunities for individuals to develop intellectual abilities despite different starting points, and to promote social mobility by enabling further educational opportunities according to the individual's choice (Borcan et al., 2015). Meritocracy is related to this definition of equality in the sense that the system seeks to reward intellectual ability as opposed to socio-economic background and/or family income. Within this discourse, obstacles to equality and meritocracy are said to include fees, neighbourhood segregation, and unequal access to quality education at primary, secondary and higher education levels (ibid.). The introduction of mandatory CCTV in school exit exams and the recommendations to do so in other mandatory and non-mandatory examinations and standardised testing drew my attention to the ongoing expansion of surveillance practices in Russian education (Piattoeva, 2016).

The rhetoric of equality offers a powerful justification narrative for the introduction of standardised examinations. For instance, the development of standardised testing across the USA was justified by strong claims of equality, asserting that compulsory standardised tests would help to reduce educational inequality, for example by improving assessment objectivity (Hursh, 2005). The authorities thus often promote an image of exams as fair and meritocratic, with the core messages of equality and social mobility asserting that the brightest and most hardworking succeed if exams are assessed impartially. There is evidence to suggest that national examinations can potentially function as a vehicle for social mobility (e.g. Heyneman & Ransom, 1990), as well as an abundance of contrary evidence that the standardised testing actually implemented has only served to exacerbate racial, gender and social inequality (e.g. Hursh, 2005; Au, 2007).

On the macro level, standardised tests are called for to make the achievement gap more transparent, enabling quality control and quality improvement through timely interventions. As a consequence, standardised examinations offer a means of state intervention into and control over the otherwise heterogeneous and loosely connected points of the education system that are only partially legible to the eye and discipline of the state at both personal and institutional levels. Exams produce data that are used for control purposes, just as quantification and statistics have long served as instruments of state power (see Shore & Wright, 2015; Porter, 1994; Miller & Rose, 1990).

As I have argued elsewhere (Piattoeva, 2015), it is important to make an analytical distinction between exams as an individualising technique, and exams as a means of producing aggregate data on education that is used in turn for the purposes of discipline and control (see e.g. Monahan & Torres, 2010). By analysing the exam from both angles, this chapter is concerned with the interventionist and controlling aspect of examinations, viewing them as being part of and enabling the expansion of surveillance practices in compulsory schooling, while capitalising on the rhetoric of equality. In other words, I place the discussion on the intensification of testing and the introduction of surveillance techniques within the context of the escalating governance of the public sector and education through data, based on complex monitoring systems and the production of information on performance and productivity (Ball, 2003).

The chapter is based on diverse types of data: existing research, Russian education policy documents, and articles and interviews from the Russian media. I analyse how the examination system authorised by the agendas of equality and justice feeds off these arguments to expand its surveillance capacities. Referring particularly to the case of contemporary Russia, I show how the discourse of in/equality is used to expand surveillance practices in both depth and width.[1] Working from the notion of surveillant assemblage the chapter examines one of the discursive elements of the emerging surveillance structure, emphasising particularly how the seemingly benign project of promoting meritocracy and equality is connected to the growth of surveillance. In line with the conceptualisation of surveillance assemblage, I assert that surveillance is powered by manifold interests and narratives, with equality as one of its elements.

I start the chapter by describing the role and nature of surveillance in the digital age and how examinations contribute to surveillance practices. I then describe the concept of surveillant assemblage—a situated accumulation of different and often mutually contradictory discourses, practices, technologies etc. I show how the emerging surveillant assemblage of the Russian school has expanded greatly since the decree in 2014 that ordered compulsory installation of surveillance appliances during graduation exams. I continue by problematising the notion of cheating in the exams and explore how rising inequalities in society and education need to be taken into account when trying to understand how and why cheating occurs in the examinations. Existing research on surveillance tools in general and CCTV in particular has shown how CCTV is often ascribed panacean attributes despite a lack of sufficient evidence (Taylor, 2010). In the Russian context and often elsewhere, cheating is presented as a practice that jeopardises equality of opportunity, and surveillance tools are then introduced as simplistic means to eliminate cheating and aid progress in social and educational equality. Equality thus functions as a kind of mythology that gives meaning and legitimacy to surveillance practices and their proliferation (Monahan, 2017). In this chapter I take issue with the logic of the expansion of surveillance by revealing its narrow and flawed basis. I argue that cheating and falsifications need to be understood in the context of the already existing inequalities and the practices of performance measurement and evaluation that hold risky high-stakes and impose controversial expectations on many actors.

SURVEILLANCE IN EDUCATION IN THE DIGITAL AGE

Surveillance is a dominant organising logic of modern institutions, shaping all their operations (Lyon, 2007). It can be defined as "watching, monitoring, tracking and data analysing for the purposes of control" (Monahan & Torres, 2010, p. 6). In this manner, surveillance is a form of knowledge production, but also functions as a productive means of self-discipline and development of modern selves (Monahan & Torres, 2010). Both state and non-state actors are involved in a connected manner in massive efforts of technologised forms of observation. Thus digital monitoring and surveillance systems are introduced for various reasons, e.g. security, transparency as a prerequisite for accountability and voice, efficiency, and discipline. In this manner surveillance is maintained by different desires and logics: control, governance, security, profit, entertainment etc.

The literature on surveillance presents two complementary views on the dynamics of surveillance. On the one hand, surveillance is defined as an exchange between a demarcated surveillor and a surveilled. On the other hand, the individualisation and multiplication of surveillance in the past years have meant that surveillance is co-produced by multiple "coveillant agents" (Ganesh, 2016, p. 174). The contemporary understanding of surveillance highlights its hybrid nature and shows how practices of surveillance, countersurveillance and sousveillance (using surveillance to challenge the authority and compromise the elites) are co-enacted and appear as a cycle of moves and countermoves.

The contemporary digital structure of surveillance has a number of characteristics that distinguish it from earlier forms. In the contemporary system the subjects of surveillance are not always aware of it, as acceleration of the use of electronic systems allows for a discreet monitoring of individuals in a variety of social contexts (Lyon, 1993). We also increasingly witness the "free submission" to surveillance on the part of the public (Facebook, Instagram, loyalty cards, etc.). Second, surveillance is better understood as dataveillance, implying that instead of direct, unmediated observation, surveillance is enabled by different streams of digitally produced data, and the surveillor is often unidentifiable. This means that surveillance "is not so much immediately concerned with direct physical relocation of the human body, but with the transforming of the body into pure information, such that it can be rendered more mobile and comparable" in the centres of observation and calculation (Haggerty & Ericson, 2000, p. 613). The digital qualities of contemporary surveillance explain why they often leave a digital record and what can be called an information surplus (Haggerty & Ericson, 2000). Dataveillance promotes self-discipline, that is, it is aimed at compliance in accordance with what is perceived as successful or required (measured) performance and thus instils a power relation through pre-defining the dimensions of measurement and attaching rewards and punishments on the basis of the results. Third, the transmission of surveillance has become much easier than in previous generations in terms of efficient and fast methods of storing, viewing, and recalling information (Ganesh, 2016).

School examinations are clear examples of the practice of surveillance in that they monitor behaviour and evaluate particular individual and institutional results, thus intervening in subjectivities and inner operations. Examinations are said to both "construct" and "discipline" those examined. In Foucault's terms:

> The examination combines the techniques of an observing hierarchy and those of normalising judgment. It is a normalising gaze, a surveillance that makes it possible to qualify, to classify, and to punish. It establishes over individuals a visibility through which one differentiates them and judges them. That is why, in all the mechanisms of discipline, the examination is highly ritualised. (Foucault, 1984, p. 197, quoted in Graham & Neu, 2004, p. 300)

The visibility imposed by the examinations on the examinees enmeshes them in particular relations of power. Self-discipline and intervention into the subjectivity of the examinees are enacted, for instance, by ordering or guiding them to write down particular things, but not others. For instance, when people or organisations are requested to make the work of their institution transparent to the public in a particular format, this practice is a kind of intervention, as it urges them to '[t]hink about and note certain aspects of their activities according to certain norms' (Rose & Miller, 1992, p. 200). It teaches them to be docile and to accept norms of behaviour dictated by the authorities. In addition to students, teachers and other participants in the examination process are also subjected to measurement and forms of standardised, regulated behaviour. The meticulous requirements of how exams should be administered, and the publication of the exam results in league tables as representations of education quality, are all means to discipline a wider range of participants apart from the students (see Graham & Neu, 2004). The accumulation of documentary traces enables another layer of intervention beyond the act of being examined. The disciplining power of these techniques lies in the uncertainty of their use. As Ball (2003) notes, monitoring engendered by performativity nurtures ontological insecurity and instability. He defines these as fear or expectation of being constantly judged in different ways by different means, according to different criteria, through different agents and agencies. No one knows in advance how this information can or will be used, and the fear is not ungrounded, as I will demonstrate in the empirical section on the case of Russia.

In sum, domination involves the exercise of a form of intellectual mastery made possible by those at a centre having information about persons and events distant from them (Miller & Rose, 1990, p. 9). Examinations produce material traces—examinations results—that can be entered into different calculative practices, thus enabling further surveillance and control on the spot and at a distance (Piattoeva, 2015, 2016). The essence of this mode of governance, anchored in the works of Michel Foucault and Actor-Network-Theory scholars, is that modern government functions by a diffuse network of indirect power. Direct control is substituted or is enmeshed with indirect means of administrative and at least superficially benign, as opposed to coercive, techniques that create cooperative and self-disciplining citizens (Graham & Neu, 2004, p. 295). Calculations at one place are linked to actions at another, not through a direct imposition, but through a delicate affiliation of a loose assemblage of agents and agencies into a functioning network.

SURVEILLANT ASSEMBLAGE

Due to the proliferation and extension of surveillance and its various forms, researchers warn that it is increasingly hard to say anything general and decontextualised about it. What has been called "situated surveillance" is based on the insight that empirical investigation of specific instances of surveillance are needed to shed light on the phenomena (Gad & Lauritsen, 2009). Scholars of surveillance have capitalised on the notion of assemblage to explore and explain the fundamental qualities of surveillance in contemporary times, i.e. the exponential multiplication of visibility, reliance on digital technologies, levelling of the surveillance hierarchy, involvement of state and non-state actors powered by different motivations and desires, and the overall multiplicity of the heterogeneous objects that work in concert to enable surveillance through multiple connections across technologies and practices (see Haggerty & Ericson, 2000). The notion of assemblage is linked to the conceptualisation of contemporary states as "evaluative states", exercising power through the multiplication of the levels of oversight solicited from and produced in new networked structures whose distinct parts are intertwined in a complex arrangement of observation, data production and calculation, and exist through the intersection of various media that can be connected for diverse purposes (Neave, 1998). Also the state increasingly capitalises on commercial agencies of control that emerge from the market (Hope, 2015). At the same time Ong and Collier write that assemblages are relational and are produced by "multiple determinations that are not reducible to a single logic" (Ong & Collier, 2005, p. 12). For our case these conceptual and empirical observations mean that different discourses, methods and purposes of surveillance can be integrated and capitalised on in complex ways.

Unravelling the surveillant assemblage from the perspective of situated surveillance requires one to scrutinise the human and non-human actors, and their interconnections, that constitute the surveillance assemblage in a specific geopolitical and historical moment. The range of desires, objects and techno-scientific practices that constitute the surveillance assemblage emphasise the different nature of the materials and linkages, e.g. some emergent and unstable, even ad hoc, others institutionalised and bounded. Assemblages weave together actors with diverse abilities that they would not otherwise have, assembled in and through practices and the relations being exercised in those practices. Nevertheless, the idea of assemblage points to eminent uncertainty because practices work in different ways and holding them together is a juggling act, thus assemblage is a perpetual work in progress (Srivastava, 2013). Surveillance regimes typically include efforts to combine and coordinate different monitoring systems that have diverse capabilities and purposes. However, part of the power of surveillance derives from the ability of institutional actors to integrate, combine, and coordinate various systems and components. Hence, while "powerful institutions do not control the entire spectrum of surveillance, they are nonetheless relatively hegemonic in the surveillant assemblage to the extent that they can harness the surveillance efforts of otherwise disparate technologies and organisations" (Hagerty & Ericsson, 2006, p. 5). In this chapter, I utilise the idea of surveillant assemblage to interrogate and trouble the discourse of equality as a constitutive element of the assemblage that plays an important role in the growth of societal surveillance in general and school surveillance in Russia in particular.

THE EXPANSION OF SURVEILLANCE AND THE QUESTION OF INEQUALITY OF ACCESS TO EDUCATION

Russian education policy documents often mention the problem of unequal access to quality education as one of the main challenges of social and education policy in the future. More often than not they mix and match two approaches to equality. One stresses nation-wide standards and equal access to high quality education requiring equal and fair treatment of all students, attention to and support for children with special needs, and availability of free-of-charge education. The provision of equal access to education regardless of geographical location or income is often highlighted. The other approach emanates from the individualisation, commodification and marketisation of education and stresses diversity of education "services", education on demand by families, extra fee-based services offered by education institutions, and the overall prerogative for educational establishments to attract extra, non-budget funds. Consequently, the rise of private institutions and commercial educational activities is perceived as both a positive form of diversification, and as a necessary but risky development that may lead to low or inconsistent education quality and the rise of social inequality. In the education policy documents issued at the beginning of the 2000s quality measurement was not mentioned among the first methods of achieving equality. Now it has taken one of the primary positions (see policy documents, RFG, 2000, 2013; MOES, 2001).

The state-wide standardised graduation examination described below was introduced as an important instrument for ensuring some kind of equality in an education system that had become increasingly diverse and contingent on socio-economic status. Its introduction was justified in terms of equality of access and anti-corruption, and manifests one of the greatest educational reforms of the post-Soviet period. The Unified State Exam (USE) started as an obligatory graduation exam for upper secondary school in 2009. The graduation diploma is awarded to those who pass at least two compulsory exams, that is, Russian and math. In addition, school graduates sit exams in the subjects required for entering tertiary education in the study field of their choice. The list of obligatory exams required for entering different higher education disciplines is mandatory and originates from the Ministry of Education and Science (MOES). The USE helps to standardise education content on the national scale, as its introduction goes hand in hand with the new national curriculum and the intensification of control over the authorised textbooks (Piattoeva, 2015). The USE also fosters cohesion by defining meticulously how the exam should be administered, from the uniform timetable applicable throughout Russia (http://www.ege.edu.ru/), which has proven difficult in a country with multiple time zones, to the practical exam arrangements, the physical environment in which the exams take place and finally, the way to handle exam answers and complaints (MOES, 2011).

The architects of the Russian USE claim that they saw its value in promoting social mobility and justice, that is, enabling students from less fortunate families and those living far from university centres to receive a university place without a need to travel for entry exams, and fighting various forms of corruption in the higher education sector, e.g. private tutoring and bribery (see e.g. TASS, 2017). Luk'yanova (2012, p. 1894) suggests that:

> The introduction of the USE was also presented as a way to eliminate the gap between the levels of knowledge provided at school and demanded from university entrants, thereby ensuring equality of access to higher education across all strata in society. Indeed, since Soviet times, preparation for university entry tests offered by various avenues of access (…) has been of uneven quality and more easily accessible for those living in urban areas. Therefore, regional and socio-economic inequalities were replicated in access to higher education, negatively affecting the opportunities of school leavers from the countryside and small towns, and of working class students. (Rutkevich, 2002; Shubkin, 1970)

Recently, Prime Minister Dmitri Medvedev said that "The USE has succeeded in making entrance to universities more open and honest, expanded opportunities for schoolchildren from the most remote areas, who completed school successfully, to receive education in regional and federal higher education institutions" (Rossiiskaia Gazeta, 2015a).

Since the initial implementation, the exam scores have been applied in an 'elastic' manner to steer the quality of education in schools and universities, and the distribution of rewards and sanctions to both high and low achievers respectively. Thus the USE examinations are no longer only a means of individual evaluation but provide data for policy-making beyond student selection and inform pedagogy and policy, hold regions, schools and teachers accountable and monitor education quality (Piattoeva, 2015; Tyumeneva, 2013). They have also become a key component in the publicised school quality rankings (Gurova & Piattoeva, forthcoming). Taken together, the exam results hold increasingly high stakes for a great number of actors in the education system and beyond (see Piattoeva, 2015).

The new legislation on obligatory surveillance during the USE exam was introduced in 2014. This was said to have become necessary due to repeated incidents of exam cheating revealed by unusually high scores in a number of regions and made visible by statistical comparisons between the grades achieved and the grade distribution predicted by the "ideal exam model". In this vein, statistical thinking plays an important role in legitimising surveillance practices and regulates the problematic relation between the possible and the real. Video surveillance was first introduced on a regional level. According to some sources, the Chechen Republic—led in a dictatorial fashion by a former warlord Ramzan Kadyrov—was among the first places to introduce a strict surveillance regime. In 2013, Chechnya, still under reconstruction after two devastating wars, achieved the lowest results in the obligatory school graduation exam in Russian language. The low achievements of the Chechen students are said to have triggered necessary precautions from the authorities in order to prevent cheating. The then Minister of Education of Chechnya, Anzor Muzaev, now holds office in Moscow as a vice-head of the Federal Service for Supervision in the Sphere of Science and Education (*Rosobrnadzor*), to which he was appointed in 2013 after what was seen by the centre as a successful implementation of regional education reforms (Izvestiia, 2013).[2]

One of Muzaev's main accomplishments was the "maximal objectivity in the exam procedures" (Izvestiia, 2013). Muzaev stated in an interview that he introduced video surveillance in 2009 because of concerns about the objectivity of the exam. Each auditorium in the 64 examination locations operated under video surveillance with the operators monitoring each individual examinee online (Izvestiia, 2013). This model of regional surveillance matches the system now functioning on a national scale, encompassing different layers of observation on the spot and from a distance, and relying on digital technology and volunteer observers/proctors (Piattoeva, 2016). Muzaev argued that with time 'the high level of objectivity' of the exam helped to improve educational achievements of the students, noting that only 12 per cent of the graduates, as opposed to the earlier 36 per cent, now leave the school without a graduation certificate (Izvestiia, 2013).

Obligatory CCTV is now introduced at different sites connected to the exam, e.g. examination rooms, offices where exam papers are stored prior to the exam and stored/dispatched and/or scored after its termination. Markers of the examination likewise work under surveillance. The other means of surveillance include metal detectors, mobile signal jammers and security guards at the entrances to the exam facilities. Control rooms operate locally and nationally, enabling different officials to observe the exam in real time from different locations through modern on-line surveillance systems. A squad of voluntary online observers watch the examination rooms on personal PCs, while public observers monitor the activities of students, teachers and exam administrators on the spot. There is a standardised chain of command that dictates how potential violations are to be investigated, e.g. the notes of the online observers on the suspected wrong-doing trigger re-examination of video footage by *Rosobrnadzor* and local and regional examination committees to verify irregularity, while the footage is stored by *Rostelekom* (Piattoeva, 2016).

Rostelekom is one of Russia's leading telecommunications corporations and an "absolute market leader in providing telecommunications services to Russian government departments and corporate users at every level" (www.rostelecom.ru/en/about/info/). *Rostelekom* is also the chief operator of the CCTV, which it first introduced for the 2012 presidential elections, and then found new use for as a technology that guarantees the "informational security" of the USE (www.rostelecom.ru/projects/ege/). In addition to being involved in exam preparation and implementation, the company is responsible for the collection and storage of video footage. *Rostelekom* presents itself as an advocate of equality by describing its activities in terms of closing the digital gap and ensuring similar conditions of exam completion across the country (e.g. Rostekelom, 2016), making a commercial actor an indispensable partner in the state's "equality through surveillance" project.[3]

Due to the high technical sophistication and coverage of the surveillance system, the costs of "catching" a single cheater are high. In 2014 the federal authorities invested 600 million Russian roubles in surveillance technology and support functions alone (RFG, 2014), exceeding the earlier total costs of the exam by at least 100 million Russian roubles (Rostelekom, 2014). It is yet unclear how much of the local educational budget is spent on surveillance, while one NGO estimates the cost of one detected exam violation at more than 1.2 million roubles (Obrnadzor, 2014). Despite the high costs, the arguments that emphasise the efficiency of surveillance cameras are hard to disprove. Reported violations are said to demonstrate that cameras help to identify and penalise violators, while the absence of violations is interpreted as proof of the efficiency of the new system which has prompted the examinees and other parties to pass the exam honestly, thus improving the quality of education by shifting attention from gaming to genuine learning and teaching (Kommersant, 2015).

Compulsory video surveillance and recording of the exam, the scoring of the exam answers and the storing of the examinations papers all leave a digital record that can be used at will, and perhaps, unexpectedly, if needed. Thus in 2015, for instance, the authorities posted a short video clip to remind the examinees that "over 4000 on-line observers and 35,000 public observers and federal and regional experts will challenge them should they violate the rules of the exam" (Rosobrnadzor, 2015). This clip is a collage of irregularities identified and recorded by on-line observers and as such it does not hesitate to circulate the images of rule breakers, whose faces are easily recognisable on the video (Rosobrnadzor, 2015). Thus from the perspective of regulation and surveillance, the rapid, nation-wide standardisation and control of school examinations constructs new grounds for the penalising interventions of central authorities in the name of objectivity, equality and commensurability (Piattoeva, 2015, 2016). The former head of the Federal Service for Supervision in the Sphere of Science and Education was sacked after failing to prevent cheating on a massive scale in various regions of the Russian Federation (Lenta, 2013). The Russian media often report similar abrupt dismissals of teachers, school principals and local authorities for either failing to clear their constituencies of corruption or failing to produce sufficiently high examination results (e.g. Rossiiskaia Gazeta, 2015b), revealing the complex hierarchies and controversial expectations inherent in the system (see Gurova & Piattoeva, forthcoming).

The proliferation and universal application of surveillance enable and function through new modes of classification and hierarchy, and new forms of inclusion and exclusion (Lyon, 2007). The complex surveillance assemblage constructed around the Russian examinations system is sustained by and produces new classifications and hierarchies, both crystallising and blurring them in different contexts. Certain groups, such as teachers, are no longer outside the practice of routine monitoring. Individuals at every location are scrutinised, but at each level this monitoring is accomplished by a particular, customised set of techniques and technologies and for both general and specific purposes. The paradox of surveillance is that it both singles out, affecting some more than others, and equalises, as it affects those previously untouched by surveillance regimes. At the same time, surveillance leads to what I call 'blurred' or 'uncertain' classifications, e.g. as the examiners, too, become the targets of surveillance through performance measurement and thus assume a position similar to that of the (student) examinees. This connects to Foucault's theory of disciplinary power as not referring to observation per se, but to the potential for observation and its implied (self-)disciplinary effects. Such effects rely on reshaping individual subjectivities through the promise of omniscient observation, with individual and social implications. Transparency practices thus produce uncertainty or suspicion vis-à-vis institutions and the people working in them, thereby undermining trust (Strathern, 2000).

In the Russian case, the surveillant assemblage can be seen to produce different effects, i.e. the new hierarchical social sorting and classifications systems in the name of promoting social equality and education quality, and blurred classifications that can be used interchangeably for both rewards and sanctions. For example, the high and low achieving schools can be singled out for more control. The high achievers (both individual students and schools) are easily suspected of exam cheating, especially in the areas with previously low achievements or where the exam results were falsified in earlier years, as in the region of Chechnya mentioned earlier. A recently introduced USE testing for first-year university students, although alleged not to carry any personal consequences, seeks to compare students' original results in the test to the scores achieved while repeating the graduation exam a year later (Moskovski Komsomolets, 2014). This examination of 'knowledge retention' is simultaneously a means to see how much cheating still happens in the school graduation exams. The individual students who are expected to achieve low scores in the USE are sorted out prior to the exam as endangering the average scores of the school, or are intensively targeted for special intervention to ensure that they pass (Gurova, 2016). Equally, universities or disciplines that accept students with low USE scores are singled out as institutions of poor or suspect education quality, and necessitating extra inspection by the federal authorities (Piattoeva, 2015).

PROBLEMATISING THE LINK BETWEEN SURVEILLANCE AND IN/EQUALITY

The putative and interventionist nature of examinations is obscured under the rhetoric of meritocracy and equality, while particular meanings are attached to these. Moreover, this rhetoric evades questions such as what happens to those individual students, or teachers, or schools, or regions, who fail (in comparison with others). Why do they fail? Does hard work always bear fruit? What structural inequalities are there that preclude students from 'working hard' and 'succeeding'? These questions are brought to the fore in the critical studies on exam cheating on the one hand (e.g. Borcan et al., 2015; Buckner & Hodges, 2016), and research on data fabrication and falsification in the organisational contexts embedded in and accountable to rigid performance measurement and audit on the other (e.g. Ball, 2003; Shore & Wright, 2015). For instance, research on exam cheating in high-stakes tests in Morocco and Jordan (Buckner & Hodges, 2016) has shown how students who engage in deception have low trust in the fairness and impartiality of the examination system and public education in general. They rightly question the uneven quality of education provided by schools located in regions where low socio-economic conditions and poor resources prevail. They refuse to let the state determine their life chances in a context where the state has failed to equalise these life chances despite its promise.

Existing studies on educational inequality in Russia have pointed out that inequality has increased drastically in the post-Soviet period and researchers attribute this trend to the post-Soviet education policy that failed to account for the specificities of the social context to which the policies were applied, e.g. change in the system of social stratification, the widening of the wealth gap, severe deprivation in some territories, and the influx of migrants (Kosaretsky et al., 2014, p. 15). Russian evidence suggests a strong effect of social background on e.g. allocation to different types of schools, track choice, aspirations towards higher education, and the chances of succeeding in high-quality higher education institutions, leading scholars to argue that "Russia's educational system cannot offset the perpetuation of social advantage and is therefore not completely efficient in providing equality of educational opportunity" (Kosyakova et al., 2016, p. 1; also Bessudnov & Malik, 2016; Kosaretsky et al., 2014). Interestingly, the meritocratic strategies of the state are said to have focused on "satisfying the demands of the more powerful social strata and education institutions which were prepared to seize new opportunities and utilise them for their own benefit" (Kosaretsky et al., 2014, p. 16).

Moreover, as our ongoing study documents, the system of performance measurement that has evolved in recent years often diverts attention from the needs of different students, while teachers concentrate on the activities most valued by the indicators of good quality and the criteria listed in the conditions for receiving personal bonus pay (Gurova & Piattoeva, forthcoming). For instance, they focus on preparing the already successful students for specialised subject contests, while other students have to study for the national examinations in their own time, with the better off students turning to private tutoring. The extensive reporting required by performance audits takes time away from both teaching and professional development, often meaning that reporting on the activities expected by the local administration supplants the very organisation of these activities, producing one reality on paper and something very different in the actual schools and classrooms. At the same time the new system of performance measurement renders individual teachers and schools accountable for the failures of individual students, while the resources of the teachers to tackle different learning needs remain scarce and vary between the schools. When the cost of low achievement is high, and the teachers have lost other means to help the students manage in life after school, deception seems to present a way to help the students at risk, and a means to help the school personnel to survive the system of rigid and consequential performance monitoring. In this context it is perhaps not surprising that one teacher in our research interview data recalled her former tutor saying that teachers "have to choose whether to sin against the children or against the Ministry". And another teacher interviewee told us that she would prefer her classwork to be monitored by constant video observation to the devastating piles of paperwork on her desk (Gurova & Piattoeva, forthcoming).

It is illuminating to connect these brief observations on the diagnosis of educational inequality and the 'terrors of performativity' (Ball, 2003) to the critical scholarly discussion on corruption in the post-socialist context, especially in Russia. Ledeneva (2013, p. 318) in her critique of the "global corruption paradigm" being accepted as a legitimate interpretative frame to understand practices of corruption in post-socialist contexts says that corruption often manifests as an expression of "entitlement associated with people's expectation regarding social (in)justice and compensation for poverty or deprivation". Informal practices are thus surprisingly and contrary to the dominant political and scientific rhetoric driven by the logic of justice and equalising effect on society rather than mere personal gain. Moreover, sometimes corruption becomes a means to get things done in a context of weak or dysfunctional formal rules (Lovell, 2008, pp. 373–388, quoted in Ledeneva, 2013, p. 318). In this manner, corrupt forms become the means of everyday resistance to ineffective or unjust governance practices by state institutions, and/or a reaction to political corruption.

Moreover, neoliberal transformation of the post-socialist societies that promoted the privatisation of public assets paved the way for corruption, as employees had to make ends meet amidst increased job insecurity and reduced, precarious income (Hirt et al., 2013). The analysis of the fragile post-socialist political institutions and crumbling safety nets amidst strong neoliberal policies has caused some observers to conclude that corruption flourishes because contemporary Russia is more neoliberal than many other Western countries in which the institutions that uphold democracy, control markets and continue to guarantee social security have stronger roots (Olimpieva & Pachenkov, 2013). If we understand corruption as a maximisation of private gain, then post-socialist corruption is a legitimate neoliberal practice (Olimpieva & Pachenkov, 2013). Olimpieva and Pachenkov (2013, p. 1367) conclude with a paradoxical interpretation that post-socialism is neoliberalism's purification, that is, neoliberalism in its "purest, cleanest and most unmediated form". In this context, a legitimate question to ask would be—If education is for sale, shouldn't the exam items and scores be too (see Buckner & Hodges, 2016)?

The above elaboration on the different ways of understanding the link between inequality, corruption and exam cheating offers an important, though only cursory critical mirror to the official rhetoric on cheating as a barrier to equality and meritocracy, and examinations and their rigid surveillance as a cure for these ills. An extensive study on Romania (Borcan et al., 2015), where surveillance cameras and other monitoring and penalising practices were introduced to combat exam corruption and promote meritocracy, reports that surveillance measures actually increased the achievement gap, showing how surveillance and tightened control proved beneficial only to well-performing, flourishing students. Such unique studies reveal the tenuousness of the evidence for a link between surveillance, cheating and inequality and make the analysis of the logic of surveillance timely.

CONCLUSION

In understanding how and why surveillance technologies spread and grow in volume, it is important to consider the promises made about their need and impact (Hope, 2015). While earlier research on the proliferation of surveillance has shown how it is justified in terms of better security and efficiency, this chapter adds to these findings by discussing how the narrative of equality promotes the expansion of surveillance in the sphere of education. The normalisation of surveillance in the school system is thus reinforced by the rationale of equality and quality education. This is how the surveillant assemblage relies on the unassailable moral and ethical elements that foil the project in the promise of a better, fairer future for all. At the same time by capitalising on the rhetoric of petty corruption in examination practices the state not only refuses to see alternative interpretations and more deep-seated causes, and thus fails to consider other ways to intervene, but shifts the blame onto grassroots actors, who merely react to the unjust, dysfunctional and inherently controversial system sustained by the authorities. By referring to the ostensibly well-meaning project of promoting equality, surveillance tightens its grip over education, while the legitimacy of this project is hard to question.

What we are witnessing is an expansion of the "surveillance school" that has emerged around the globe and incorporates multiple technologies, practices and discourses to "identify, verify, categorise, and track pupils in ways never before thought possible" (Taylor, 2014, p. 1). Different interconnected surveillance tools and discourses together constitute a surveillant assemblage that makes education increasingly invasive and invaded. The different techniques and technologies of surveillance come together for a more encompassing, deeper and wider, control of the education system, e.g. traditional examinations merge with on-the-spot and online observation of behaviour, and the new forms of dataveillance produce and use performance-related data for disciplining multiple actors. The school space affected by the politics of performance measurement can be seen as combining different forms of surveillance while accepting and normalising a culture of invasive surveillance (Hope, 2015).

Fast developing technologies combined with governmental prerogatives and commercial interests, with the three being increasingly entangled, nurture new modes of surveillance, making surveillance expansion hard to follow, analyse or regulate (Lyon, 2007). However, as technology expands the options for surveillance, it also develops technological advances to circumvent surveillance, leading to a cycle of new technologies and tighter controls. In the Russian case, and predictably elsewhere, cheating in exams is perpetrated with the help of the latest affordable technology, e.g. smart phones and the Internet, requiring other technological means to respond to the opportunities for countersurveillance afforded by these tools. The irony is that in order to meet the new criteria for effectiveness and objectivity in the name of equality, to counter its failure, the assemblage has to become even more intrusive, implying that its further success and expansion are contingent upon failure.

NOTES

[1] A strand of surveillance research investigates the impact of surveillance practices and technologies on social inequality, e.g. in terms of social sorting and surveillance of the marginalised (see e.g. Monahan, 2008). However, this is not the foci taken up in this chapter.
[2] Rosobrnadzor was established in 2004 under the auspices of the Ministry of Education and Science. Its main functions are control and surveillance in the sphere of education and science including the administration of USE (Unified State Exam) and other procedures of state control of education quality. *Rosobrnadzor* maintains databases on educational achievement and is responsible for monitoring the implementation of federal education legislation on the regional level (http://www.obrnadzor.gov.ru).
[3] The argument of "equal conditions" is central to the USE, but many critical voices have pointed out that these are biased because the strict rules concerning the conditions of the examination locations mean, for instance, that students in rural areas have to make long bus journeys to the examination locations that fulfil all the criteria (see e.g. *Uchitelskaia Gazeta*, 2015).

REFERENCES

Au, W. (2007). High-stakes testing and curricular control: A qualitative metasynthesis. *Educational Researcher, 36*(5), 258–267.

Ball, S. J. (2003). The teacher's soul and the terrors of performativity. *Journal of Education Policy, 18*(2), 215–228.

Bessudnov, A., & Malik, V. (2016). Socio-economic and gender inequalities in educational trajectories upon completion of lower secondary education in Russia. *Voprosy Obrazovaniya/Educational Studies, 2016*(1), 135–167. Retrieved from https://vo.hse.ru/en/2016--1/178801763.html

Borcan, O., Lindahl, M., & Mitrut, A. (2015). *Fighting corruption in education: What works and who benefits?* (Working Papers in Economics 612). Gothenburg: University of Gothenburg, School of Business, Economics and Law. Retrieved from https://gupea.ub.gu.se/bitstream/2077/38272/1/gupea_2077_38272_1.pdf

Buckner, E., & Hodges, R. (2016). Cheating or cheated? Surviving secondary exit exams in a neoliberal era. *Compare: A Journal of Comparative and International Education, 46*(4), 603–623.

Collier, S. J., & Ong, A. (2005). Global assemblages, anthropological problems. In S. J. Collier & A. Ong (Eds.), *Global assemblages: Technology, politics, and ethics as anthropological problems* (pp. 3–21). Malden, MA: Blackwell.

Gad, C., & Lauritsen, P. (2009). Situated surveillance: An ethnographic study of fisheries inspection in Denmark. *Surveillance & Society, 7*(1), 49–57.

Ganesh, S. (2016). Managing surveillance: Surveillant individualism in an era of relentless visibility. *International Journal of Communication, 10*, 164–177.

Graham, C., & Neu, D. (2004). Standardized testing and the construction of governable persons. *Journal of Curriculum Studies, 36*(3), 295–319.

Gurova, G. (2016, March 9–11). *The effects of school quality evaluation practices on social segregation in Russia*. Unpublished paper presented at the Nordic Educational Research Association (NERA) conference, Helsinki.

Gurova, G., & Piattoeva, N. (forthcoming). A post-Soviet audit culture: Changing practices and subjectivities of school teachers in a Russian region. In L. M. Carvalho, L. Levasseur, L. Min, R. Normand, & D. Oliveira Andrade (Eds.), *Education policies and the restructuring of educational professions*. Dordrecht: Springer.

Haggerty, K. D., & Ericson, R. V. (2000). The surveillant assemblage. *British Journal of Sociology, 51*(4), 605–622.

Haggerty, K. D., & Ericson, R. V. (2006). New politics of surveillance and visibility. In R. V. Ericson & K. D. Haggerty (Eds.), *The new politics of surveillance and visibility* (pp. 3–25). Toronto: University of Toronto Press.

Heyneman, S. P., & Ransom, A. W. (1990). Using examinations and testing to improve educational quality. *Educational Policy, 4*(3), 177–192.

Hirt, S., Sellar, C., & Young, C. (2013). Neoliberal doctrine meets the Eastern Bloc: Resistance, appropriation and purification in post-socialist spaces. *Europe-Asia Studies, 65*(7), 1243–1254.

Hope, A. (2015). Governmentality and the 'selling' of school surveillance devices. *The Sociological Review, 63*, 840–857.

Hursh, D. (2005). The growth of high-stakes testing in the USA: Accountability, markets and the decline in educational equality. *British Educational Research Journal, 31*(5), 605–622.

Izvestiia. (2013, March 9). *In the battle for the quality of the USE the Chechen experience will be useful*. Retrieved June 14, 2017, from http://izvestia.ru/news/556358 [in Russian].

Kommersant. (2015). *I let my daughter study in the first grade of a regular Russian school, not abroad*. Retrieved June 14, 2017, from https://www.kommersant.ru/doc/2768820 [in Russian].

Kosaretsky, S., Grunicheva, I., & Pinskaya, M. (2014). *School system and educational policy in a highly stratified post-soviet society: The importance of social context* (Working Paper WP BRP 22/PA/2014). Moscow: HSE. Retrieved from https://publications.hse.ru/preprints/139205999

Kosyakova, Y., Yastrebov, G., Yanbarisova, D., & Kurakin, D. (2016). The reproduction of social inequality within the Russian educational system. In H.-P. Blossfeld, S. Buchholz, J. Skopek, & M. Triventi (Eds.), *Models of secondary education and social inequality: An international comparison* (pp. 323–342). Northampton, MA: Edward Elgar Publishing.

Ledeneva, A. (2013). A critique of the global corruption 'paradigm'. In J. Kubik & A. Lynch (Eds.), *Postcommunism from within: Social justice, mobilization, and hegemony* (Social Science Research Council) (pp. 297–332). New York, NY: New York University Press.

Lenta. (2013). *Medvedev dismissed the head of Rosobrnadzor Murav'iev.* Retrieved June 16, 2017, from https://lenta.ru/news/2013/07/31/rosobr/ [in Russian].

Luk'yanova, E. (2012). Russian educational reform and the introduction of the unified state exam. A view from the provinces. *Europe-Asia Studies, 64*(10), 1893–1910.

Lyon, D. (1993). *The electronic eye: The rise of surveillance society.* Minneapolis, MN: University of Minnesota Press.

Lyon, D. (2007). *Surveillance studies: An overview.* Cambridge: Polity Press.

Miller, P., & Rose, N. (1990). Governing economic life. *Economy and Society, 19*(1), 1–31.

MOES. (2001). *The concept of modernisation of Russian education for the period until 2010 no. 393.* Retrieved June 14, 2004, from http://www.edu.ru/db/mo/Data/d_02/393.html [in Russian].

MOES. (2011). *Decree on approving the procedure of holding a unified state exam.* Retrieved January 15, 2013, from http://www.edu.ru/abitur/act.31/index.php [in Russian].

Monahan, T. (2008). Editorial: Surveillance and inequality. *Surveillance & Society, 5*(3), 217–226.

Monahan, T. (2017). Regulating belonging: Surveillance, inequality, and the cultural production of abjection. *Journal of Cultural Economy, 10*(2), 191–206.

Monahan, T., & Torres, R. D. (2010). Introduction. In T. Monahan & R. D. Torres (Eds.), *Cultures of surveillance in public education* (pp. 1–18). New Brunswick: Rutgers University Press.

Moskovski Komsomolets. (2014, October 30). *Students' knowledge retention will be tested.* Retrieved June 15, 2017, from http://www.mk.ru/social/2014/10/30/u-studentov-proveryat-ostatki-znaniy.html [in Russian].

Neave, G. (1998). The evaluative state reconsidered. *European Journal of Education, 33*(3), 265–284.

Obrnadzor. (2014). *USE-2014: Final results: A public-expert report.* Moscow: Obrnadzor. Retrieved June 14, 2017, from http://Обрнадзор.рф [in Russian].

Olimpieva, I., & Pachenkov, O. (2013). Corrupt intermediaries in post-socialist Russia: Mutations of economic institutions. *Europe-Asia Studies, 65*(7), 1364–1376.

Piattoeva, N. (2015). Elastic numbers: National examinations data as a technology of government. *Journal of Education Policy, 30*(3), 316–334.

Piattoeva, N. (2016). The imperative to protect data and the rise of surveillance cameras in administering national testing in Russia. *European Educational Research Journal, 15*(1), 82–98.

Porter, T. (1994). Objectivity as standardization: The rhetoric of impersonality in measurement, statisitics, and cost-benefit analysis. In A. Megill (Ed.), *Rethinking objectivity* (pp. 197–238). Durham: Duke University Press.

RFG. (2000). *National doctrine of education in the Russian Federation no. 751.* Retrieved November 6, 2009, from http://elementy.ru/Library9/Doctrina.htm [in Russian].

RFG. (2013). *State programme of the Russian Federation 'development of education' for 2013–2020.* Retrieved May 22, 2015, from http//:www.минобрнауки.рф/документы/3409 [in Russian].

RFG. (2014). *Decree dated 18 April 2014 no. 631*-p [in Russian].

Rose, N., & Miller, P. (1992). Political power beyond the state: Problematics of government. *The British Journal of Sociology, 43*(2), 173–205.

Rosobrnadzor. (2015). *Rosobrnadzor prepared a video clip about violations during the USE.* Retrieved May 20, 2015, from http//:www.obrnadzor.livejournal.com/162973.html [in Russian].

Rossiiskaia Gazeta. (2015a, February 13). *Exam with the prime minister: No. 6602(31).* Retrieved June 14, 2017, from https://rg.ru/2015/02/13/ege-site.html [in Russian].

Rossiiskaia Gazeta. (2015b, June 16). *Took a gadget out of the pocket: No. 6700(129).* Retrieved June 14, 2017, from https://rg.ru/2015/06/16/shkolniki.html [in Russian].

Rostelekom. (2014). *Journalists from Kostroma saw the transparency of the USE.* Retrieved June 14, 2017, from http://www.rostelecom.ru/press/news_fill/d435690/ [in Russian].

Rostelekom. (2014). *Summary of the USE in 2014.* Retrieved May 5, 2015, from http//:www.rostelecom.ru/projects/ege/ege_2014/ege_results_2014.pdf [in Russian].

Shore, C., & Wright, S. (2015). Governing by numbers: Audit culture, rankings and the new world order. *Social Anthropology/Anthropologie Sociale, 23*(1), 22–28.

Srivastava, S. (2013). Assembling international organizations. *Journal of International Organizations Studies, 4*(3), 73–85.
Strathern, M. (2000). Introduction. In M. Strathern (Ed.), *Audit cultures: Anthropological studies in accountability, ethics and the academy* (pp. 2–18). London: Routledge.
TASS. (2017). *Exam with a track record.* Retrieved June 14, 2017, from http://tass.ru/obschestvo/4007906 [in Russian].
Taylor, E. (2010). I spy with my little eye: The use of CCTV in schools and the impact on privacy. *The Sociological Review, 58*(3), 381–405.
Taylor, E. (2014). *Surveillance schools: Security, discipline and control in contemporary education.* Basingstoke: Palgrave Macmillan.
Tyumeneva, Y. (2013). *Disseminating and using student assessment information in Russia.* Washington, DC: World Bank.
Uchitel'skaia Gazeta. (2015, June 23). *Why happy childhood disappears from the school? The promise of unity remains a promise: No. 25.* Retrieved June 14, 2017, from http://ug.ru/archive/60829 [in Russian].

Nelli Piattoeva
Faculty of Education
University of Tampere
Finland

SEZEN BAYHAN

10. CONTESTING THE CITIES

A Comparative Perspective on the Geographically Specific Tendencies in Urban Education Policies

INTRODUCTION

Drawing on multi-year fieldwork on urban education in Istanbul, the purpose of this chapter is to discuss education policy in Turkey by situating it in urban education literature and theory produced internationally, with particular focus on the UK, United States, and Australia. Considering the worldwide scholarship on urban education, the chapter points to two geographically situated tendencies in the way urban education policy is implemented in the case of Turkey. The first one is that while studies on urban education in Western scholarship point to the racial displacement implicated in school relocations and closings, the findings presented in this chapter suggest that de-secularisation is involved in the context of Turkey. The second differing trajectory is the operationalisation of school choice discourse. While there is a lack of engagement with school choice discourse in the case of Turkey, a large body of scholarship produced in the West points to the production of common sense around school choice as an aspect of implementing neoliberal urban education policies. Deploying the theories of critical geography and critical theories of education, the chapter focuses on school relocations in Istanbul, discussing it with reference to its counterparts in various locales across the world, including, inter alia, Chicago, Sydney, London, and New Orleans. The data for this chapter were collected through a multi-year fieldwork on Istanbul school relocations. Policy discourses, official documents, media images, ethnographic narratives of school communities, and interviews with school communities have been deployed to theorise the issue. The chapter concludes by emphasising that spatial and educational justice issues are quite alike across contexts despite the differing ways that urban education policies are put into practice in specific locales.

SCHOOL RELOCATIONS AND RACIAL DISPLACEMENT
IN INTERNATIONAL CONTEXT

A growing body of urban education research, particularly in the context of US, Australia, and England, has demonstrated the increasingly important role neoliberal urban restructuring has played in shaping education policy and pointed to the interconnection between neoliberal urbanism and education policy. Most of these studies have emphasised the nexus of race and class, arguing that neoliberal urban restructuring and education policy with which it interacts have racial implications and tend to disadvantage non-white poor and working class communities.

Critics of neoliberal education reform point to the intertwined relationship between housing markets and neoliberal education policy. Since school is a key criterion shaping the housing purchase decisions of middle class parents (Billingham & Kimelberg, 2013; Stovall, 2013), schools can be seen as instruments to market the city to middle-class families (Cucchiara, 2008; Stovall, 2013). To understand school closings in Chicago within the scope of *Renaissance 2010* Project, Lipman (2011a) explored the forces that interacted with the reform. In her analysis, she points to the interrelationship between housing and education policy by emphasising how the HOPE IV urban project and the Renaissance 2010 education project worked in a co-constitutive manner. Lack of investment in African American and Latino/a working class communities precipitated the gentrification of these neighbourhoods, dispersal of community residents, and dispossession of their schools (p. 13). One example of such gentrification took place in midsouth region, where decades of neglect and disinvestment were followed by mass demolishment of public housing units largely populated by African American communities (Lipman, 2011a).

Selective closing of schools on the pretext of low enrolment is another instance that shows the convergence of housing and education policies. For example, many schools became depopulated with the dismantling of public housing in Chicago and then phased out or closed due to low enrolment (Lipman, 2011a; Stovall, 2013). An overwhelming majority of the schools closed in accordance with Renaissance 2010 plan were predominantly attended by African American or Latino/a students (Stovall, 2013). To give an example, out of the 101 schools that were closed, phased out, or declared as turnaround, 99 were predominantly African American or Latino/a schools (Lipman et al., cited in Stovall, 2013, p. 37). Grant, Arcello, Konrad, and Swenson (2014) state that the history of restrictive housing policies for black populations in Chicago dates back to the early 1900s, when white covenant associations were established to deter blacks from settling in white neighbourhoods, and continued until the late 1900s. Grant et al. (2014) further argue that these ideologies are still deeply embedded in the state's education system. The students of schools that were closed on the pretext of low enrolment or achievement levels often ended up in low-performing schools (de la Torre & Gwynne, 2009, cited in Grant et al., 2014). A 2009 report showed that 42% of students who left closed schools continued to be educated in schools with very low academic achievement (de la Torre & Gwynne, 2009, quoted in Grant et al., 2014, p. 672). Gulson's (2006, 2007, 2011) work on the interplay between urban renewal practices and neoliberal education policies in the context of inner-city Sydney describe how neoliberalising education policies seek to attract middle classes to inner city government schools. He explores how inner city school reform influenced the Aboriginal population and changed the demographic characteristics of the region by closing down, on the pretext of low enrolment, the inner city schools predominantly attended by Aboriginal students while keeping those with primarily white student populations despite their having lower enrolment (Gulson, 2011). Disruption of neighbourhood schools might function as mechanisms for rupturing black spaces and spatially reorganising the city (Lipman, 2011a; Pedroni, 2011). According to Pedroni (2011), in Detroit, "schools slated for closure have, like other neighbourhood schools across the city, functioned as anchors of the local community; as one of the only remaining public spaces in the community" (p. 210).

Rebranding and marketing the neighbourhood school is also a strategy for attracting middle class parents to the city. A large body of urban education studies point to the efforts to reorganise and improve urban public schools in order to attract middle class families to the city centre in Philadelphia (Cucchiara, 2008), Chicago (Lipman, 2004, 2011a), Sydney (Gulson, 2007a), and Boston (Billingham & Kimelberg, 2013). Such a policy of marketisation results in the marginalisation of low income and minority parents, who are treated implicitly as unwanted others while upper-middle classes and knowledge workers are seen as valued patrons capable of contributing to the school and changing its ethos (Cucchiara, 2008, 2013; Gulson, 2007a; Lipman, 2011a). Meanwhile, whiteness is constructed as an "invisible norm" (Gulson, 2006, p. 271) and a desirable quality (Gulson, 2007a).

SCHOOL CLOSINGS/RELOCATIONS AND SCHOOL CHOICE

The role of school choice policy emerges as a dominant theme in many studies dealing with the relationship between urban transformation and education policy. Since the late 1980s, public education systems have been fundamentally restructured, in part through the dismantling of centralised educational bureaucracies and their replacement with decentralised systems involving significant degrees of institutional autonomy and more diversified forms of administration (Whitty, 2000). Such shifts have often been linked to the promotion of discourses of parental choice and competition between different forms of educational institutions (Whitty, 2000).

Promotion of choice discourse and diversification of educational supply came alongside a new emphasis on public-private partnerships in the provision of education (Lipman, 2011a; Whitty & Edwards, 1998). Charter schools in the United States (Andréy-Bechely, 2007; Lipman, 2011b; Lipman, Person, & Kenwood Oakland Community Organization, 2007; Stovall, 2013) and grant maintained schools and city technology colleges (announced in 1986) in England (Dale, 1989; Whitty, 1990, 1997; Whitty & Edwards, 1998) are high-profile experiments aimed at extending publicly funded choice into the private sector. Similarly, in Australia, the 1990s were marked by a shift from comprehensive schooling to a system based on choice and diversity (Gulson, 2007b).

Although the origins and meaning of charter schools and choice discourse are closely linked to neoliberal ideologies, they enlisted significant support from progressive forces, school communities, and people of colour (Lipman, 2011a;

Whitty, 1997). The public acceptance they solicited was rooted in the desire of communities to address persistent educational problems and to gain a voice in educational decisions (Lipman, 2011a; Stovall, 2013; Whitty, 1997). In the case of England, policies promoting greater parental choice and institutional autonomy seemed to be favoured initially by progressive forces such as left-leaning teaching unions, inspectors, and teachers (Whitty & Wisby, 2016). The emergent policy preference for school choice in Western education systems came with the conservative governments of the time, such as the Thatcher government in England (see Dale, 1989; Whitty, 2000; Whitty & Edwards, 1998) and Bush administration in the US. These governments did not create an illusion or false consciousness. Instead, they spoke to the immediate problems and discomfort of people from a populist perspective (Apple, 2014). By pointing out problems in public education, school choice was advocated in many contexts of education as a solution. Neoliberals, who are the most powerful group within the power bloc supporting conservative modernisation (Apple, 2001a), successfully advocated the notion of parental school choice, framing choice in a consumer-oriented manner and promoting the extension of publicly-funded choice into the private sector (Whitty & Edwards, 1998).

Although choice policy garnered popular support by appealing to the aspirations of disadvantaged populations for a better system, an analysis of the policy reveals that they turned out to be far from increasing the opportunities for the disadvantaged. A large body of inquiry examined the ways in which the policy emphasis on choice and institutional autonomy further disenfranchised the already disadvantaged communities by opening the way for a further marketisation of education (Ball et al., 1996; Carnoy, 1993; Reay & Lucey, 2003; Whitty, 2000, 2002; Whitty & Edwards, 1998). Choice policies reinforced the existing hierarchy of schools, which remains shaped by "academic test results and social class" (Whitty, 1997, p. 14). Also, the policy created a competition among schools (Whitty, 1997). A cream-skimming effect became a major issue (Smith & Meier, in Whitty, 1997), and a large fraction of students, those from low-demand families in particular, tended to be worse off (Reay & Lucey, 2003; Whitty, 1997) while middle class parents were "more likely to have the knowledge, skills and contacts to decode and manipulate what are increasingly complex and deregulated systems of choice and recruitment" (Apple, 2001b, p. 415). Deregulation provides a space to apply informal procedures, with the middle class, on the whole, "better at moving their children around the system" (Ball et al., quoted in Apple, 2001a, p. 73). In this regard, research suggests that unrestricted choice gives rise to further stratification (Ball, Bowe, & Gewirtz, 1995), of which charter schools are an example (Frankenberg, Siegel-Hawley, & Wang, 2011).

Studies on school closings and relocations unfolding in the context of neoliberal urban renewal indicate that the number of public schools decreased at the expense of a vibrant growth in charter and contract schools (Lipman, 2011a; Stovall, 2013). Lipman (2011a), who worked extensively on Chicago school closings, argues that charter schools in Chicago are concentrated in impoverished African American and Latino/a neighbourhoods in which public schools have been shuttered. "As their students transfer to charters, neighbourhood public schools lose additional funding. In some areas of Chicago, so many schools have been closed that charter schools are parents' 'only choice'" (p. 127). However, after the transformation of public housing in these neighbourhoods and introduction of competitive selection criteria, not all children of African American or Latino/a parents could easily get into the charters (Stovall, 2013). Although some receiving schools remained in low-income black neighbourhoods, some charter schools such as those run by Educational Management Organisations enrolled the children of the higher-income residents, which means choice was not available to low income African American community members (Stovall, 2013). While charter schools were promoted as much better alternatives to conventional neighbourhood schools, not much attention was paid to the neighbourhood children whose access to the redeveloped charter schools were restricted due to the newly introduced selection criteria (Stovall, 2013). These instances show that educational reforms justified by the failure of public schools and treating the failure as a phenomenon that occurred in a vacuum (Apple, 2005) has the potential to create further inequalities.

Following Hurricane Katrina, policy makers advocated for a new system in New Orleans, where all schools were redeveloped into charter schools. Buras (2013) discusses how entrepreneurs sought to take advantage of Hurricane Katrina and how "targeted state disinvestment in black communities prepared the ground for white entrepreneurs to capitalise on public schools and create an urban space economy that serves their accumulative interests through dispossession of working-class communities of color" (p. 19). While there were plans prior to Katrina, a bill was passed right after the disaster in 2005, giving the control of an overwhelming majority of city's schools to the state, and charter schools became the chief strategy for restructuring public education (Jabbar, 2016). In this way, market-based reforms were implemented with much less resistance and public schools in the city were privatised.

ISTANBUL PUBLIC SCHOOLS, URBAN RENEWAL, AND DE-SECULARISATION

Neoliberal restructuring in Istanbul has dramatically changed the texture of the city. For Bartu-Candan and Kolluoglu (2008), "we are witnessing with awe, horror or indifferent familiarity an Istanbul changing rapidly in terms of its spaces, the relations it comprises and its imaginary, as the city has undergone a neoliberal restructuring over the past two decades" (p. 5). What was restructured was not only the material structures in the city, but also the ways various actors experienced it. The neoliberal phase of Istanbul's transformation was a result of the socioeconomic developments occurring in the 1980s (Çaliskan et al., 2012). The current neoliberal urban regime has its roots in the aftermath of the 1980 military coup d'etat, which also initiated economic liberalisation in Turkey (Önis, 1991, in Kuyucu & Unsal, 2010). As part of the central government's vision to position Istanbul as a world metropolis, a number of legal measures were taken to enable urban renewal projects and real estate investments. Mayor Dalan (1984–1989) played an important role in this transformation (Aksoy, 2012; Keyder & Öncü, 1993; Rutz & Balkan, 2009), linking economic prosperity to the cultural industry—in particular the city's Byzantine and Ottoman heritage—in order to invoke an image of a city as the centre of power, commerce, and culture (Rutz & Balkan, 2009). "Urban growth coalitions" in the city have had sustained interest in transforming Istanbul into a global city through policies seeking to turn it into a gentrified city appealing to the "tourist gaze" (Keyder, 2005, p. 128) and into a space of consumption and "tourist commodification" (Aksoy, 2012, p. 93). Çaliskan et al. (2012) state that a new phase was initiated in the late 1990s and became more evident in 2002, with the ascent to power of the ruling Justice and Development Party (JDP). Urban transformation processes of this era effected deep-rooted changes in the urban texture of the city and urban capital accumulation processes were articulated to capitalism in an unprecedented way (Çaliskan et al., 2012).

There has been a convergence of urban and education policies, and neoliberal urbanism and education policy have become inextricably intertwined. This chapter describes how educational policy is constitutive of urban restructuring processes that Brenner and Theodore (2002) discuss while theorising the relationship between cities and neoliberalism. The co-constitutive relationship between cities and neoliberalism is characterised by "a marked urbanisation of neoliberalism" since "cities have become strategic targets for an increasingly broad range of neoliberal policy experiments, institutional innovations, and politicoideological projects" (p. 376). In a similar vein, the chapter describes how education policy is central to neoliberal restructuring in the city and vice-versa.

The issue of school relocations dates back decades, but the first solid, albeit unofficial, proposals came in 2006 (see "1 Yerine 10 Okul", 2006; Kireçci, 2006). Print media covered the government's idea of selling 45 Istanbul inner-city public schools with high real estate value (Uçar, 2009). The Ministry of National Education (MoNE) stated that the lands of schools in historical buildings or those actively providing education services would not be subject to the policy of redevelopment (MoNE Press Release, 2009). According to the Ministry only schools in areas that lost residential district character would be considered for redevelopment although further developments and the statements of the Istanbul Director of the MoNE contradicted the Ministry's official explanation. When the names of 22 schools-for-sale in Istanbul were announced in newspapers ("Okul Satışlarına Protesto", 2010), the Director stated that this would be a bartering process whereby, in return for school lands, the MoNE would receive many more schools in other districts of the city (Ögünç, 2010). The legal framework had already been changed in 2008 to make possible the transfer of schools that were not "needed" into private bodies with the approval of the MoNE ("Istanbul'un Tarihi Okulları", 2009). Union leaders claimed that the number of schools was many more and reported phasing out of certain schools (Personal interview, 2012). In the face of public reaction, the government backed away from this plan of mass selling as it was not yet politically palatable.

However, since 2011, many of the schools that were listed publicly as for-sale schools, as well as various others that were not publicised, have been destabilised through various mechanisms such as the new compulsory schooling system and earthquake strengthening schemes.

One of the characteristics of the interplay between education policy and neoliberal urban restructuring in Istanbul is the drive towards de-secularisation. Sweeping changes in school systems and curricula have recently become entangled with urban renewal practices in various districts of Istanbul. Some of these changes are the compulsory school (grades 1–8) system reform, changes in high school (grades 9–12) system, and the introduction of elective religion courses. Law No 6287 changed the compulsory school system (grades 1–8) and initiated a massive reorganisation of school spaces. During the same period, all high schools (grades 9–12) were converted into selective enrolment schools with the introduction of a nationwide high school placement exam. Coupled to these changes was an overall conservative policy trend in public schools, resulting in a range of entanglements with urban renewal practices.

Law No 6287 mandated that the eight-year uninterrupted compulsory schooling introduced in 1997 be extended to an intermittent 12-year system, which is commonly called as 4+4+4 system. Prior to eight-year uninterrupted schooling, compulsory schooling consisted of a 5-year elementary school education (grades 1–5; ages 7–11), and a 3-year middle school education (*ortaokul* [grades 6–8; ages 12–14]) which was optional for those who wanted to continue their education. The 8-year uninterrupted schooling system closed autonomous middle schools and made them a part of primary schooling, merging them with what was called primary schools (*ilkokul*). This meant the closure of selective enrolment middle schools and religious (*Imam Hatip*) middle schools. In other words, students would be able to enter an exam-based selective enrolment school or a religious school only from age-14 on, which was severely criticised by Islamic parties and groups of the time. Middle school sections of religious (hereafter *Imam Hatip*[1]) schools and public (secular) middle schools were opened with the 4+4+4 reform while exam-based enrolment middle schools were not. In a way, a dual system of public education, religious and secular, was initiated. The Law now stipulates that each type of school (elementary, middle, high school) be established in separate buildings unless conditions dictate otherwise. This has meant the conversion of existing schools providing 8-year education for *either* a secular elementary school, a secular middle school, or an *Imam Hatip* middle school.

With the implementation of Law No 6287, education policy became intertwined with urban restructuring processes in secular districts of Istanbul. Fieldwork data suggest that secular schools in some neighbourhoods were converted into *Imam Hatip* middle schools despite community reaction and lack of demand.[2] A central agenda of neighbourhood solidarity forums established in 2013 following the urban uprising of June 2013 was to stop school conversions or relocations. During the span of 2-year fieldwork, I followed the struggles around the conversion of three secular schools in Kalimni district centre, with a particular focus on one school. Two of the schools, Gordon High School and Greenfield Middle School,[3] were located in secular middle class neighbourhoods where contractor-led urban transformation was in force. Another school, Meryem Primary School, was located in a mixed-income neighbourhood nearby a state-led urban transformation zone and became depopulated due to urban transformation, separation of its 5 to 8 grades into a middle school, and changes in its catchment.

Meryem Primary School, which was in a newly-built large building, first shared some of its classes with the students of the newly established girls' *Imam Hatip* middle school that was re-opened after the 6287 school reform. Parents and neighbourhood activists who wanted to learn what would happen to the school received vague answers each time they visited the MoNE authorities. Their claim that their school would be relocated was denied by authorities. However, at one of their meetings, they were told by the MoNE director of Kalimni district centre that they needed to increase student numbers in order to retain their schools, although it is in no way a community responsibility. MoNE authorities attributed the decrease in student numbers to urban transformation, but they would not mention the role of school reform and changes in the school's catchment. After a two-year process, the school was closed and converted into an *Imam Hatip* middle school. Although parents were told to increase student numbers to keep their schools, when they asked MoNE District Office why they were opening *Imam Hatip* schools in a district where demand was not high, they received the answer that if four parents gave a petition asking for an *Imam Hatip* school when neighbourhood catchment lacked one, MoNE was responsible for opening it. As in most other relocation cases in Kalimni, selective neglect of secular public schools was the case. Educational policy can draw on geographical aspects to legitimise the restructuring of state schools, to constitute new subjects, and to reposition the schools in the education market (Gulson, 2007a). The case of Meryem Primary school not only illustrates how a secular public school was transformed into a religious school on the pretext of urban transformation; but it also exemplifies how parents trying to keep their schools were treated as an undesired population left to submit to the new educational conditions or create their own solutions.

Greenfield Middle School case is a good example of how a well-performing urban public school in a salubrious district of Istanbul was closed despite public opposition. Greenfield was located in a staunchly secular district that was undergoing contractor-initiated urban transformation. The school was to be converted into an *Imam Hatip* school, and Greenfield students were to be relocated to a nearby school that was previously included in the for-sale list that was leaked to the press. According to parents and neighbourhood residents reacting against the plan, the school's closure and conversion was a deliberate attempt to change and punish the neighbourhood. Drawing on his interactions with policy makers regarding the situation of Greenfield, Hayri Poza, an MP from the secular opposition party, who was involved in school activism, alluded on various occasions that the school closure/conversion plan was a deliberate policy. He summarised his encounters with MoNE authorities as follows:

[Every time I see them] they keep saying that there's demand [for an *Imam Hatip* school]. I tell them, 'how is that possible? How can there be demand in a neighbourhood where we get 92 percent of the votes?'" (Fieldnotes, 2014). *Imam Hatip* schools have both a cultural and class dimension. Neighbourhood residents were spatially defensive and expressed their reaction to the MoNE by using the argument that these schools were not in high demand in their community and that the overwhelming majority of the students were bussed for free from other districts of Istanbul. At organisation meetings, they largely attributed school conversions to attempts to change the composition of the neighbourhood. On the one hand, as contractor-led urban transformation changed the physical environment, there was a change in the social composition of the area since existing residents moved out, never to return. Some would sell their houses to contractors; some would find the neighbourhood too noisy, dirty, and unsafe due to construction; others would find their new house and neighbourhood less affordable. Remaining residents thought that the new Imam Hatip schools' changed the face of their neighbourhood. Although the state does not provide free school-bussing or lunch in public schools, it was not an uncommon practice in *Imam Hatip* schools. MoNE authorities who were questioned about these facilities would explain that it was not the state or the MoNE, but, rather, charities that provided this support. Although the conversion of Greenfield was stopped in 2014, the school was not able to accept new students in the next term. The MoNE did not allocate adequate cleaning staff to the school, and parents had to hire one by collecting money among themselves. In 2015, Greenfield was closed and converted into a science and arts centre.

In the Greenfield case, as with most other conversion cases in Kalimni, a key concern was the promotion of private schooling. As soon as the news of Greenfield's conversion was released, private schools phoned a number of parents and invited them to talk about enrolment conditions, giving tests to students who would need fee discounts. Some parents who were anxious about the future met with private school management and allowed their children sit these exams. Considering that self exclusion can be a middle class strategy at stages of educational transition, albeit used primarily by those who are rich in both cultural and economic capital (Reay, 2004), one could reason that the new institutional structure described here contributes to the increasing marketisation of education, as well as its stratification. In light of research that claims that parents' views on public education are a chief factor in shaping their school choice (Aratemur-Cimen, 2015) and the claims of school communities that public schools are destabilised through various 'reform' mechanisms, it is possible to argue that the middle classes will further withdraw from public provision. Additionally, that these developments have been accompanied by the private school incentive system signals a further shift from the publicly funded comprehensive schooling as we know it.[4] As of the 2014–2015 academic year, and in line with the protocol signed between the Ministry of Finance and the Ministry of Education, the state was to grant financial support to 250,000 students who were already attending or who wanted to enrol in a private school. The subject matter law came at a time when many parents were unprepared and disgruntled with the rapid pace of the reforms, making them think that financial aid to private schools was paradoxical in light of the neglected situation of public schools. This new institutional structure, where middle class parents are excluded from consensus mechanisms and encouraged to voluntarily exclude themselves from public education, further encourages them to act in pursuit of their own children's interest, which resonates with the neoliberal ideal of creating rational, profit-seeking and self-reliant individuals.

The turn to *Imam Hatip* schools also signals a hegemonic turn in Turkish education policy. Aware that economic power does not necessarily mean political power or vice versa, neoliberal Islamism in Turkey seeks to create the conditions for the reproduction and perpetuation of its class interests. The perpetuation of power in the economic domain requires political, social, and cultural authority or leadership (Gramsci, 2012). The government's promotion of further religionalisation in education can be considered as a strategy similar to what Clarke (2010) describes in the context of Britain, "there has been a continuing search for the conditions that would enable a new hegemony—one which would rest on increasingly segmenting populations through dynamics of inclusion and exclusion" (p. 348).

CHOICE DISCOURSE IN TURKEY'S EDUCATION POLICY

School choice options vary depending on the local conditions in which they are implemented, and therefore, in order to understand the effects of choice policies, one first needs to attend to the local context in which choice discourse unfolds (Andrey-Bechely, 2007). In the context of Turkey, where there is no local level policy making and thus the practices in Istanbul can be viewed as similar to other regions, cities and local communities, choice discourse was not operationalised in the same manner and at the same level of emphasis.

The discourse of choice in Turkish education has not been in the forefront of the policy agenda as it has been in the US and Western Europe, which can partly be explained historically. Literature suggests that although discourses about school choice and institutional autonomy are separate, they are promoted simultaneously and intersect to consolidate each other (see Lipman, 2011a; Whitty, 1997). Whitty (2002) describes school autonomy as referring to "moves to devolve various aspects of decision making from regional and district offices to individual public schools, whether to site-based professionals, community-based councils, or a combination of both" (p. 3). Expansion of charter schools in the name of individual choice can be traced to the "roll out of 'local control'" (Lipman, 2011a). As mentioned in the previous sections, public acceptance of charter schools had to do with them promising more freedom to choose and autonomy to parents, teachers, and schools. An understanding of the autonomy model as described above contrasts in some aspects, albeit not completely, with the dictates of Turkish education policy. The World Bank (2005) describes the Turkish education system as the most centralised system in Europe and its schools as having little autonomy, which it attributes to "legitimate historical reasons, including issues of culture, nation building, and social unity" (p. 27). The centralised character of the education system has also been problematised by non-governmental organisations and human rights groups and is attributed to the particular political climate in the country.

One reason for the strict commitment to a centralised education system despite the contrary trajectory internationally is that education in mother tongue has long been one of the central demands of the Kurdish political movement but met with the resistance and unwillingness of the state. Kurds are not officially recognized as minorities in the Lausanne Peace Treaty, which defined minority rights and concepts in the new republic established in 1923. The Lausanne Peace Treaty was also responsible for drawing the present borders of the Turkish Republic (except Hatay). Although the League of Nations defined minorities in religious, ethnic, or linguistic terms, the Turkish delegate to the Lausanne Treaty had reservations about this comprehensive definition, preferring instead that only non-Muslims would be defined as minorities (Oran, 2007). Hence, although any community could seek minority status by recourse to one or more of these three categories, thus ensuring the right to establish schools and use mother tongue language for instruction, Kurds, as Muslims, were excluded from doing so by legislation. Although this definition of minority status is at odds with current political thinking about the status and definition of minorities, the Turkish state insisted on using this definition (Oran, 2007) and invoked it in international agreements when minority rights were under consideration. Although Turkey has signed international treaties pertaining to minority and cultural rights, it has put reservations on provisions that are relevant to minorities' rights to education in their mother tongue (Kaya, 2009). Even expression and dissemination of thought in Kurdish was prohibited by law until late 2001[5] (Hale, 2003).

It was in 2001, with the need to comply with the European Union democratisation criteria, that the clauses that banned the expression of thoughts and publication in Kurdish were completely removed. However, Kurdish education in public schools is still a contested issue. Although the JDP seemed to adopt a more liberal approach to the Kurdish issue until 2015, rather than acknowledging the difference and rights of Kurds, its policy relied heavily on stressing the similarities—Islamic brotherhood in particular—between the Kurds and Turks. Although Kurdish activism for the right to mother tongue education has a long history, it was only legalised in *private* education in 2014 and remains prohibited in public schools. Despite global tendencies to the contrary, the localisation and devolution of responsibilities to individual bodies remains a limited aspect of Turkish education policy. Here, the obvious implication of local control in education—meaning increased municipal control in the context of Turkey—would be culturally-sensitive education that took account of the desire for mother tongue instruction. However, due to the central character of policy development in the National Assembly, the capacity for decision-making that responds to the issues of cultural and linguistic relevance—an issue of particular importance to the Kurdish community—is side-lined. As such, the priorities of urban education in Turkey, and thus the ethnic majority, set the direction for the remainder of the country. As a consequence, urban education in Turkey follows its own different path.

It can be said that compared to what is described by international literature, there was lack of engagement with choice discourse in Turkish education policy. In cases when choice was articulated, it was done to promote publicly funded religious education, which was provided in *Imam Hatip* schools. As explained earlier, Law No 6287, which was hurriedly passed in 2012 despite the uproar it caused among NGOs and unions, changed the 8 years of uninterrupted basic education system to a 4+4+4 model, and *Imam Hatip* middle schools were re-opened. The notion of choice, which was not present in the preceding version, entered the Basic Law on National Education No. 1739. With an amendment to Article 25 of the Law No. 1739, middle schools were defined as follows: "Primary education institutions consist of (…) four-year compulsory middle schools and *Imam Hatip* middle schools, making it possible to choose among different types of educational programs" (Law no 1739). Because only middle school sections of *Imam Hatip* schools were reopened while those of other school types such as Anatolian middle schools that were closed in 1997 were not, it can be inferred that the phrase "different types of educational programs" included in the law refers to religious education. What happened in most cases was that rather than opening new middle schools, existing secular primary or secondary schools were converted into *Imam Hatip* middle schools. Additionally, the law introduced two more elective religion courses: the 'Koran' and 'The Life of Prophet Mohammed' while defining non-religion courses as "other elective courses", with no specific mention of them. An MP from the ruling party expressed his admiration for the new policy at an alumni gathering of an *Imam Hatip* high school:

> Now we have gotten a chance. We will surely increase the enrolment at these [*Imam Hatip*] schools. But [what is more important is that] we have gotten the chance to turn all schools into *Imam Hatip* schools. We have gotten this chance thanks to the elective courses on the Koran and the Life of Our Prophet introduced by the 4+4+4 system. (Boga, 2012)

As a result of all these developments, secular parents and citizens vented their frustration and anger via various street events. In numerous districts of Istanbul, for example, citizens organised forums, demonstrations, and press statements so that they could make their voices heard.

The history of *Imam Hatip* schools is rooted in complex power struggles between right-wing political thought and a secular republican establishment, each seeking to institutionalise their own version of religiosity since the establishment of Turkish Republic. Whilst it is beyond the scope of this chapter to address these struggles in detail, choice and demand discourses in relation to *Imam Hatip* schools can only be understood in relation to them. Indeed, choice and demand are politically, socially, and economically generated (see Çakir, Bozan, & Talu, 2004).

Despite the geographically specific tendency in Turkey with respect to choice, a common tendency across multiple spaces of education policy is the perpetuation of existing hierarchies and inequalities or the creation of new ones through the promotion of certain school types and values in education. Although a lack of engagement with choice discourse might seem to be a barrier to marketisation in education, it is precipitated in various ways as described above.

CONCLUSION

This chapter has described two geographically situated tendencies in urban education policy in Istanbul, situating it in international body of scholarship. While international literature points to the destabilisation of black and minority neighbourhoods and their schools in the nexus of urban renewal and education policy change, the argument of this chapter has been that a central character of the interaction between urban renewal and school reform in Istanbul has been the destabilisation of traditional middle class public schools and a concomitant de-secularisation of the education system. Rather than an anomaly, this difference is described as the outcome of existing power relationships and the specific cultural character of Turkey's neoliberalisation. Neoliberalism is a political project that is institutionalised through contextually specific strategies and interacts with inherited regulatory structures (Brenner & Theodore, 2005).

The relative lack of engagement with choice discourses in Turkish education policy has been described as an outcome of historical conditions, and a framing of parental choice in terms of being able to choose a religious school where a single interpretation of Islam is taught. Unsurprisingly, this has been described as part of an attempt to create new hierarchies in education. Just like charter schools or grant maintained schools that attempt to extend publicly funded choice into the private sphere, *Imam Hatip* schools in Turkey have been promoted and endorsed by policy makers themselves. This policy stands in sharp contrast to the spatial and material neglect of secular public schools and has a potential for pushing middle class parents towards private education. The deteriorating situation of the traditional middle class, however, does not open space for the disadvantaged. On the contrary, it might contribute to the deterioration of the conditions in public schools and a widening of the disparities and inequalities in education. Neglecting secular public schools or converting them to *Imam Hatip* schools is constitutive of a cultural social control whereby the hegemony of a particular belief is instituted. Here, the economic power of a group of elites is sustained and made legitimate.

NOTES

[1] Imam means "prayer leader", and hatip means "preacher" in Turkish.
[2] The author is aware that "demand" in education is a construct that needs to treated with caution. In the case described in this chapter, lack of demand is determined drawing on field notes and field observations, which documented neighbourhood residents reporting low demand for the school from its vicinity and students being bussed for free to many schools converted to Imam Hatip schools, which is not a service provided in mainstream public schools. Free bussing to an urban school in the context of Istanbul is an indication that the school is not on high demand by neighbourhood residents but enrolment in this school is promoted.
[3] All the names of schools and research participants in this chapter are pseudonyms.

⁴ This shift may not necessarily involve retrenchment of public sources in education, but may entail redrawing the boundaries between the public and private (see Clarke, 2004a, 2004b).
⁵ The law did not explicitly refer to Kurdish language but defined it in an indirect way.

REFERENCES

1 Yerine 10 Okul. (2006, August 11). *1 yerine 10 okul* [10 schools for 1]. Retrieved August 17, 2013, from http://hurarsiv.hurriyet.com.tr/goster/haber.aspx?id=4906044&tarih=2006-08-11

Aksoy, A. (2012). Riding the storm: "New Istanbul". *City, 16*(1–2), 93–111. doi:10.1080/13604813.2012.662373

Andrey-Bechely, L. (2007). Finding space and managing distance: Public school choice in an urban California district. *Urban Studies, 44*(7), 1355–1376. doi:10.1080/00420980701302304

Apple, M. W. (2001a). *Educating the right way: Markets, standards, god, and inequality*. New York, NY & London: Routledge & Falmer.

Apple, M. W. (2001b). Comparing neo-liberal projects and inequality in education. *Comparative Education, 37*(4), 409–423. doi:10.1080/03050060120091229

Apple, M. W. (2005). Audit cultures, commodification, and class and race strategies in education. *Policy Futures in Education, 3*(4), 379–399. doi:10.2304/pfie.2005.3.4.379

Apple, M. W. (2014). *Official knowledge: Democratic education in a conservative age* (3rd ed.). New York, NY: Routledge.

Aratemur-Çimen, C. (2015). *Differentiating children through education: School choices and educational practices of middle-class families in neoliberal times* (Unpublished doctoral dissertation). Bogazici University, Istanbul.

Ball, S. J., Bowe, R., & Gewirtz, S. (1995). Circuits of schooling: A sociological exploration of parental choice of school in social class contexts. *The Sociological Review, 43*(1), 52–78.

Ball, S. J., Bowe, R., & Gewirtz, S. (1996). School choice, social class, and distinction: The realization of social advantage in education. *Journal of Education Policy, 11*, 89–112.

Bartu-Candan, A., & Kolluoglu, B. (2008). Emerging spaces of neoliberalism: A gated town and a public housing project in Istanbul. *New Perspectives on Turkey, 39*, 5–46.

Billingham, C. M., & Kimelberg, S. M. (2013). Middle-class parents, urban schooling, and the shift from consumption to production of urban space. *Sociological Forum, 28*(1), 85–108. doi:10.1111/socf.12004

Boga, A. (2012). *Address of MP Ali Boga on 24 August 2012* [Newspaper Report]. Retrieved from http://www.milliyet.com.tr/-okullari-imam-hatip-yapma-sansi-yakaladik-/siyaset/siyasetdetay/24.08.2012/1585614/default.htm

Brenner, N., & Theodore, N. (2002). Cities and the geographies of 'actually existing neoliberalism'. *Antipode, 34*, 349–379.

Brenner, N., & Theodore, N. (2005). Neoliberalism and the urban condition. *City: Analysis of Urban Trends Culture, Theory, Policy, Action, 9*, 101–107. doi:10.1080/13604810500092106

Buras, K. L. (2013). 'We're not going nowhere': Race, urban space, and the struggle for king elementary school in New Orleans. *Critical Studies in Education, 54*, 19–32. doi:10.1080/17508487.2013.741072

Çakir, R., Bozan, I., & Talu, B. (2004). *Imam Hatip liseleri: Efsaneler, gercekler* (Imam Hatip schools: Myths and realities) [Adobe Digital Editions version]. Retrieved from http://www.tesev.org.tr/assets/publications/file/IH%20Efsaneler-Gercekler.pdf

Çaliskan, C. O., Cilgin, K., Dundar, U., & Yalcintan, M. C. (2012, December 6–7). *Istanbul donusum cografyasi* [Transformation Geography of Istanbul]. Paper presented in the Urban and Regional Studies Symposium, Ankara, Turkey.

Carnoy, M. (1993). School improvement: Is Privatization the answer? In J. Hannaway & M. Carnoy (Eds.), *Decentralization and school improvement: Can we fulfill the promise?* (pp. 163–201). San Francisco, CA: Jossey-Bass.

Clarke, J. (2004a). *Changing welfare changing states*. Thousand Oaks, CA: Sage Publications.

Clarke, J. (2004b). Dissolving the public realm? The logics and limits of neo-liberalism. *Journal of Social Policy, 33*(1), 27–48.

Clarke, J. (2010). Of crises and conjunctures: The problem of the present. *Journal of Communication Inquiry, 34*(4), 337–354. doi:10.1177/0196859910382451

Cucchiara, M. B. (2008). Re-branding urban schools: Urban revitalization, social status, and marketing public schools to the upper middle class. *Journal of Education Policy, 23*, 165–179.

Cucchiara, M. B. (2013). *Marketing schools, marketing cities: Who wins and who loses when schools become urban amenities.* Chicago, IL: The University of Chicago Press.

Dale, R. (1989). The thatcherite project in education: The case of the city technology colleges. *Critical Social Policy, 9*(27), 4–19. doi:10.1177/026101838900902701

Frankenberg, E., Siegel-Hawley, G., & Wang, J. (2011). Choice without equity: Charter school segregation. *Education Policy Analysis Archieves, 19*, 1. Retrieved October 3, 2015, from http://epaa.asu.edu/ojs/article/view/779

Gramsci, A. (2012). *Selections from prison notebooks of Antonio Gramsci* (Q. Hoare, Ed. & G. N. Smith, Trans.). New York, NY: International Publishers.

Grant, C. A., Arcello, A. F., Konrad, A. M., & Swenson, M. C. (2014). Fighting for the 'right to the city': Examining spatial injustice in Chicago public school closings. *British Journal of Sociology of Education, 35*, 670–687. doi:10.1080/01425692.2014.919844

Gulson, K. N. (2006). A White veneer: Education policy, space, and 'race' in the inner city. *Discourse: Studies in the Cultural Politics of Education, 27*, 259–274. doi:10.1080/01596300600676243

Gulson, K. N. (2007a). Repositioning schooling in inner Sydney: Urban renewal, an education market and the 'absent presence' of the 'middle classes'. *Urban Studies, 44*, 1377–1391. doi:10.1080/00420980701302379

Gulson, K. N. (2007b). 'Neoliberal spatial technologies': On the practices of educational policy change. *Critical Studies in Education, 48*, 179–195. doi:10.1080/17508480701494226

Gulson, K. N. (2011). *Education policy, space, and the city: Markets and the (in)visibility of race.* New York, NY: Routledge.

Hale, W. (2003). Human rights, the European Union and the Turkish accession process. *Turkish Studies, 4*(1), 107–126. doi:10.1080/714005714

Istanbul'un tarihi okulları. (2009, July 8). *Istanbul'un tarihi okullari satiliyor mu?* [Are historical schools of Istanbul being sold?] Retrieved March 21, 2014, from http://www.cnnturk.com/2009/turkiye/07/08/istanbulun.tarihi.okullari satiliyor.mu/534205.0/

Jabbar, H. (2016). The visible hand: Markets, politics, and regulation in post-Katrina New Orleans. *Harvard Educational Review, 86*(1), 1–26. Retrieved from http://dx.doi.org/10.17763/0017-8055.86.1.1

Kaya, N. (2009). *Forgotten or assimilated? Minorities in the education system of Turkey* (Report by Minority Rights Group International). Retrieved from http://www.ecoi.net/file_upload/1002_1237662172_mrg-turkey.pdf

Keyder, C. (2005). Globalisation and social exclusion in Istanbul. *International Journal of Urban and Regional Research, 29*(1), 124–134.

Keyder, C., & Öncü, A. (1993). *Istanbul and the concept of world cities.* Istanbul: Friedrich Ebert Foundation.

Kireçci, T. (2006, October 10). *Istanbul'da 8 okulun yeri satiliyor* [Land belonging to 8 schools in Istanbul are on sale]. Retrieved January 5, 2013, from http://www.milliyet.com.tr /2006/10/10/ekonomi/eko03.html

Kuyucu, T., & Unsal, O. (2010). Urban transformation as state-led property transfer: An analysis of two cases of urban renewal in Istanbul. *Urban Studies, 47*(7), 1479–1499.

Lipman, P. (2004). *High stakes in education: Inequality, globalization, and urban school reform.* New York, NY: Routledge Falmer.

Lipman, P. (2011a). *The new political economy of urban education: Neoliberalism, race, and the right to the city.* New York, NY: Routledge.

Lipman, P. (2011b). Contesting the city: Neoliberal urbanism and the cultural politics of education reform in Chicago. *Discourse: Studies in the Cultural Politics of Education, 32*(2), 217–234. doi:10.1080/01596306.2011.562667

Lipman, P., Person, A. S., & Kenwood Oakland Community Organisation. (2007). *Students as collateral damage: A preliminary study of Renaissance 2010 school closings in the Midsouth* [Report]. Retrieved March 12, 2016, from http://ceje.uic.edu/wp-content/uploads/2013/11/collateral-damage-midsouth-report-1-31-07.pdf

MoNE Press Release. (2009). *Sahibinden satilik mektep haberiyle ilgili basın açıklaması* [Press statement regarding the news "School for sale from the owner"]. Retrieved August 5, 2013, from http://www.meb.gov.tr/duyurular/duyuruayrinti.asp?ID=6545

Ögünç, P. (2010, December 15). *Ogrenciden temiz, kelepir okul* [Cheap and clean schools for sale by students]. Retrieved March 5, 2012, from http://www.radikal.com.tr/Radikal.aspx?aType=RadikalDetayV3&ArticleID=1032650&CategoryID=41

Okul satışlarına protesto. (2010, July 2). *Okul satislarina protesto* [Protesting school sales]. Retrieved March 30, 2012, from http://egitim.milliyet.com.tr/okul-satislarina-pretesto/egitimdunyasi/haberdetay/02.07.2010/1258228/default.htm

Oran, B. (2007). The minority concept and rights in Turkey: The lausanne peace treaty and current issues. In Z. F. Kabasakal-Arat (Ed.), *Human rights in Turkey* (pp. 35–56). Retrieved from https://books.google.com.tr/books?hl=tr&lr=&id=AWIUBAAAQBAJ&oi=fnd&pg=PA35&dq=Lausianne+treaty&ots=6GLsm3pBOS&sig=91x7Q_IYiWwOUIZOsqgENKXk0p8&redir_esc=y#v=onepage&q=Lausianne%20treaty&f=false

Pedroni, C. T. (2011). Urban shrinkage as a performance of whiteness: Neoliberal urban restructuring, education, and racial containment in the post-industrial, global niche city. *Discourse: Studies in the Cultural Politics of Education, 32*(2), 203–215. doi:10.1080/01596306.2011.562666

Reay, D. (2004). Exclusivity, exclusion, and social class in urban education markets in the United Kingdom. *Urban Education, 39*(5), 537–560. doi:10.1177/0042085904266925

Reay, D., & Lucey, H. (2003). The limits of 'choice': Children and inner city schooling. *Sociology, 37*, 121–142. doi:10.1177/0038038503037001389

Rutz, H. J., & Balkan, E. M. (2009). *Reproducing class: Education, neoliberalism, and the rise of new middle class in Istanbul.* New York, NY: Berghahn Books.

Stovall, D. (2013). Against the politics of desperation: Educational justice, critical race theory, and Chicago school reform. *Critical Studies in Education, 54*, 33–43. doi:10.1080/17508487.2013.739192

Uçar, S. (2009, July 8). *Sahibinden satilik mektep* [School for Sale from the Owner]. Retrieved July 11, 2014, from http://www.haberturk.com/gundem/haber/157690-sahibinden-satilik-mektep

Whitty, G. (1990). Creeping privatization and its implications for schooling in the inner city. *The Urban Review, 22*(2), 101–114.

Whitty, G. (1997). Creating quasi-markets in education: A review of recent research on parental choice and school autonomy in three countries. *Review of Research in Education, 22*, 3–47. Retrieved from http://www.jstor.org/stable/1167373

Whitty, G. (2000). Sociology of education and urban education policy. In K. A. McClafferty, C. A. Torres, & T. R. Mitchell (Eds.), *Challenges of urban education* (pp. 79–97). Albany, NY: State University of New York Press.

Whitty, G. (2002). *Making sense of education policy: Studies in the sociology and politics of education.* London, Thousand Oaks, CA, & New Delhi: Sage Publications.

Whitty, G., & Edwards, T. (1998). School choice policies in England and the United States: An exploration of their origins and significance. *Comparative Education, 34*, 221–227. doi:10.1080/03050069828289

Whitty, G., & Wisby, E. (2016). Education in England: A testbed for network governance? *Oxford Review of Education, 42*(3), 316–329. doi:10.1080/03054985.2016.1184873

World Bank. (2005). *Turkey- education sector study* (Report No. 32450-TU). Retrieved from http://siteresources.worldbank.org/INTTURKEY/Resources/361616-1142415001082/ESS_Main_Report_V1.pdf

Sezen Bayhan
School of Foreign Languages
Istanbul Technical University
Turkey

MARCELA RAMOS

11. PARENTAL INVOLVEMENT IN DISADVANTAGED DISTRICTS OF SANTIAGO

Intergenerational Consequences for Equity of a Market-Driven Educational System

INTRODUCTION

Chile is known worldwide as a paradigm of market-based education. During the 1980s, under the military dictatorship of Augusto Pinochet, an open market system whereby funding follows students to their schools of choice (vouchers policy) was established. The Chilean market design was expected to prove that, through competition, the average school results would improve (Contreras et al., 2010; Jofre, 1988). To make this market more transparent and competitive, a national test (SIMCE) was created for assessing 'educational quality' by measuring students' learning outcomes. However, competition did not generate better results. Instead, schools responded to these incentives by grouping, selecting or even rejecting students (Hsieh & Urquiola, 2003; Hsieh & Urquiola, 2006). A selective and segregated education system was instituted in Chile and policies driven during democracy somehow deepened the process (Bellei, 2015). Indeed, after the return to democracy, in 1990, the vouchers policy remained unchanged and a shared funding scheme that allowed private subsidised and secondary public schools to charge parents a fee in addition to the state voucher was established. As a result, the number of families that paid for their children's school and the privatisation of the school system as a whole increased considerably (Elacqua et al., 2013). In short, after the return to democracy, the reforms undertaken 'complemented, guided, refined but not replaced' the market logic that underpins the Chilean education system since the 1980s (Bellei, 2015, p. 15).

For the persistence of its market narrative, the Chilean education system could be considered, comparatively, a case of interest. Seen abstractly, it constitutes an example of what Robertson (2016) has defined as an education sector 'dominated by neoclassical economists and their ideas' (Robertson, 2016, p. 824). Within such a scheme, certain beliefs, aspirations and values in relation to education are prompted and developed. This chapter seeks to illuminate an area of that subjective space. Specifically, the purpose is to discuss beliefs and aspirations in relation to education of a group qualitatively meaningful: urban lower middle-class Chilean parents who grew up embedded in the neo-liberal narrative of personal effort and who, from the year 2000 onwards, have participated in their children's education within a context of expanded opportunities.

Within education literature, the market logic and its influence on middle-class parents' constructions and reflections in relation to their children's education have been approached mainly through the study of school choice practices at a national (Raczynski et al., 2010; Falabella et al., 2015; Elacqua et al., 2006; Canales et al., 2015) and international level (Ball, 2003; Gewirtz et al., 1995; James et al., 2010; Vincent et al., 2012). They have also been studied through the relationship they have with schools and schools' procedures (Crozier, 1997; Crozier & Davies, 2007; Lareau, 1989, 2000). This study seeks to contribute to the understanding of the influence of the market narrative of education in a less explored space: the *hows* and *whys* of parental involvement in their children's education. From an intergenerational perspective, to explore parental constructions about education and their involvement possibilities is particularly meaningful taking into account that what happens at home is central to children's development (Biggeri, 2007; Biggeri & Santi, 2012; Desforges & Abouchaar, 2003; Fantuzzo et al., 2004; Hartas, 2008; Hartas, 2011; Jackson & Remillard, 2005; Weiss et al., 2009; Zellman & Waterman, 1998).

PARENTAL INVOLVEMENT IN THIS STUDY

An area of parental involvement literature has focused on parent-school relationships and how parents can positively influence their children's academic performance (Epstein, 1990; Epstein & Dauber, 1991; Epstein, 1995; Sheldon & Epstein, 2005; Grolnick & Slowiaczek, 1994). This 'school centric' focus (Jackson & Remillard, 2005) can be considered useful for the development of educational policies. For instance, the OECD recommended that governments encourage parental participation practices, as this may help to reduce performance differences across socio-economic groups (Borgonovi & Montt, 2012). However, the idea that a causal relationship between parental participation and children's school results may exist has been problematised both at a methodological level (Mattingly et al., 2002; Domina, 2005; Gorard & See, 2013) as well as from a social justice perspective (Crozier, 1997; Crozier & Davies, 2007; Nakagawa, 2000). The focus on results may favour certain forms of participation and, as a consequence, certain groups of parents, to the detriment of others (Bakker & Denessen, 2007; Crozier, 1997; Lareau, 2000; Nakagawa, 2000).

Beyond the arguments that have already been made, within this study it is considered that the emphasis on the outcomes or results aspects of education in general, and in terms of parental involvement in particular, might promote a limited way of understanding education. This would consist of a view that emphasises its instrumental aspect, as if the purpose and meaning of education were the results associated with it. However, as Biesta (2009) highlights, education has different perspectives and spaces of influence (personal, social, institutional) and this comprehensive way of addressing it could be particularly relevant when it has to do with children's educational development.

The usefulness of this perspective is also stressed in the light of debates that emphasise the need to approach parental involvement not as a "laundry list of good things that good parents do for their children's education" (Barton et al., 2004, p. 3), but on the basis of the quality and meaningfulness that, above all, might underpin a positive process of involvement (Pomerantz et al., 2007; Jackson & Remillard, 2005). Following this train of thought, the study approaches the topic of parental involvement using the capability approach (Sen, 1979, 1992, 1999; Nussbaum, 2006, 2011) as the main theoretical framework. How and why this framework is used in this research and the spaces it can illuminate when it comes to studying parental involvement will be explained below.

PARENTAL INVOLVEMENT FROM A HUMAN CAPABILITY APPROACH

The capability approach is a normative framework that can be applied in the evaluation of well-being, the design of policies and the assessment of proposals about social change (Robeyns, 2006a). When approaching education, it is understood as an alternative framework to human capital theory (Robeyns, 2006b; Walker, 2006), which understands education primarily as a means to access better opportunities: better salaries and better jobs (Schultz, 1961; Lanzi, 2007). According to Sen, further training can make a person more efficient, more productive and, as a result, have access to a better salary. However, even if his/her salary is not increased, the education received may enable the development of other capabilities: being able to discuss and expose an idea, choosing in a more informed way and being taken more seriously by others. Following Sen's logic, placing the emphasis on the economic aspects is to highlight just a section of the picture, since individuals "are not merely means of production (even though they excel in that capacity) but also the end of the exercise" (Sen, 1997, p. 1960). From a capability approach perspective, education should be acknowledged both because of its instrumental and intrinsic value (Sen, 1997), since it allows people not only to develop different capacities and access better opportunities, but also to flourish.

Functionings and capabilities are two central concepts in the capability approach (Sen, 1992). Functionings are achieved beings and doings. There are basic functionings, such as feeding, moving from one place to another, riding a bike; and more complex, such as playing a musical instrument, debating and writing essays. Capabilities, meanwhile, represent the space of the possible: what people are able to do and to be (Robeyns, 2011). From an evaluative and comparative perspective, distinguishing between these two concepts is relevant, since one of the central features of the capability approach is its focus on what people can genuinely achieve. As Dreze and Sen (1995) highlight, the idea of capability "is essentially one of freedom—the range of options a person has in deciding what kind of life to lead" (Drèze & Sen, 1995, p. 11). The distinction between functionings and capabilities is significant to this study because it provides the theoretical tools to critically address both the beings and doings when it has to do with parental involvement practices (the space of functionings) and also the different possibilities and opportunities of becoming involved (the space of capabilities). Secondly, according to the capability approach, an individual's opportunities or capabilities depend not only on the persons' abilities but also on contextual factors and access to certain resources or services. Therefore, through the capability approach it is possible to acknowledge the centrality the context may play in individuals' possibilities, particularly among less advantaged groups.

In sum, the capability approach is used as the main theoretical framework in this study for three reasons: (i) because education is understood and valued from its intrinsic and instrumental perspective; (ii) for the importance it attaches, while addressing social phenomena, to people's freedom and their real possibilities to choose what they value (namely, individuals' capabilities); and (iii) its relational ontology (Smith & Seward, 2009), which recognises that personal and contextual factors may promote or limit people's possibilities of being and doing (in this case, parental involvement capabilities).

The next section will give details of the chosen methods for the research, explaining briefly how the capability approach was translated into the methodological design.

THE RESEARCH DESIGN

The study from which this chapter draws is an exploratory and critical qualitative study. Data was collected through two rounds of semi-structured interviews that were conducted with a sample of 14 urban lower middle-class parents. Based on Chilean literature (Barozet, 2006; Barozet & Fierro, 2014; Franco et al., 2011; Rojas & Falabella, 2013), urban lower middle-class parents are defined as mothers or fathers that live in certain districts of Santiago, the Chilean capital city, that have more years of schooling than their own parents and after finishing school have pursued technical or vocational studies. In terms of income, it has been defined as a vulnerable group because, despite the fact that they live in better economic conditions, an illness or a long period of unemployment on the part of the head of the household can affect the economic stability of the family. These are groups who tend to work in the private sector, which distinguishes them from the traditional Chilean middle-classes (Rojas & Falabella, 2013).

The research was carried out, first, with the help of a purposive sample strategy (Cohen et al., 2007). The idea was to look for urban lower middle-class Chilean parents with certain characteristics in order for potential different experiences/views on their children's education and their own role in that process to subsequently be grasped. The following criteria were considered: parents or mothers with at least one child between the age of 6 and 15 who attend subsidised private schools (for which they paid a monthly fee until a policy amendment in 2016) or emblematic schools (highly selective free public secondary schools). The latter is based on evidence highlighting that in Chile children from urban lower middle-class families attend those kinds of school (Valenzuela, 2008). The parents/mothers interviewed share some socio-economic characteristics (income level, neighbourhood) but are of a different age, and have different educational backgrounds and children at different stages in the school system and attending different schools. In sum, it seeks to conform to a purposive 'strategic' (Mason, 2002, p. 124) or 'maximum variation sampling' (Cohen et al., 2007, p. 157), including a range of experiences, characteristics and examples. Finally, to gain access to some of the parents interviewed, a snowball sampling strategy was followed, but carefully attending to the variation criteria, to maintain differences among the sample (Punch & Oancea, 2014). The majority of the interviewees were contacted through professional or personal contacts, some of which acted as gatekeepers (Cohen et al., 2007, p. 116). In some cases, my contacts sent me the email addresses of potential interviewees, and in others, their telephone numbers. I sent emails or called all of them in order to introduce myself and briefly explain the research topic, objectives and the issues I wanted to discuss in the interview related to their children's education and how they get involved in this process. Both mothers and fathers were interviewed, but proportionally fewer fathers.

In this study parental involvement is understood broadly (Georgiou, 1997), comprising parenting behaviours at home and parent–school relationships, but with particular attention to parents' beliefs, aspirations and values in relation to their children's education, including, but not limited to, schooling (Bakker & Denessen, 2007). The main instrument of data collection was qualitative semi-structured interviews. Following Jackson and Remillard's (2005) parental involvement framework two spaces of involvement were privileged within the interview schedules: "involvement in children's learning", understood as the way parents support their children's learning in diverse contexts, namely, not just those that are related to schools; and "involvement in children's schooling", defined as the ways parents actively participate in support of their children's development in school. Among the purposes of this research was to gain access to parents' reflections and experiences in relation to their children's education. Prompt cards (Robson, 2011) were used to stimulate conversation, to elicit responses and provide the means for parents to think freely and reflect on parental involvement and the activities they carry out or not with their children, and to explore what sorts of beings and doings in relation to parental involvement they achieve or would value undertaking. The interview schedule included topics related to activities and also parental reflections on their practices and beliefs about education, in order to understand if there is room for criticism, reasoning or the possibility of distinguishing between the different values of education. In this way, both the space of parental involvement functionings and capabilities might be acknowledged.

Thematic analysis (Braun & Clarke, 2006) was used to identify recurrent themes within the interviews conducted. Themes and patterns were identified both inductively (data driven) and using a theoretical thematic analysis. Specifically, after transcribing the data, repeated rounds of reading were conducted to identify the salient cross-cutting themes and patterns in interviewees' accounts. Following this logic, all interviews were coded and coding was developed considering both semantic and latent content (Braun & Clarke, 2006). Themes were built as was done previously with the coding of the interviews: the researcher read through the codes (nodes/child nodes in NVivo) looking for patterns, structures, differences, similarities and unexpected reflections. The quotes and reflections cited below represent examples from some of the themes that emerged from the analysis.

THE 80S: A CONTEXT OF NARROW OPPORTUNITIES AND ASPIRATIONS

The 14 parents interviewed in this research were born in Santiago in the 1970s and 1980s. During those years huge transformations that reshaped the country politically, economically, culturally and socially were taking place. In 1973 a military coup overthrew the democratically elected government of President Salvador Allende. Then, over a period of 17 years, Chile was ruled by a military dictatorship, a tough period characterised by persistent human rights violations.[1] A profound transformation was experienced during those years. The ideas of neo-liberalism underpinned a series of reforms that resulted in the introduction of market principles in education, housing, health and social security systems. The way Chilean social policy was conceived and delivered changed.

Compared to their children, the parents interviewed in this research lived in a very different country when they were young, characterised by high and extended levels of poverty and underdevelopment within an atmosphere of severe restrictions in terms of freedom of expression and political participation. MA, mother of two, for instance, recalled that she used to live in a peripheral and poor *poblacion* in Santiago, called La Bandera, 'a place where the dictatorship and all that was lived and was felt very intensely'. In fact, MA claimed that in La Bandera the dictatorship, the issue of fear, of having little information, 'lasted much longer' than in other places in Chile.[2] This is an issue that at the same time left some traces in her partner and herself, still manifesting in the way they face certain challenges regarding their children's education. 'In that respect R and I have had to change the "switch", have no fear, try to be more open minded... Maybe that's why I'm always feeling afraid and insecure, questioning if I am doing right or wrong...'.

Unlike their children, during their childhood, most of the parents interviewed attended public schools, free of charge, with precarious facilities. Overall, the goals of their households during their adolescence were structured around basic needs: having food, protecting oneself against illness, finishing school, finding a job:

> My mother emigrated from the south of Chile, hardly finished school herself... She came from a family of many children; she wasn't even brought up by her parents. She lived in a fantasy world; for her what mattered is that we were happy, she wanted us to be good brothers and sisters, good persons. But for her education was not an issue; she did not encourage us to study, get good grades, work hard at school, find out about possible scholarships.... (MA, mother of two)

> What I had was not poverty, but we had to live through difficult situations as a family. We didn't even have our own house. It was a very very very complex situation. The bathroom ceiling was damaged and, when it rained, your head would get wet. My students think I've always had a car, but getting to where I am now has involved a lot of sacrifices. That's why I also have a tough character. Because in the end all you've been through leaves marks on you (…) No one ever said to me 'study'. (CG, mother of three)

Fundamentally, the youth of the parents interviewed was characterised by a context of few opportunities, cultural constraints and economic limitations, where the possibility of planning and therefore projecting themselves in educational terms, was limited. Within those constrained opportunities, the 'machismo'[3] experienced in their families is one of the factors that limit the personal projections of some of the mothers interviewed.

> When I finished school my dad said to me 'we will give you some vocational training'. And at the door of the college he said 'ok, you will enrol in computing'. I was not very good at numbers but I said 'fine'. I had no option to choose or to ask anything. I could have enrolled in Biology teacher training at the UPLA University, which I liked. (But my father) would not let me go. No chance at all. So I pursued computing, without any arguments. In the end, early in your life you learn that things are like that, so you don't get frustrated. I knew that, as a woman, there would be no university for me because there were economic constraints and that's the way things were in the 80s. (LC, mother of two)

Other parents attribute the restrictions to a lack of financial resources:

> I studied Computing in a training college. I followed that path because I have a brother who is almost my age; there are just 11 months between us, and we finished school together, so we followed parallel paths. Besides, our father did not have the resources to enrol us in university or to provide better professional perspectives for us. (MO, mother of two)

> I am a pharmacy assistant, which is the one who serves people that buy medicines. (Being a pharmacy assistant) implies having a broad knowledge of medicines, to offer products (…) Because of family financial constraints, and because my sister had to complete her studies, I followed a one-year training course to become a pharmacy assistant. Something had to be done, in terms of me getting any specific skill, and my friends gave me advice in looking for this option. (PA, mother of two)

These conditions started to change dramatically upon the return of democracy to Chile. From the parents' accounts, it would appear that their constrained background also interacted with an open economy, which, from the middle of the 1990s onwards, led some of the interviewees to adopt a sort of 'strategic' logic regarding their own opportunities and also in relation to their children's educational trajectories. This is manifested, for instance, in parental enrolment in vocational studies and in the search for new educational opportunities for their children. The policy context where the parents educate their children could explain these parental priorities. As Falabella (2013), Falabella and Opazo (2014) and Kosunen and Carrasco (2016) have raised, a growing emphasis on assessment and the promotion of competition between schools through the public dissemination of standardised tests rankings and results characterised the Chilean school policy. Within that scenario, the parents interviewed tend to position themselves more strategically regarding their children's education, with some of them acting as managers of their children's educational path.

> When I listen to myself (talking about my daughters) it sounds like it was what I wanted to do. But it's not like that. It has to do with what I want her to be, or the tools I want her to access and which I never had. Maybe I could have continued studying, even though my family had no resources. But the thing is that I had no idea that there were scholarships; I had no idea that if I tried a little harder I could have been able to continue studying. In that sense, I do feel some frustration and I don't want this to happen to her (…). For me it is pretty clear that in this respect my mom was wrong, perhaps unconsciously, but she was wrong, and somehow what I want is to give my daughters both what my mom gave and what she failed to give me. (MA, mother of two)

The following section will analyse the practical manifestation of this logic and how it translates into new forms of relationships with education, specifically into the deployment of certain parental involvement functionings and capabilities, distant and sometimes critically reflective regarding their own educational experiences.

PARENTS AS MANAGERS OF CHILDREN'S EDUCATION

All the parents interviewed in this study could have enrolled their children in free municipal schools but they chose to pay because the vast majority of them considered that doing otherwise would have negative consequences on their children's future opportunities. This has to do mainly with the fact that those who attend free municipal primary schools in Chile generally come from poor families, with less advantaged educational backgrounds (Falabella et al., 2016; Garcia-Huidobro & Bellei, 2003; Garcia-Huidobro, 2007). Paying a monthly fee for their primary education appears to be the first decision taken by the parents interviewed when thinking of their children's educational future. Later, for some of them, a second key moment occurs as a consequence of their children's good academic results at primary school level. Some of them, due to their children's levels of achievement, decide to apply for a place in an emblematic school. This involves paying for at least one year the cost of specific training for selection tests applied by these highly selective schools.

> My kids went to *BC*, an ordinary but not so good primary school. Indeed my older son had excellent grades but when he applied to the *Instituto Nacional*

(emblematic school) he failed to pass the exam: he was 8 points below the minimum required. Then people advised me that, prior to the admission exam, he needed to be prepared and brought up to the required level. I looked for a private tutor, with experience in preparing for emblematic schools. She covered all the contents the primary school had not taught him and in the end he entered an emblematic school in *Primero medio* (Year 10). In the case of my daughter, I did the same but in Year 7. (M, mother of two)

The different parents interviewed in this research demonstrate concern and interest in their children's school achievements and, particularly, in their future educational pathways, understood mainly as what is going to happen to them after finishing school and whether they are going to be enrolled in a traditional (not private) university to study a career that will somehow assure them a successful professional life. For the majority of the interviewees (apart from five cases), the latter means a career that, above all, guarantees their economic independence and their ability to have '*lucas*', Chilean slang for 'money'.

We want my daughter to study at the university, to get a good career. I tell her "so you do not have to do what I do, running around the whole day driving a school van, selling cups, stickers, whatever". (The idea is for the two of them) to have good professions and live well. (MO, mother of two)

Among all but three of the parents interviewed, the relationship with their children's education seems to be built on some powerful and aspirational thinking: that their children will become 'something better', 'more than me', as LC, one of the mothers interviewed claimed. Almost all of them work hard to contribute to a family goal built around the idea that education means access to certain credentials.

I worked in a vocational training centre. Because I am a teacher there, my children are eligible for a full scholarship. Based on that, someone told me: "Lucky you, your twins have their future sorted out ...", but I looked at that person and I said "What?" And this person said "But you studied there". "Yes, precisely. Do you know how difficult it was for me to reach my colleagues' standards?" One of the characteristics of this institution is that 90 per cent of students belong to the first generation in their family that pursued post-school studies. But my daughters... No... They have been prepared for something different. This vocational centre is the place for those who have no aspirations other than passing exams. (CG, mother of three)

In the case of MO, she also has concrete plans for her daughter. Her husband works in the mining sector, and he knows how well professionals are paid in that sector. Both of them would like their daughter to become a geologist or a mining engineer. The conversation with MO is particularly enlightening.

As a parent, you want them to study the best careers, so that they get a good job, have enough lucas (money), enjoy a good standard of living.

R: The issue of salary is important. But so is to be pleased and satisfied with the work one does...Regarding this topic, another interviewee told me as follows: 'I don't really care what my son studies, above all I want him to be happy and fulfilled'...What do you think about that?

Of course it is important (to be happy), but maybe that person is better off than we are (...) Although we do not have huge financial problems, I would define us as middle class, maybe lower middle-class, don't know really (...) Therefore we strive to give them the best, so they can pursue a university career and not be like us (...) My husband's job is tough and far away from home. We don't want this stuff for them. Therefore, for us what they study does matter. (MO, mother of two)

When trying to understand parents' reasons for the emphasis on certain careers and the economic security attached to them, their own stories, experiences and concerns emerge, for example, the idea that becoming an artist is a luxury, a risk, which their families can't afford. LC is pretty clear on this matter:

My dad is a musician. Music is his art, his passion, but he can't live on music (...) Children need to be taught about these kinds of issues. Show them, for instance, that in certain professions you work little and earn a lot; and that there are others in which you work a lot and receive a salary that is just enough to keep you alive. And finally there are other professions where one has to work extremely hard and earn the minimum. You have to open the range of options and show them the different alternatives, what we as parents have learned, things that our own parents didn't tell us (...). (LC, mother of two)

The confidence most of the parents interviewed demonstrated in education as a space for social mobility is somehow deepened by a market narrative that transforms the educational terrain into a space for competition and strategies that seems to be meaningful for the majority of the parents interviewed, since they nourish those kinds of middle-class differentiating practices which critical sociology has documented extensively (Ball, 2003; Ball et al., 1996; James et al., 2010; Crozier et al., 2011; Crozier, 1997; Bellei, 2015).

However, such a confidence in the power of education lacks empirical support in Chile. Urzúa (2012) analyses the relationship between university enrolments, employment opportunities and wages earned and concludes that the data does not show that access to higher education produces the results families expect: greater social mobility, better jobs, less poverty and better income distribution. This is explained as a result of three factors: high dropout levels from those who are the first generation in their families to have access to higher education; high levels of debt associated with the payment of university fees; and, finally, enrolment at poor-quality universities, which do not ensure access to better jobs. In relation to mobility, Torche (2008) analyses what happens between different income groups in

Chile and concludes that, while in the first four quintiles there is fluidity between groups, for them, entering the fifth quintile is highly complex and this complexity is associated with other kinds of barriers. "While reproduction of the non manual Chilean elite is largely mediated by educational attainment, hierarchical barriers to mobility are determined by factors other than the ability of parents to afford human capital accumulation by offspring" (Torche, 2008, p. 190).

At an international level, the relationship between education and better opportunities has also been a debatable issue (Brown et al., 2011). Robertson (2016) highlights how the overvaluation of the instrumental aspect of education seems to blur the influence power structures and political conditions have on individuals' opportunities as inherent aspects of educational spaces.

Although a linear relationship between education and social mobility is debatable, parental aspirations seem to place a veil over the context in which their children are growing. This is relevant for the current study since it may place limits on the development of parental capabilities of acknowledging and reflecting on the relational factors that play a key role in children's futures, particularly in a highly segregated society such as the Chilean one. With the exception of P, who openly disbelieves the meritocratic path, most of the parents interviewed cling to that promise as a route that somehow gives meaning and purpose to their participation in their children's education. This is challenging from an intergenerational perspective since, by averting the influence of these factors, achievements as well as difficulties are assumed as a result of personal effort or decision making, which may end up overloading families, as though everything depended on them.

CG's narratives and plans are representative of the support network created by some of the interviewees. Prior to entering the emblematic school, her daughters were trained for one year in a specialised academy. Once enrolled, CG hired two private teachers, to reinforce their English and Maths learning and to help them maintain good grades. When they enter high school in a year's time, CG's plan is to enrol them in a pre-university programme, to support them in their PSU preparation (the Chilean university entrance exam). Another option is to strengthen the preparation for the PSU with an extra year at pre-university level after finishing school.

> I tell my daughters 'you know, if your PSU scores are not so good, I'm willing to do a new year of pre-university (here, CG speaks in the first person) for them to achieve the goal (of entering the university). (CG, mother of three)

Ule et al. (2015) document similar patterns in European countries that have undergone the transformation of their educational systems now guided by market logic. The neoliberal context, the researchers claim, has transformed the parental role in relation to their children's educational trajectories, giving new form and meaning to parental tasks particularly among lower-middle and working-class families.

REPERTOIRES OF INVOLVEMENT

The conversations that take place at home, the books that are read together and the shared experiences may also constitute spaces through which parents play a role in their children's educational development, for instance, by opening doors for their children to explore their capabilities, develop their imagination, exercise critical thinking and give shape to their opinions. In order to explore whether these possibilities, more related to the intrinsic aspect of education, are meaningful for the parents researched, and whether they are embedded within their routines, prompt cards were used during the interviews to engage and stimulate the interviewees' spontaneous reflections and memories regarding those activities. The interviewees were asked to look at images that showed children and their parents reading together, visiting a library, riding bikes, playing in parks and visiting museums, or children playing musical instruments or talking with their parents. Then they were asked if they recognised activities that they used to do or were still doing with their children. The cards were also an excuse to talk about their spare time and the kinds of activities they valued.

Listening to music and going to the cinema were among the activities that most parents usually did with their children in their leisure time. None of the interviewees had been to the theatre to see a play with their children, and two of the mothers interviewed defined their children as active users of their districts' public libraries. The majority of the families interviewed liked music, but none had considered the possibility of their children taking lessons in musical instruments. Somehow this type of instruction seemed to be out of the realm of their possibilities because of the lack of financial resources and because in the schools their children attended, particularly in the early years, music lessons and performing arts instruction appeared to be limited. None of these kinds of activities were naturally considered positive for children's education. In this vein, the following reflection from MC, one of the fathers interviewed, is noteworthy: 'In my view, the humanities aren't more important than mathematics but equally important. I think the humanities, history, impact on people's nature, how you are going to be as a person. This is in addition to the values that your parents and the environment bring to you. In fact, in my house all of us are more interested in the humanities'.

According to CB, her son is highly gifted in visual arts and drawing. However, those capabilities seem not to be acknowledged in his school, where students are mainly prepared in mathematics and language, the subjects assessed by the SIMCE tests.

> They don't make the most of children who have other types of skills. Indeed, only at the end of the year do they perform more artistic activities, and my son painted a mask, really beautiful. He made it like a painting. I couldn't believe it; it was very impressive. (CB, mother of one)

In MO's house, when they have time, they sing together. That is their way of having a good time together.

> Here (at home) we have the whole equipment: mixer, speakers, and microphones. We download music from YouTube and put videos and karaoke. With my daughters we go to music concerts to see our favourite singers and they sing and shout. So yes, we're totally on the music side. (MO, mother of two)

Most of the parents interviewed (three of them did not see it this way) tended to associate reading a book with school duties, or other activities associated with personal abilities. MO, for instance, said she does not read too much because of time constraints but also because she has no ability to do it, unlike her sister. 'My sister, who studied at university, can easily read. She downloads books and, because she travels a lot, anywhere she goes, she pulls out her phone and reads, reads, reads … I'd love to do that. In fact I have bought books or she has lent some books to me, and I get excited but then I have no time', claims MO. As a result of time constraints, LC, B, MC and CG are not in the habit of reading.

> I read, but I can't continue (the story) as a result of my daily routine. I have very little leisure time. I work a lot and when I get home, I want to rest. This semester, in fact, I said I'll have a decent academic schedule, only on Mondays and Tuesdays I will get home by 23:30 pm, but the next semester that will be my schedule every single day; and I work on Saturdays too. (CG, mother of three)

Unlike other parents interviewed in this research who tended to understand reading as a school task and therefore a task that needs to be fulfilled, AM promotes the idea of reading for pleasure among her children.

> Reading builds up your vocabulary, enhances your comprehension and stimulates the imagination. I used to tell them that reading is wonderful because you can imagine what you are reading but not necessarily what you imagine is going to be what someone else visualises (…) I am especially interested in encouraging the topic of imagination among them. (AM, mother of three)

However, in most cases, reading a book for the pleasure of it, visiting a library and holding a conversation with their children about education were somehow beyond the interviewed parents' own experiences.

CONCLUSIONS

This research found that, within a continuum, and subject to their own histories and their children's age, school stage and results, urban lower middle-class Chilean parents tend to position themselves as managers of their children's educational trajectories. Following a neoliberal logic (Ule et al., 2015), the parents interviewed seem to believe that their children's current and future possibilities are highly attached to their personal effort. In that scenario, parents privilege the development of certain parental involvement capabilities, such as being informed, being strategic, being watchful of opportunities and planning their children's educational future. Nurturing and deploying these capabilities seems to be valuable and meaningful for the majority of the interviewees, particularly for those who critically analyse the limitations that marked their youth, their own history, and thus aim to give their children opportunities they did not have access to.

However, based on the conceptual tools offered by the capability approach and supported by a critical epistemology, this research also sheds light on the limitations that characterise the development of parental involvement functionings and capabilities within a market narrative such as the one that characterises the Chilean educational system. For instance, the reflections and practices of the parents interviewed show that, driven mainly by aspirations of social mobility, they exercise agency and try to challenge their own history. But, at the same time, it is an agency understood mainly as individual effort that underestimates the contextual factors, which is problematic from a social justice perspective because those factors are also relevant in determining individuals' possibilities. Secondly, the testimonies show that, when becoming involved in their children's education, rather than being prompted by a reasoned or free process of choice, their patterns of involvement are shaped by a policy context that has transformed education into a contending terrain. This form of involvement challenges the development of parental involvement capabilities in the way that the capability approach understands it: based on what people have reason to value.

From the above, it is possible to conclude that the capability approach illuminates the relational nature of parental involvement, allowing the researcher to analyse opportunities for participation within a space of possibilities that depends not only on parental agency but also on a context that influences and shapes, as well as sets some limits. At the same time, this framework allows reflection on and problematising of parental involvement opportunities from a less explored angle: the value assigned to education, and the doors that different perspectives may open or close.

Specifically, when access to educational opportunities is thought to be mediated by the deployment of certain capabilities and the economic capacity of the families, for instance, certain parental involvement spaces are privileged. As a consequence, a narrow view of education is promoted, as if its sole purpose were to ensure employability. From a capability approach perspective, this limited view of education constrains parental involvement opportunities and narrows the parental capability of being involved. For instance, while focusing on the instrumental aspect of education, meaningful involvement spaces associated with the intrinsic value of education are set aside: supporting children in developing capabilities and skills such as the joy and taste of learning, the development of imagination, voice and critical reflection. This could have intergenerational effects, taking into account that (i) education is a foundational capability (Terzi, 2007) and (ii) parents are central to the development of their children's capabilities (Biggeri et al., 2006; Biggeri, 2007). Finally, the increasing responsibilities placed on families by the state and schools could end up overloading parents. This pressure is unfair, particularly for vulnerable groups. At the same time this tends to mask structural inequalities that go beyond parental control, such as social mobility or labour market conditions, all of which are crucial to both children's and parents' present and future opportunities.

NOTES

[1] According to official data, there were 28,259 victims of political imprisonment and torture; 2,298 were executed and 1,209 people were detained and disappeared.
[2] Pinochet's dictatorship ended in March 1990.
[3] Spanish word for 'sexism'.

REFERENCES

Bakker, J., & Denessen, E. (2007). The concept of parent involvement: Some theoretical and empirical considerations. *International Journal about Parents in Education, 1*(0), 188–199.
Ball, S. (2003). *Class strategies and the education market*. London: RoutledgeFalmer.
Ball, S., Bowe, R., & Gewirtz, S. (1996). School choice, social class and distinction: The realization of social advantage in education. *British Journal of Sociology of Education, 11*(1), 89–112.
Barozet, E. (2006). Middle class, social integration and differentiation in Chile. *Revista de Sociologia, 20*.
Barozet, E., & Fierro, J. (2014). La clase media en Chile implicancias sociales y políticas. *Revista Paraguaya de Sociología, 51*(145), 147–158.
Barton, A., Drake, C., Perez, J. G., St. Louis, K., & George, M. (2004). Ecologies of parental engagement in urban education. *Educational Researcher, 33*(4), 3–12. Retrieved May 28, 2014, from http://edr.sagepub.com/cgi/doi/10.3102/0013189X033004003
Bellei, C. (2015). *The great experiment: Market and privatization of the Chilean education* (El gran experimento: Mercado y privatización de la educación chilena). Santiago: LOM Ediciones.
Biesta, G. (2009). Good education in an age of measurement: On the need to reconnect with the question of purpose in education. *Educational Assessment, Evaluation and Accountability, 21*(1), 33–46.
Biggeri, M. (2007). Children's valued capabilities. In M. Walker & E. Unterhalter (Eds.), *Amartya Sen's capabiliity approach and social justice in education*. New York, NY: Palgrave MacMillan.
Biggeri, M., Libanora, R., Mariani, S., & Menchini, L. (2006). Children conceptualizing their capabilities: Results of a survey conducted during the first children's world congress on child labour *. *Journal of Human Development, 7*(1), 59–83. Retrieved May 29, 2014 from http://www.tandfonline.com/doi/abs/10.1080/14649880500501179
Biggeri, M., & Santi, M. (2012). The missing dimensions of children's well-being and well-becoming in education systems: Capabilities and philosophy for children. *Journal of Human Development and Capabilities, 13*(3), 373–395. Retrieved from http://dx.doi.org/10.1080/19452829.2012.694858\n
Borgonovi, F., & Montt, G. (2012). *Parental involvement in selected PISA countries and economies* (OECD Education Working Papers No. 73). Paris: OECD.
Braun, V., & Clarke, V. (2006). Using thematic analysis in psychology. *Qualitative Research in Psychology, 3*(2), 77–101.
Brown, P., Lauder, H., & Ashton, D. (2011). *The global auction: The broken promises of education, jobs, and incomes*. Oxford: Oxford University Press.
Canales, M., Bellei, C., & Orellana, V. (2015). *El Soporte Cultural para el Mercado Educacional: Disposiciones Culturales y Prácticas de las Familias Chilenas Referidas a La Elección de Escuelas*. Fondecyt 1130430. Santiago.
Cohen, L., Manion, L., & Morrison, K. (2007). *Research methods in education* (6th ed.). New York, NY: Routledge.

Contreras, D., Sepúlveda, P., & Bustos, S. (2010). When schools are the ones that choose: The effects of screening in Chile. *Social Science Quarterly, 91*(5), 1349–1368. Retrieved from https//:doi.org/ 10.1111/j.1540-6237.2010.00735.x

Crozier, G. (1997). Empowering the powerful: A discussion of the interrelation of government policies and consumerism with social class factors and the impact of this upon parent interventions in their children's schooling. *British Journal of Sociology of Education, 18*(2), 187–200. Retrieved June 3, 2014, from http://www.tandfonline.com/doi/abs/10.1080/0142569970180203

Crozier, G., & Davies, J. (2007). Hard to reach parents or hard to reach schools? A discussion of home–school relations, with particular reference to Bangladeshi and Pakistani parents. *British Educational Research Journal, 33*(3), 295–313. Retrieved May 29, 2014, from http://doi.wiley.com/ 10.1080/01411920701243578

Crozier, G., Reay, D., & James, D. (2011). Making it work for their children: White middle-class parents and working-class schools. *International Studies in Sociology of Education, 21*(3), 199–216.

Desforges, C., & Abouchaar, A. (2003). *The impact of parental involvement, parental support and family education on pupil achievement and adjustment: A literature review* (Research Report No. 443). Nottingham: DfES Publications.

Domina, T. (2005). Leveling the home advantage: Assessing the effectiveness of parental involvement in elementary school. *Sociology of Education, 78*(3), 233–249. Retrieved from http://soe.sagepub.com/ content/78/3/233.full.pdf+html

Drèze, J., & Sen, A. (1995). *India: Economic development and social opportunity*. Delhi: Oxford University Press.

Elacqua, G., Montt, P., & Santos, H. (2013). *Evidence to—gradually—eliminate the shared funding* (Evidencias para eliminar–gradualmente–el financiamiento compartido). Santiago: Instituto de Políticas Públicas, Universidad Diego Portales. Retrieved from http://politicaspublicas.udp.cl/ media/publicaciones/archivos/356/Evidencias_para_eliminar_gradualmente_el_Financiamiento_ Compartido.pdf

Elacqua, G., Schneider, M., & Buckley, J. (2006). School choice in Chile: Is it class or the classroom? *Journal of Policy Analysis and Management, 25*(3), 577–601.

Epstein, J. L. (1990). School and family connections. *Marriage & Family Review, 15*(2), 99–126. Retrieved from http://dx.doi.org/10.1300/J002v15n01_06

Epstein, J. L., & Dauber, S. L. (1991). School programs and teacher practices of parent involvement in inner-city elementary and middle schools. *The Elementary School Journal, 91*(3), 289–305.

Epstein, M. (1995). Caring for the children we share. *The Phi Delta Kappa International, 76*(9), 701–712.

Falabella, A. (2013). *Accountability policy effects within school markets, A study in three Chilean municipalities* (Unpublished doctoral dissertation). University of London, London.

Falabella, A., Leyton, D., & Rojas, M. (2016). Madres de clases medias emergentes frente al mercado educativo en Chile: Decisiones y dilemas. In J. Corvalán, A. Carrasco, & J. E. García-Huidobro (Eds.), *Mercado escolar y oportunidad educacional: Libertad, diversidad y desigualdad* (pp. 231–263). Santiago: Ediciones Universidad Catolica.

Falabella, A., & Opazo, C. (2014). *System quality assurance and process improvement: A view from the educational management*. Research Report, Ministry of Education, UNESCO.

Falabella, A., Seppanen, P., & Raczyinski, D. (2015). Growing tolerance of pupil selection: Parental discourses and exclusionary practices in Chile and Finland. In H. Seppänen, P. Rozas, A. C. Kalalahti, M. Rinne, & R. Simola (Eds.), *Contrasting dynamics in education politics of extremes: School choice in Chile and Finland* (pp. 1–17). Rotterdam, The Netherlands: Sense Publishers.

Fantuzzo, J., McWayne, C., Perry, M., & Childs, S. (2004). Multiple dimensions of family involvement and their relations to behavioral and learning competencies for urban, low-income children. *School Psychology Review, 33*(4), 467–480.

Franco, R., Hopenhayn, M., & León, A. (2011). Crece y cambia la clase media en América Latina: Una puesta al día. *Revista de la CEPAL, 103*, 7–26. Retrieved from http://repositorio.cepal.org/ handle/11362/11446

Garcia-Huidobro, J. (2007). Educational inequality and school system segmentation: Reflections upon the Chilean case. *Revista Pensamiento Educativo, 40*(1), 65–85.

Garcia-Huidobro, J., & Bellei, C. (2003). Desigualdad educativa en Chile (Educational inequality in Chile). In R. Hevia (Ed.), *La education en Chile Hoy* (pp. 87–114). Santiago: Universidad Diego Portales.

Georgiou, S. N. (1997). Parental involvement: Definition and outcomes. *Social Psychology of Education, 1*(3), 189–209.

Gewirtz, S., Ball, S., & Bowe, R. (1995). *Markets, choice and equity in education.* Bukingham: Open University Press.

Gorard, S., & See, H. B. (2013). *Do parental involvement interventions increase attainment? A review of the evidence.* London: Nuffield Foundation.

Grolnick, W., & Slowiaczek, M. (1994). Parents' involvement in children's schooling: A multidimensional conceptualization and motivational model. *Child Development, 65*(1), 237–252.

Hartas, D. (2008). Practices of parental participation: A case study. *Educational Psychology in Practice, 24*(2), 139–153.

Hartas, D. (2011). Families' social backgrounds matter: Socio-economic factors, home learning and young children's language, literacy and social outcomes. *British Educational Research Journal, 37*(6), 893–914. Retrieved from http://dx.doi.org/10.1080/01411926.2010.506945

Hsieh, C., & Urquiola, M. (2003). *When schools compete, how do they compete? An assessment of Chile's nationwide school voucher program* (Working Paper No. 10008). Cambridge, MA: National Bureau of Economic Research.

Hsieh, C.-T., & Urquiola, M. (2006). The effect of generalized school choice on achievement and stratification: Evidence from Chile's voucher program. *Journal of Public Economics, 90*(8–9), 1477–1503.

Jackson, K., & Remillard, J. (2005). Rethinking parental involvement: African American mothers construct their roles in the mathematics education of their children. *School Community Journal, 15*(1), 51–73.

James, D., Reay, D., Crozier, G., Beedell, P., Hollingworth, S., Jamieson, F., & Williams, K. (2010). Neoliberal policy and the meaning of counterintuitive middle-class school choices. *Current Sociology, 58*(4), 623–641. Retrieved from http://eprints.uwe.ac.uk/11498/1/neoliberal_policy.docx

Jofre, G. (1988). *The education subsidy system: The Chilean experience* (El sistema de subvenciones en educación: La experiencia chilena). Santiago: CEP. Retrieved from http://www.opech.cl/bibliografico/Doc_Financiamiento/sistema_subvenciones_educacion_chilena.pdf

Kosunen, S., & Carrasco, A. (2016). Parental preferences in school choice: Comparing reputational hierarchies of schools in Chile and Finland. *Compare: A Journal of Comparative and International Education, 46*(2), 172–193. Retrieved from http://dx.doi.org/10.1080/03057925.2013.861700

Lanzi, D. (2007). Capabilities, human capital and education. *Journal of Socio-Economics, 36*(3), 424–435.

Lareau, A. (1989). *Home advantage.* London: Falmer Press.

Lareau, A. (2000). *Home advantage, social class and parental intervention in elementary education.* Lanham, MD: Rowman & Littlefield Publishers.

Mason, J. (2002). *Qualitative researching* (2nd ed.). London: Sage Publications.

Mattingly, D. J., Prislin, R., McKenzie, T., Rodriguez, J., & Kayzar, B. (2002). Evaluating evaluations: The case of parent involvement programs. *Review of Educational Research, 72*(4), 549–576. Retrieved from http://rer.sagepub.com/cgi/doi/10.3102/00346543072004549

Nakagawa, K. (2000). Unthreading the ties that bind: Questioning the discourse of parent involvement. *Educational Policy, 14*(4), 443–472.

Nussbaum, M. (2006). Education and democratic citizenship: Capabilities and quality education. *Journal of Human Development, 7*, 385–395.

Nussbaum, M. (2011). *Creating capabilities, the human development approach.* Cambridge, MA: The Belknap Press of Harvard University Press.

Pomerantz, E., Moorman, E., & Litwack, S. D. (2007). The how, whom, and why of parents' involvement in children's academic lives: More is not always better. *Review of Educational Research, 77*(3), 373–410. Retrieved June 3, 2014, from http://rer.sagepub.com/cgi/doi/10.3102/003465430305567

Punch, K., & Oancea, A. (2014). *Introduction to research methods in education* (2nd ed.). London: Sage Publications.

Raczynski, D., Salinas, D., de la Fuente, L., Hernandez, M., & Lattz, M. (2010). *Hacia una estrategia de validación de la educación pública-municipal: Imaginarios, valoraciones y demandas de las familias*. Santiago: Ministerio de Educación.
Robertson, S. L. (2016, October). Piketty, capital and education: A solution to, or problem in, rising social inequalities? *British Journal of Sociology of Education, 37*(6), 823–835. Retrieved from http://dx.doi.org/10.1080/01425692.2016.1165086
Robeyns, I. (2006a). The capability approach in practice. *The Journal of Political Philosophy, 14*(3), 351–376.
Robeyns, I. (2006b). Three models of education: Rights, capabilities and human capital. *Theory and Research in Education, 4*(1), 69–84.
Robeyns, I. (2011). The capability approach. In E. N. Zalta (Ed.), *Stanford encyclopedia of philosophy*. Retrieved from http://plato.stanford.edu/archives/*sum2011*/entries/*capability-approach*
Robson, C. (2011). *Real world research* (3rd ed.). Hoboken, NJ: John Wiley & Sons Ltd.
Rojas, M., & Falabella, A. (2013). Estrategias educativas de las clases medias: Opciones y dilemas. In A. Candina (Ed.), *La frágil clase media: Estudios sobre grupos medios en Chile contemporáneo*. Santiago: LOM Ediciones. Retrieved from https://www.academia.edu/10125125/Estrategias_educativas_de_las_clases_medias_opciones_y_dilemas
Schultz, T. (1961). Investment in human capital. *The American Economic Review, 51*(1), 1–17.
Sen, A. (1992). *Inequality re-examined*. Oxford: Clarendon Press.
Sen, A. (1997). Editorial: Human capital and human capability. *World Development, 25*(12), 1959–1961.
Sen, A. (1999). *Development as freedom*. Oxford: Oxford University Press.
Sheldon, S. B., & Epstein, J. L. (2005). Involvement counts: Family and community partnerships and mathematics achievement. *The Journal of Educational Research, 98*(4), 196–207.
Smith, M. L., & Seward, C. (2009). The relational ontology of Amartya Sen's capability approach: Incorporating social and individual causes. *Journal of Human Development and Capabilities, 10*(2), 213–235.
Terzi, L. (2007). The capability to be educated. In M. Walker & E. Unterhalter (Eds.), *Amartya Sen's capabiliity approach and social justice in education* (p. 275). New York, NY: Palgrave MacMillan.
Torche, F. (2008). Social mobility and education in contemporary Chile. In H. Ishida (Ed.), *Social stratification and mobility in late-industrializing countries SSM research series*. Sendai: SSM.
Ule, M., Živoder, A., & du Bois-Reymond, M. (2015). "Simply the best for my children": Patterns of parental involvement in education. *International Journal of Qualitative Studies in Education (QSE), 28*(3), 329–348. doi:10.1080/09518398.2014.987852
Urzúa, S. (2012). La rentabilidad de la educacion superior en Chile. *Estudios Publicos, 125*, 1–52.
Valenzuela, J. P. (2008). *Evolución de la segregación socioeconómica de los estudiantes chilenos y su relación con el financiamiento compartido* (Evolution of the socioeconomic segregation of Chilean students and it relation to the shared financing system). Santiago: Ministerio de Educación.
Vincent, C., Rollock, N., Ball, S., & Gillborn, S. (2012). Being strategic, being watchful, being determined: Black middle-class parents and schooling. *British Journal of Sociology of Education, 33*(3), 337–354.
Walker, M. (2006). Towards a capability-based theory of social justice for education policy-making. *Journal of Education Policy, 21*(2), 163–185. Retrieved June 3, 2014, from http://www.tandfonline.com/doi/abs/10.1080/02680930500500245
Weiss, H., Bouffard, S. M., Bridglall, B. L., & Gordon, E. (2009). *Reframing family involvement in education: Supporting families to support educational equity*. New York, NY: Columbia University Press. Retrieved May 10, 2016, from http//:www.equitycampaign.org/i/a/document/12018_equitymattersvol5_web.pdf
Zellman, G. L., & Waterman, J. M. (1998). Understanding the impact of parent school involvement on childrens educational outcomes. *The Journal of Educational Research, 91*(6), 370–380.

Marcela Ramos
School of Education
University of Bristol
Bristol, England

MARIANNA PAPASTEPHANOU

12. INTERROGATING EQUITY DISCOURSES

Conceptual Considerations and Overlooked Complexities

INTRODUCTION

In a burgeoning, related literature, the term 'equity' crops up in likely and unlikely places. In some cases, it is found in the title, abstract and conclusion, but is missing in the rest of the paper. In other cases, equity is stated or employed in the discussion or in the literature review sections of empirical works as if it were the most self-evident and unproblematic concept. Many researchers do not feel that any theoretical unpacking of this notion is required, even when references or claims to equity are juxtaposed with difficult conceptual bedfellows such as efficiency and improvement. Co-opted and asserted where it is least expected equity typically emerges as a fashionable, positive and somewhat facile educational objective.

Equity plays a variety of roles in educational discourses. It is often employed interchangeably with equality, inclusion, tolerance, social justice or diversity; or, it forms with such concepts strings of nouns that operate in justificatory, normative-prescriptive and comparative ways. For instance, as David Bridges (2006, p. 386) explains, "considerations of inclusiveness, equity, and equal valuing" justify, at least in part, "the diversification of practice that characterises contemporary higher education". Equity has normatively been pursued "as a key issue in the educational policy agendas of both developing and developed countries" (Wang, 2013, p. 46). The prescriptive discursive operations of equity become manifest in the commitment of educational institutions and policy makers "to prevent, redress, or reduce existing inequalities and to create, promote and enhance equal education and desirable outcomes" (ibid.). Its comparative discursive operations stand out when some educational work "aims to shed light on how each country is able to grapple with the issue of equity" (ibid.) and to carry out "comparative analysis of what can be learned from each country" on this issue. However, beyond the 'country' rhetoric, as part of hegemonic discourses in global educational 'policyscapes' (Carney, 2010), equity also figures as a notion in whose name many measures and introduced practices find legitimisation.

Generally, equity is a cherished goal, although it is rather unclear what it signifies and how it differs from kindred notions that, along with it, demarcate the scope of educational ideality. However, I argue from a philosophical-educational perspective, an important first step in the relevant literature should be a search for a more precise meaning of equity. This argument does not reflect a modernist obsession with conceptual order and neat categorisations. On the contrary, it is based on the assumption that the search for more precision reveals the multiplicity of meanings that equity has taken in its rich conceptual history and helps us overcome semantic constraints that reproduce equity's modernist confines. Avoiding conceptual work for fear of falling prey to a modernist passion for classification ironically enforces modernist understandings of equity which thus remain unchallenged and maintain their conceptual sway over equity discourses.

Unease about the terminological vagueness of equity may motivate us toward an exploration of diverse theories and toward a critical engagement with alternative approaches to this notion. Such unease may contribute to our becoming more attentive to a neglected issue of academic endeavour: the possibility that any empirical or philosophical investigation of equity may first require discursive equity. With 'discursive equity' I theorise openness toward, and fair treatment of, diverse discourses on a topic. We treat worldviews, outlooks and theoretical standpoints with discursive equity when we take into consideration not only the discourses that enjoy social currency and secure academic visibility but also, and more, non-hegemonic discourses, even those originating in a remote past or space. Such equity has also a temporal dimension in need of exploration, as we make time for the unfashionable and the unknown, and we dedicate time to searching for or in it. We should resist the managerial pressures to invest our time on endeavours that most likely pay off by guaranteeing academic distinction and by reiterating established positions that usually go down well in academic contexts. We should enable more theoretical diversity and hybridity and avoid fortifying the walls that confine us to established strongholds or lead us to turning contestations of power into new meta-narratives and hegemonies.[1]

This approach to equity involves a complex and often improbable dialectic. A search for some semantic precision that does discursive justice to theoretical diversity discloses complexities of the issue of equity that have been overlooked. The interrogation of current equity discourses requires conceptual considerations that reveal such complexities and invite further theoretical pollination, investigatory effort and interpretive challenge. I illustrate how a retrieval of alternative conceptual considerations of equity intersects with largely overlooked complexities by brief reference to Aristotle's notion of equity and to the African notion of *Ubuntu*. But, first, I indicate how a vague treatment of equity overlooks complexities and bypasses persistent problems.

CONCEPTUAL CONSIDERATIONS BEYOND MODERNIST CONFINES

As indicated above, equity often becomes a placeholder of other normative concepts or, worse, a stopgap notion signifying anything positive in the social sphere. It thus remains unpacked—a vague, though mythologised, reference point of much scholarship. That equity as a value requires for its exploration some specification of what counts as equity's dialectical opposite, namely, inequity, also escapes attention. Definitions of the inequity that is identified as a major problem in our societies are revealing of the dependence of equity on diagnoses of pathologies that it comes to remedy. If "inequity is the presence of systematic and potentially remediable differences among population groups defined socially, economically, or geographically" (Starfield, 2011, p. 1), then, I think, equity cannot just be a matter of ameliorating individual achievement and the fate of the autonomous subject, as the liberal view often seems to assume. This admission further leads us to ask what counts as remediable difference among collectivities and through what kind of off-setting mechanisms could it possibly be remedied. A consideration of equity along with inequity may shed a different light on current standpoints and, therefore, it could be another fertile ground for interrogating established discourses and for acknowledging the complexity of the issue of equity.

It also remains under-theorised and obscure how meanings change when the noun 'equity' becomes qualified through adjectives that make it either more specific (e.g. ecological, social) or more discipline-related (educational). As concerns the topic of the conference which offered the opportunity for the present chapter, namely, 'Equity In and Through Education',[2] its history has not only been one of practical shifts and developments but also of theoretical contestations of what counts as 'equitable education'. For instance, 'dramatic attempts to promote social equity' have defined 'the history of American schooling'. The relevant examples, i.e. "the common schools movement of the mid 1800s, the Progressivist movement of the mid 1900s, and the legal crusade for equal educational opportunity of the 1950s–1970s" (Kurth-Schai, 1992, p. 147) attest to the semantic shifts of equity from democratiation to equal access, processes and opportunities.

Important conceptual distinctions and qualifications have been added throughout the years. Concerning higher education, for instance, it became evident that "higher access to university for some groups" misfired when followed by higher numbers of academic failures, dropout or course repetition rates for those groups (Ridge & Waghid, 2001, p. 82). The conceptual and normative passage from equity-as-access to equity-of-outcomes enables positions such as Hans-Georg Kotthoff's (2011), which explore equity as correlation of performance and social origin. 'The correlation between socio-economic background and achieved performance levels' allows assessments of improvement in the German education system and of degrees to which gaps among social groups are narrowed.[3] From a very different viewpoint, such as Robin Attfield's (2010, p. 103) environmental ethics, equity is specified as "equity between species", focuses on cross-generational ethical responsibilities, and, again, emerges as a paramount ethico-political relational notion beyond mere individual access to goods.

Still, most such diverse perspectives have not yet infiltrated educational discourses let alone inspired further conceptual explorations and possibilities. Despite contestations and shifts, as Elaine Unterhalter (2009, p. 416) remarks, "underspecified definitions make understanding the normative assumptions of equity difficult and this has consequences for implementation". We encounter a similar conclusion, deriving from a most diverse discursive standpoint, when philosophers Bryson and De Castell (1993, p. 341) argue that equity remains an "inherently contradictory project" in need of "substantial conceptual clarification" before "any useful work can be done in its name".

Approaches that take equity as conceptually and theoretically unproblematic and turn it into a generality fail to revisit modernist undertones that pin down the meaning of equity to egalitarian formalism and liberal individualism. For, if equity is either equal treatment of equals (horizontal version) or unequal treatment of unequals (vertical version), with no further specifications of the subject positions of the equals and unequals, the basic liberal assumptions about the self and society remain operative, and so do many related problems. The next section registers some such problems to show that conceptual considerations of what counts as equity reveal frequently overlooked complexities.

SOME PROBLEMS

Let me unpack this complex point and let us mention some relevant problems. In its horizontal version,[4] equity as equal treatment of equals mistakes the ideal of political equality for an accomplished reality. And it also conflates symmetry of rights with existential symmetry, as if the latter is a direct effect of acknowledging the former. But having equal rights and opportunities does not in reality entail that such opportunities can actually be seized by all, irrespective of one's existential condition (geographical and social position, family background, etc.). Certainly, horizontal equity is an important legislative measure as a springboard for addressing equitable education. But, left on their own, such perspectives on equity overlook that the individuals to be treated educationally as equals are not just individuals but also members of groups, some of which have long been disadvantaged. One specific and extreme liberal assumption, namely, that there is no society other than as the sum total of individuals and their families, is particularly compatible with this kind of equity. In its context, all that is owed to individuals is a common curriculum and learning material, same teaching strategies, and equal treatment. Thus, such equity is exhausted in an egalitarian formalism.

This may justify the claim that "the primary barriers on the path toward equity are philosophical rather than material or technical in nature" (Kurth-Schai, 1992, p. 147). But philosophy has also initiated the overcoming of some such barriers. It was mainly a specific philosophy, John Rawls' theory of justice with its difference principle (Wang, 2013), that set on course a departure from horizontal equity toward a vertical equity that acknowledged disadvantage and prescribed unequal treatment of unequals. Because different groups have different starting points they require differentiated treatment.

However, in my view, a major problem with vertical equity is that much depends on how 'the starting point' is interpreted and causally connected with individual performance. I name this the 'interpretation of performance' problem and define it as conflation of existential asymmetry with natural-endowment or 'character' difference. Because of this conflation the problem comes up bifurcated, that is, in a 'naturalisation of difference' version and a 'character' version. The 'naturalisation of difference' version singles out natural endowment as a different starting point. Elsewhere, I have examined how Rawls' essentialist notion of natural endowment harms his difference principle and the concomitant notion of equitable education (Papastephanou, 2005) and so will not cover the same ground here. Let me just indicate how the 'naturalisation of difference' problem leads back to liberal individualistic interpretations of who the unequals are.

Some of the unequals are those who, according to Rawls, are naturally endowed and should enjoy some kind of favourable inequality in order to be motivated to avail their talents to all for the common good. Other unequals are those who have not been favoured in the natural lottery as concerns intelligence and should receive an off-setting educational attention. Implicit in this discourse are naturalist explanations of performance. Such interpretations of performance make it too easy for a liberal education to bypass socio-cultural and political explications of educational failure and to resort to facile equations between low outcomes and supposedly natural inability of individuals. Thereby, such equity discourses aspire only to amelioration, since it is assumed that some students will inevitably lag behind due to natural inadequacies for which education cannot do much. Then educational discourses focus on those who have improved and turn them into proof of the success of the equity project, rendering those who have not improved and the true reasons for this invisible. I single out this problem as one of the ways 'in which institutionally structured discourses of amelioration function more as blinders than as lenses' as one source has it, blinders which "render actual differences invisible", and thence "entitle only those who conform to pre-established conditions of entitlement, while disenfranchising the rest who have by this means become invisible" (Bryson & De Castell, 1993, p. 346).

I theorise a related problem in interpreting performance as the 'character' problem. Character education and virtue-epistemology appear at first sight as rivals of liberal education in their emphasis on the virtuous learner and their shift away from knowledge transmission. In an aretaic model, those lagging behind may not have tried enough, may not have displayed the intellectual and ethical virtues that would have secured them achievement. But such discourses make common cause with liberal discourses: by presenting low outcomes as individual lack of motivation and character failure to develop the intellectual and ethical virtues that secure epistemic success; and by thus obfuscating that performance and success at what society cherishes depend on existential dissimilarities (e.g. social origin, family, language, narrativity, identification, the relational position of one's race or nation in the wider social context) about which nature or character are either minimally or not at all informative. Naturalising and individualising low performance and reducing expectations from some students goes hand in hand with an exculpation of social order concerning some learning difficulties and with a dissociation of equity from more radical demands for social change. No-child-left-behind then becomes a vital educational precondition of distinction, so that those who will eventually lag behind in a competitive world of socially constructed unequal positionings and gains will be those who could not meet the standards. They are seen as destined to lag behind either due to inherent inferiority or due to lack of motivation and strength of character. Despite appearances, educational systems do not address all in order to avoid the creation of an élite class. By addressing all educational systems ultimately exclude 'undeserved' membership in élite classes and legitimate this exclusion in presenting it as self-exclusion.

Material conditions shaping existential asymmetries are left untouched on varying arguments. Chief among those arguments is the TINA (there is no alternative) assumption that any aspiration to radical social and global change ignores human realities that confirm our world as the best possible. There is also the liberal-contextualist assumption that any aspiration to radical change imposes one conception of the good and violates pluralism. "A contextualist picture of schooling and social justice resists the reduction of educational value to any single good" and endorses the value-pluralist view "that there is no One Best Way to live a worthwhile human life" (Blacker, 2007, p. 102). True, there is no One Best Way to live a worthwhile human life; however, there are too few ways (material and symbolic ways that enable real and conscious choice) to become capable of approaching what seems to you worthwhile. This escapes the liberal scope which, in my view, runs yet another risk of 'hollow rhetoric' (Unterhalter, 2009). In their formalist (and ultimately uniform) treatment of the good, many educational discourses fail to make higher demands on society other than simply expanding access or undoing the correlation of individual performance and social origin. They empty equity of any broadly positive material consequence, and turn it into an elusive and abstract idea. Discursive rhetoric and practices that (perhaps unwittingly) serve technologies of normalisation and social order rather than change end up hijacking and domesticating equity. It is thus forgotten that the recipients of our equitable educational reforms (the poor, the disadvantaged) are created by the society that ultimately exonerates its self-image in promoting such reforms and measures.

Other, largely overlooked, complexities concern how the identity of target-groups is construed in institutionally mandated projects that promote equity and in related theoretical works. What we may call the 'identity problem' has been addressed by Judith Butler among others. Following Butler, critics of established theories and practices charge them with inherent contradictions and contrast to them a 'democratic activism' in the pursuit of another 'species of equity'. Standard conceptions of equity rely on categories of identity that are engendered, naturalised and immobilised by consolidated structures that should be critiqued instead of reproduced (Bryson & De Castell, 1993, p. 345). The above-mentioned naturalisation of low performance and of talent through assumptions of endowment entail fixed identities. They still are ideological pillars of some educational discourses which perpetuate what Pierre Bourdieu called the 'racism of intelligence' (see Papastephanou, 2005). Likewise, identity-classifications of developed and developing countries overlook: genealogies that produce and perpetuate these very categories; and discourses that deconstruct them. In so doing, they contradict the equity that they supposedly promote. Bryson and De Castell state such consequences concerning policies which "make particular identity-classifications a prerequisite to 'equity' (for example, *gender* equity)". Such policies "necessarily function to *deny* rights more than to *affirm* them" (Bryson & De Castell, 1993, p. 344).

A concomitant problem is the indirect promotion of sameness and of One Best Way to live a worthwhile life (in other words, the reintroduction through the back door of the uniform narrative of the good that pluralist liberalism is supposed to combat): "attempts to promote educational equity through erasure, containment, or colonisation of difference" are "based upon false assumptions of shared needs and aspirations" (Kurth-Schai, 1992, p. 155). Such conceptions of equity overlook curricular gender/class/race blindness. They assimilate the diversity that they are supposed to address equitably and establish the loss of "gender/race/class identity as a prerequisite for academic success" (ibid.). Feminist thinkers such as Bryson and De Castell have detected complex operations of an equity rhetoric that ultimately serves sameness. Though, as will become evident in the next section, my position is critical of the absence of reconstructive elements in Bryson and De Castell's conceptual discussion of equity, my analysis of problems related to the conceptualisation of equity concurs with their deconstructive tactic. Hence, I illustrate an equity operation that serves sameness through reliance on their work: while equity nominally concerns 'a state of fairness and justice', it 'typically refers *in institutional programmes* to a state of sameness'. In a framework that these thinkers call a 'progressive liberal masquerade', equity operates as a term of concealment that "announces the right to be or to become like the idealised subject of 'human rights'" (Bryson & De Castell, 1993, p. 343). The sanguine discourse which stems from those PISA metrics that show improvement in the correlation of better outcomes by members of equity target-groups overlooks that the measured equity is of a specific kind. This species of equity "re-asserts traditional rules, roles, and relations by announcing the right of non-dominant, marginalised persons to 'assume the position' of dominance, to hold the same jobs, go to the same places, have the same desires, and do the same things as the normatively sanctioned bourgeois subject of human rights" (Bryson & De Castell, 1993, p. 343). The latter become, then, "rights of pseudo-membership in the group in dominance, rights to be like—but always impossibly so—those whose right it is to define the proper subjects of rights" (ibid.).

In my view, the above point to complexities of identity and sameness that affect not only horizontal but also vertical equity, not only 'access' but also 'process and outcomes' equity. But they also involve what may be called the 'social mobility' problem. This problem, emphasised by Paulo Freire amongst others, refers to the fact that equity projects seem to reflect a social mobility commitment to generating larger numbers of individuals enabled to climb up the social ladder. The meaning of equity is exhausted in achieving conditions of higher social mobility of separate individuals.

Equity is thus dissociated from demands for broader change of the structures that contribute to disadvantage and from knowledge that is often uncomfortable and does not find space in standardised tests that measure cognitive achievement. The notion that typically beautifies such equity is empowerment through knowledge. But, we must not forget that, as Bridges rightly remarks, 'people are not just generally "empowered"'. They are empowered "to do certain kinds of things and to pursue certain kinds of lives. Therefore, what kind of knowledge counts as empowering depends on what kinds of things people want to be able to do" (Bridges, 2006, p. 385). In a context where the achiever typifies the empowered subject, equity is coupled with social mobility and becomes its idealised condition of possibility.

This chimes with what I name the 'cross-purposes' problem: educational aims operate at cross-purposes concerning equity when some of them cultivate social hope and change, while other aims undermine social hope and change by cultivating the privatised hope of individual achievement in a competitive world uninterested in drastic change. On the one hand, to a degree, practices toward equity are encouraged when educational studies emphasise democratic care and condemn injustices. On the other hand, and simultaneously, educational studies echo and serve a Western culture that exhorts its members primarily to become "highly competitive, intellectually advanced, and economically sustainable" (Smeyers & Waghid, 2010, p. 467). Attachment to the latter aims renders the former aims a lip service to equity.

Finally, let me register another complexity: it can be termed the 'inclusion problematic'. Equity is often reduced to inclusion and, mainly to an inclusion in deliberative practices. This framework, which utopianises communication and democratic dialogue, operates in theories as diverse as Seyla Benhabib's notion of iterations and Deriddean notions of an all-inclusive democracy to come and cities of refuge. There is no space here for a separate critique of this framework,[5] and I am only stating the possibility of such a critique with an eye to a more demanding sense of equity. The inflated inclusion framework is unhelpful when it obscures the fact that some issues of inequity do not boil down to including the other in the dialogues of the privileged, to merely giving her voice repeatedly or to offering her your magnanimous hospitality when ashore. Some issues of equity presuppose higher demands on the Western self such as drastic redistribution of wealth, different allocation of resources, material measures beyond or prior to deliberative inclusion and an education prepared to acknowledge and to teach ethico-political debts to otherness (Papastephanou, 2017). Such acknowledgement and teaching may focus on the privileged rather than on the underprivileged, on the self-critical transformation of the former rather than on that of the latter, while also revisiting and deconstructing the dichotomy as such whenever needed.

Due to the above complexities, which remain overlooked when equity is arbitrarily associated with mere inclusion, tolerance and respect of diversity, I take issue with renegotiations of the meaning of equity along such arbitrary lines. Treating equity as an overarching notion encompassing inclusion, respect and tolerance attributes to equity undue elasticity, idealises this string of nouns that purportedly explains it and leaves untouched the liberal idealised subject, the one who tolerates, respects and includes those others who manage to merit such tolerance, respect and inclusion. Therefore, in the rest of this chapter, I briefly explore theoretical material that might contribute to a conceptual reconstruction of equity such that:

- against vagueness, equity emerges as a distinctive idea
- against the monological individual or collective self invited to distribute power equitably, equity emerges as a relational idea
- against univocal discourses recycling well-rehearsed ideas, a reconsideration of social and global equity requires discursive equity as a welcoming of a theoretical diversity that challenges insiders' talk about equity.

ARISTOTLE AND UBUNTU

The above-mentioned considerations and problems question implicit discursive assumptions about equity being theoretically unproblematic. But do they entail that equity is an inherently contradictory concept? This would render any reconceptualising effort futile. It would thus legitimise reluctance to consider alternative conceptualisations. However, even those theorists who spot contradictions in discourses on equity nevertheless make room for another species of equity (Bryson & De Castell, 1993). When critics state that a specific equity discourse "does not amount to a pursuit of equity; it is better described as a pursuit of social order" (Bryson & De Castell, 1993, p. 344), they indicate, in my view, a failure and a gap. They imply a discursive failure to be true to the conceptual potential of equity, and they also imply a gap separating hegemonic discourses on equity from possible, alternative discourses that might rescue equity from being subservient to social order. They reveal the distance from the possibility of equity being construed otherwise, a distance that is created when equity slides into, or is reduced to, social order. The logical implication is that equity is conceptually and politically distinct from social order, hence redeemable from, rather than reducible to, sameness, uniformity, entrenched ideologies and other such elements of order.

In other words, nothing prohibits that richer conceptual resources may offer richer outlooks and more appropriate responses to the problems singled out above. Equity requires not just deconstructive handlings of established discourses but also reconstructive endeavours. The two should be entangled in a critical interplay, mutually directive and corrective.[6] The year of publication of the more deconstructive Bryson and De Castell (1993) source that I have employed in this chapter was also the year that a more reconstructive article on equity by Martha Nussbaum was published. The persuasions and standpoints of the two are different, but could we treat them with discursive equity and see how we may heighten our perspective on equity by playing the one off against the other? Whilst Bryson and De Castell do not reconstruct what another species of equity might mean or be like, Nussbaum, drawing from Aristotle, explores another sense of equity, that of *epieikeia*, which relates to justice. In my view, this sense may shed a different light on ideas of justice and equality that currently underpin equity discourses. As *epieikeia*, equity bears connotations of 'flexible particularised judgment' and designates 'something mild and gentle', 'contrasted to the rigid or harsh'. Against "strict retributive justice" equity is "associated with situational appropriateness" (Nussbaum, 1993, p. 86) and with awareness that we live in a "world of imperfect human efforts and of complex obstacles to doing well" (p. 91). Nussbaum finds in Aristotle an account of the equitable 'as that which corrects or supplements—and thereby fulfils—the written law' and as 'equitable assessment, telling us that the equitable person is characterised by a sympathetic understanding of "human things"' (p. 94).

Nussbaum's Aristotelian outlook on equity provides a fertile though as yet poorly mined ground for exploring equity beyond self-congratulatory considerations of improved outcomes of those who have caught up and for turning empathetically toward those who still 'lag behind'. Attention to them requires a grasp of the particular circumstances of their situation and a harkening to their voices. Thus, we are reminded that any adequate moral or legal judgment and, closer to our issue here, any political and educational judgment requires "two features of the equitable: its attentiveness to particularity and its capacity for sympathetic understanding" (p. 105).

However, deconstructive efforts of which Bryson and De Castell's position is emblematic provide valuable insight into risks lurking in reconstructive efforts, and Nussbaum's account is not immune to such risks. Equity without the challenge to sameness may end up an arrogant and patronising notion of looking down upon the recipients of equitable treatment. And empathy does not complicate enough the positioning of the self as the arbiter of the particular circumstances of the other.

Nussbaum's equitable judgment as judgment that attends to the particulars' (1993, p. 85) is the judgement of the thinking self—in our educational context, the judgement of the policy- and decision-maker, the achiever, the researcher, after all, the judgement of the person in a position of authority and in a position to judge. If equity involves "the ability to judge in such a way as to respond with sensitivity to all the particulars of a person and situation" (ibid.), who judges the ability of the policy maker? The vague expectation to respond with sensitivity says nothing about how this sensitivity is tested or authorised. All too often, sentimentality passes for sensitivity and the particulars of a person or a situation are mistakenly thought to invite pity, aid or charity instead of recognition of her rightful claims to justice and to fair treatment. Not just any response to particularity will do, as some responses to particularities interpret them in a way convenient to the reproduction of society within a logistics of gains and losses. To indicate this risk in connection with a previous section we may refer to Rawls's assumption that the difference principle will be accepted by the privileged not out of altruism, but because some inequality will guarantee that, as the rational egoists that they are, they will be motivated by this inequality (and the prospect of further gains in the future) to avail their 'talents' to the common good (Papastephanou, 2005).

As I see it, the shift of semantic contents within the conceptual history of selfhood toward more monological than relational accounts of the I, up to the liberal conception of the rational egoist, has generally affected the modern reception of Aristotle's notion of equity too. Residues of Cartesian monologism and the placing of the self centre stage have blocked attention to some other dimensions of Aristotelian equity that may make higher and more material demands on the authoritative self. Beyond Nussbaum's reading of Aristotle, we encounter in his writings another connotation of the terms 'equity' and 'equitable'. Aristotle "speaks of the '*equitable and fair man*' as the "one who by choice and habit does what is equitable and fair, and who does not stand on his rights unduly, but is content to receive a smaller share although he has the law on his side" (Chroust, 1942, p. 127). As has been noted, "this new concept is obviously devoid of all those characteristics common to our previously gained notions of the 'Equitable', being primarily concerned with whether one stands upon his rights, or whether one by his own choice renounces these rights out of a purely altruistic motive" (ibid.). Such a conception of equity is significant not only from a virtue ethics perspective but also from a supererogatory sense of justice and from a political framework of redistribution of wealth, enlargement of capabilities and other material measures of social and global change. Those should be presupposed, emphasised and demanded by any educational endeavour that truly wishes to promote equity.

This Aristotelian interpretive possibility can become radicalised by association with another conception of equity, that of the African *Ubuntu*. Much like the Aristotelian equity, Ubuntu *inter alia* concerns: ethical and legal lenient judgment (Bennett, 2014);[7] emphasis on the particular situation and empathetic understanding of alterity; and altruism and other such notions that complicate the uniform, modern narrative of equity. I find in *Ubuntu* one of the most explicit rejections of centripetal, modern obstacles to viewing social positionings otherwise. As Mecke Nagel explains, "often, Ubuntu is linked to a famous saying by Kenyan theologian and philosopher John Mbiti" that turned the modern metaphysics "of 'I think, therefore I am' on its head" (Nagel, 2013, p. 7). Mbiti's saying goes as follows: "I am because we are, and, since we are, therefore I am". "With this statement of solidarity and interconnectedness", Mbiti "turns decidedly against the egocentric, monological Western world view" (Nagel, 2013, p. 7). Interestingly, also in the ancient Greek context, the etymological derivation of *epieikeia*, equity, from 'eiko', to give way, to yield, to make room, to allow, etc, involves a centrifugal aspect that does not only connect particularised situational judgement with leniency (as Nussbaum [1993] implies). It is also centrifugal in the implication that the self retreats in acknowledging the dissimilar other's existential condition, in granting priority to considerations that undo those confines of the self that limit a person's scope to her established outlooks and to sticking doggedly to her own prerogatives and conceptions of what counts as just. Ubuntu chimes with this equitable openness and, as Nagel remarks, it "resonates with aspects of virtue ethics and an ethic of alterity—my humanness is nothing without the other" (Nagel, 2013, p. 6).

CONCLUSION

The discursive equity that I have *inter alia* theorised in this chapter speaks for an effort to revisit what we mean by 'equity' in light of what has so far been treated as neglected 'other' within equity discourses. I have offered an illustration of this by reference to alternative conceptions of equity (Aristotle's, Ubuntu) which enrich the received view on equity while contesting the monological (self-centred) grounds that generate some of its problems. Admittedly, the illustration has been too sketchy and skeletal; it has aspired to initiate fresh connections rather than claim 'last word' intervention in the related literature. Hence, I will end this chapter with a disclaimer which, I hope, furthers discursive equity even more and does discursive justice to both the frameworks that have been targeted and the frameworks that have been suggested as possibly corrective and re-directive of our views. I have not said and I have no intention of saying that Ubuntu or Aristotle have all the answers that we need in our effort to reformulate equity. Reconstructive efforts should always go hand in hand with deconstructive work. For instance, in much relevant literature of comparative education, Ubuntu is viewed from a humanist perspective (Assié-Lumumba, 2017) which has been challenged in postmodern discourses. I am not implying that such challenges should be treated as a new master discourse; I am stating, rather, that such challenges no longer allow us an innocent, utopianising and romanticising gaze, unaware of, or unresponsive to, postmodern interrogation.

We should not exaggerate the opposition between the monological and the relational nor should we exclusively attach them to Western philosophy and to ancient and African philosophy correspondingly, let alone romanticise or utopianise the latter. Support to this cautionary remark we may find in a recent article where it is argued that Western individualism and African communitarianism are not as neat an opposition as it is often argued (Enslin & Horsthemke, 2016). Certainly, Western philosophy and African philosophy (as well as ancient philosophies such as Aristotle's) are too multivocal and multidimensional[8] to fit in such categories or to be associated with pure merit and demerit. Besides, my aim has not been to adjudicate the issue between communitarianism and individualism. Instead, my aim has, in this chapter, been to argue for the need to go beyond the opposition as such in search for elements that have largely been bypassed, though they could take us away from some of the problems that I have detected in current engagements with equity projects. Discursive equity toward spatiotemporal theoretical otherness does not invite a facile relation of substitution of one paradigm with another in a model of 'one-way transfer' comparative philosophy of education. But I hope to have indicated that discursive equity compels an acknowledgement of the need to have more complex conceptual and theoretical approaches to what counts as 'equity' and the need to be open to how a remote or different way of thought challenges, complicates and pollinates centripetal notions of equity toward more relational ones.

NOTES

1. For more on 'stronghold fortification' and frame demolition' as pathological operations of discursive and discipline polemics see Papastephanou (2010).
2. http://www.cese-europe.org/2016 'Equity in and through education: Changing contexts, consequences, and contestations'. Robert Owen Centre for Educational Change, University of Glasgow, Scotland, UK, May 31–June 3, 2016.
3. 'While the reading literacy of the students from higher social classes remained relatively high and stable, the performance levels of students from lower social classes has improved, with the result that the gap between the two groups has been reduced by a third' (Kotthoff, 2011, p. 55).
4. The theoretical distinction of horizontal equity (equal treatment of equals) and vertical equity (unequal treatment of unequals) and the philosophical plea, since John Rawls, to view horizontal equity as a precondition for tackling vertical equity has been a reference point in much educational literature on equity (see, for instance, Wang, 2013).
5. For more on this and on how it affects current outlooks on refugee crises, see Papastephanou (2017).
6. Needless to say that thinking better about equity and conceiving it in more appropriate terms does not effect—on its own—a direct practical application that would safeguard accomplishment of equity in societies. Thus, the reconceptualisations which I suggest constitute theoretical work that aims to serve theoretical purposes and cannot be said directly to lead to a 'better world'. Conceptual work of the kind that has been carried out in this chapter does not aspire to solve the time-honoured problems of theory and practice and of justification and application. It aspires to contribute to the way we think about equity, it cannot guarantee that thinking differently about equity entails equitable practice.
7. It would be interesting to explore how the legal dimension of Ubuntu that Bennett (2014) deploys converges with Aristotle's epieikeia, but this certainly goes beyond the limits of this chapter.
8. As concerns the pluriform character of African philosophy, see, for instance, Waghid and Smeyers (2012).

REFERENCES

Assié-Lumumba, N. D. T. (2017). The ubuntu paradigm and comparative and international education: Epistemological challenges and opportunities in our field. *Comparative Education Review, 61*(1), 1–12.
Attfield, R. (2008). Global warming, equity and future generations. *Proceedings of the XXII World Congress of Philosophy, 23*, 5–11.
Bennett, T. (2014). An African doctrine of equity in South African public law. *European Journal of Comparative Law and Governance, 57*, 709–726.
Bridges, D. (2006). The practice of higher education: In pursuit of excellence and of equity. *Educational Theory, 56*(4), 371–386.
Bryson, M., & De Castell, S. (1993). En/gendering equity: On some paradoxical consequences of institutionalized programs of emancipation. *Educational Theory, 43*(3), 341–355.
Carney, S. (2010). Reading the global: Comparative education at the end of an era. In M. Larsen (Ed.), *New thinking in comparative education: Honouring Robert Cowen* (pp. 125–142). Rotterdam, The Netherlands: Sense Publishers.
Chroust, A. H. (1942). Common good and the problem of equity in the philosophy of law of St. Thomas Aquinas. *Notre Dame Law, 18*, 114.
Enslin, P., & Horsthemke, K. (2016). Philosophy of education: Becoming less Western, more African? *Journal of Philosophy of Education, 50*(2), 177–190.
Kotthoff, H. G. (2011). Between excellence and equity: The case of the German education system. *Revista Española de Educación Comparada, 18*, 27–60.
Kurth-Schai, R. (1992). Ecology and equity: Toward the rational re-enchantment of schools and society. *Educational Theory, 42*(2), 147–163.

Nagel, M. E. (2012). *Ubuntu and African prison intellectuals.* Retrieved from March 5, 2016, https://lekythos.library.ucy.ac.cy/bitstream/handle/10797/6156/ISSEIEchoesNagel.pdf?sequence=1

Nussbaum, M. C. (1993). Equity and mercy. *Philosophy & Public Affairs, 22*(2), 83–125.

Papastephanou, M. (2005). Rawls' theory of justice and citizenship education. *Journal of Philosophy of Education, 39*(3), 499–518.

Papastephanou, M. (2010). The conflict of the faculties: Educational research, inclusion, philosophy and boundary discourses. *Ethics and Education, 5*(2), 99–116.

Papastephanou, M. (2017). Cosmopolitan dice recast. *Educational Philosophy and Theory, 49*(14), 1338–1350. Retrieved January 17, 2017, from http://www.tandfonline.com/doi/full/10.1080/00131857.2017.1278675

Ridge, E., & Waghid, Y. (2001). Equity and distance education. *Equity and Excellence in Education, 34*(3), 80–86.

Smeyers, P., & Waghid, Y. (2010). Cosmopolitanism in relation to the self and the other: From Michel Foucault to Stanley Cavell. *Educational Theory, 60*(4), 449–467.

Starfield, B. (2011). The hidden inequity in health care. *International Journal of Equity and Health, 10*(1), 15–25.

Unterhalter, E. (2009). What is equity in education? Reflections from the capability approach. *Studies in Philosophy and Education, 28*(5), 415–424.

Waghid, Y., & Smeyers, P. (2012). Reconsidering ubuntu: On the educational potential of a particular ethic of care. *Educational Philosophy and Theory, 44*(2), 6–20.

Wang, F. (2013). Educational equity in the access to post-secondary education: A comparison of ethnic minorities in China with aboriginals in Canada. *Interchange, 44*(1–2), 45–62.

Marianna Papastephanou
Department of Education
University of Cyprus
Nicosia, Cyprus

INDEX

A

Accreditation, 81–89, 93, 94, 120, 134
Activism, 15, 182, 185, 214
Actor-network theory, 161
African philosophy, 220
  see also Ubuntu
Agency, 10, 22, 61–63, 75, 121, 122, 141–154, 204
Apartheid, 3, 18, 25
  anti-apartheid, 18, 25
Aristotle, 210, 217–220
Aspirations, 7, 9, 10, 20, 24, 25, 60–75, 124, 125, 131, 145–152, 167, 178, 191, 195, 196, 199, 201, 204, 215
Australia, 23, 31, 175, 177

B

Bologna Process, 97, 101, 105
Bourdieu, Pierre, 61, 126, 144, 216
Britain, 30, 36–38, 101, 184
  see also United Kingdom

C

Capability approach, 22, 193, 194, 204
Caste system, 151, 154
Chile, 3, 7, 8, 10, 59–76, 191–205
China, 43–53, 140
Choice
  higher education, 61–75, 87, 124
  post-secondary, 8, 10
  school, 3, 10, 157–167, 175–187, 191, 192, 204
Citizenship, 8, 22, 37, 52, 82–86, 89, 90, 94
Class, *see social class*
Colonialism, 23, 31, 43–46
Communism, 16, 17, 20, 25, 34, 38
  anti-communist, 16

Communitarianism, 220
Competition, 4, 83, 88–94, 103, 110, 177, 178, 191, 198, 200
Content analysis, 48, 105
Copenhagen Process, 81–93, 97–106, 111
Corruption, 163, 166, 168, 169
Critical pedagogy, 23, 24
Critical theory, 94
Cultural capital, 61, 62, 75, 100, 125, 126, 132, 133, 144, 149

D

Dalits, *see caste system*
Discourse, 2–10, 30–35, 45–56, 81–93, 157–170, 175–187, 209–220
Discourse analysis, 100, 105, 143
Discrimination, 1, 7, 22, 29, 31, 43–49, 54–56, 140, 149, 151

E

Education
  adult education, 8, 25, 64, 81–94
  higher education, 8, 22, 46, 59–75, 92, 97–113, 119–136, 163, 167, 200, 209, 211
  lifelong, 8, 81–94, 97–113
  postsecondary, 7, 61–65, 97, 99, 157, 181, 182, 186, 198, 199
  primary, 157, 181, 182, 186, 198, 199
  secondary, 3, 46, 59–76, 98, 99, 109, 120, 128, 157, 163, 186, 191, 194
  university, 2, 6, 64–70, 108, 119–136, 163, 166, 197, 198, 200, 203, 211
  vocational, 8, 59, 75, 81–94, 97–113, 148, 152–154, 194, 197–199

Emigration, 17, 141, 145, 148, 152, 153
Employability, 8, 81–94, 110, 134, 204
Equity
  access, 3, 8, 10, 21–25, 59, 60, 74,
    84, 87–89, 93, 98–101, 106–109,
    112, 113, 119–136, 144–154, 157,
    162–163, 179, 193, 198–204, 211,
    214, 215
  conceptual, 209–220
  curriculum, 2, 14, 17, 19, 32, 33–37,
    43–56, 74, 113, 122, 148, 150,
    152–154, 212
  outcomes 2, 3, 8, 21, 22, 81–83,
    86, 88, 89, 94, 124, 129, 132,
    191, 192, 209, 211, 213,
    215, 218
  performance, 68, 74, 99, 102, 121,
    129, 142, 158–160, 166–170,
    192, 211–214
  resourcing, 1–3, 9, 55, 66, 75,
    89–100, 106, 109, 139–154,
    167–168, 194, 216
Ethnicity, 22, 45–52, 87, 91
  ethnic hatred, 36
  ethnic minorities, 7, 20, 43–55, 177,
    185, 187
  multi-ethnic, 7, 31, 33, 37, 38
Europeanisation, 97–100, 102, 106
European Union, 81, 83, 84, 86, 88
Examinations
  higher education, 66, 70, 75,
    109, 201
  school, 9, 48, 122, 157–170, 181,
    183, 199

F
Family, 43, 67, 72, 73, 90, 125, 131,
  133, 140, 145, 147, 151, 157,
  194, 197, 199, 212, 213
Fascism, 16
  anti-fascist, 16, 18
Feminism, 25, 215
Foucault, Michel, 4, 104, 160, 161, 166

France, 15, 30, 34–38, 54, 97–101,
  105–113
Freire, Paulo, 94, 215

G
Gender, 1, 6, 9, 14, 22, 25, 49, 51, 64,
  91, 127, 128, 140, 147, 157, 215
Genocide, *see also Holocaust*
  Bosnia, 37
  Rwanda, 37
Germany, 33–35, 38, 97–113
  West Germany, 29, 30, 32, 33, 38
Globalisation, 4, 6, 31, 46, 48, 50, 82,
  83, 88, 90, 93, 94
Gramsci, Antonio, 7, 16–21, 24, 25
Greece, 92, 93
Grounded theory, 105
Guilt, 31, 34

H
Hierarchy, 3, 142–154, 160, 161,
  166, 178
Holocaust, 29, 30, 32, 33, 36, 37
  education, 7, 29, 31–34
  museums, 32–34, 37
Hong Kong, 7, 43–56
Hope, 6, 9, 13–26, 216
Human rights, 29–38, 43, 44, 49, 51,
  108, 109, 185, 196, 215

I
Inclusion, 8, 10, 13, 70, 82, 86, 89, 91,
  92, 94, 119, 124, 166, 184, 209,
  216, 217
Individualism, 94, 142–145, 150–154,
  159, 162, 212, 213, 220
Institutions, 20–24, 45, 47, 51, 60, 75,
  83–87, 126
  institutional analysis, 60
  institutional autonomy, 177,
    178, 184
  institutional discourse, 139, 140,
    147, 213, 214

INDEX

institutionalism, 7, 98, 100, 103, 104, 107, 140, 162, 186, 187,192
institutional structures, 90, 91, 97, 98, 102, 104, 107, 113, 139, 142, 143, 147, 158, 162, 183, 184, 192
see also education
Isomorphism, 5, 102
Italy, 17, 101

J
Japan, 30, 31
Justice, 3, 5, 7, 10, 14–25, 31, 47, 55, 82, 89, 92, 94, 152, 158, 163, 168, 175, 192, 204, 209–220

L
Labour market, 59, 64, 72–75, 81, 87–94, 108, 109, 110, 113, 205
Lauwerys, Joseph, 6, 13, 14, 21, 24
Legislation, 16, 85, 86, 121, 164, 181, 183, 185, 186, 218, 219

M
Mandela, Nelson, 7, 19–21, 24
Marketisation, 3–5, 8–10, 24, 81, 88, 162, 177, 178, 183, 187, 191, 192, 196, 200, 201, 204
Massification, 60, 75
Media
   Hong Kong, 43, 44, 48, 49, 52–55
   Russia, 158, 161, 166
   Turkey, 180
Mentoring, 8, 119–136
Meritocracy, 25, 111, 157, 158, 167, 169
Michel, Louise, 7, 15, 16, 18, 20, 21, 24, 25
Middle East, 38, 54
Mobility
   educational, 98, 111, 113, 201
   geographical, 139, 140, 145, 147
   income, 140, 200
   labour, 81, 83–86, 93, 109, 205

   social, 3, 59, 62, 75, 112, 122, 139, 140, 145, 152, 157, 163, 200, 201, 204, 205, 215, 216
Multiculturalism, 7, 44–48, 52, 55, 56

N
Nazism, 29, 31–38
Neoliberalism, 2, 4–6, 10, 82, 88, 90, 94, 168, 169, 175–181, 184, 187, 191, 196, 201, 203
Nepal, 8, 139–154
Nussbaum, Martha, 217–219

P
Pakistani, *in relation to children*, 53
Parents, 2, 8, 10, 52, 60, 122, 124, 131, 176–179, 182–184, 187, 191–205
Performativity, 160, 168
Permeability, 8, 97–113
Pluralism, 44, 46–49, 214, 215
Policy, *see*
   Britain
   Chile
   China
   European Union
   France
   Germany
   Greece
   Hong Kong
   Nepal
   Russia
   Scotland
   Sweden
   Turkey
   United Kingdom
   United Nations
Post-Cold War era, 5, 29, 31, 32, 34, 37, 38
Post-socialism era, 168, 169
Post-welfare era, 88, 90
Post-World War Two era, 5, 7, 9, 14, 21, 29, 32–37, 51

Power, 13, 21, 24, 25, 62, 90, 104, 121, 140–154, 158–162, 166, 168, 178, 180, 184, 186, 187, 201, 210, 216, 217
Prisoners, 15–25
Privatisation, 5, 8, 59, 88, 92, 168, 191
Public schools, 10, 31, 34, 177–187, 191, 196

Q

Qualifications, 13, 72, 75, 99, 100, 101, 107, 122, 144, 145, 211
  European Qualifications Framework, 8, 81–94
  Scottish Credit and Qualifications Framework, 120

R

Race, 16, 22, 31, 45–47, 50, 54, 55, 176, 213, 215
Racism, 19, 36, 46, 47, 214
Relational, 18, 145, 147, 150, 152, 194, 213, 217, 219, 220
Religion, 44–55, 181, 184, 186
  anti-semitism, 34, 36, 38
  Buddhism, 34, 36, 38
  Catholicism, 13, 17, 44, 49
  Christianity, 35, 44, 48, 49, 51
  Islam, 7, 10, 43–56, 181, 184–187
  Imam-Hatip Schools, 10, 181–187
  Judaism, 29, 31–38, 48
  non-religion, 48, 186
  Sikhism, 49
Russia, 9, 157–170

S

Scotland, 119–136
Selection, 66, 70, 75, 99, 108, 122, 124, 164, 179, 181, 191, 194, 198
Sen, Amartya, 193
Social capital, 89, 126, 133, 136
Social class, 2, 14, 61–63, 91, 176, 178
  elite, 2, 30, 47, 60, 62, 69, 126, 159, 187, 201, 214
  lower middle-class, 191, 194, 200, 201
  middle-class, 2, 10, 176, 177, 182–184, 187, 192, 200, 203
  upper middle-class, 177
  working-class, 2, 87, 163, 176, 179, 201
Social inequality, 4, 22, 72, 75, 97, 98, 110, 111, 141–144, 157, 162,
Socialism, 16, 19, 20, 33
  see also post-socialism era
South Africa, 3, 18, 19, 25
Standardisation, 9, 61, 84, 122, 157–166, 198, 216
Stigmatisation, 99, 113
Structural inequality, 2, 4, 6, 8, 9, 15, 47, 49, 61–63, 75, 81, 91, 94, 97, 126, 140, 167, 205
Surveillance, 4, 9, 157–170
Sweden, 3, 30, 35, 36, 38

T

Teachers, 43–56, 129, 130, 140, 141, 148–150, 153, 160, 164–168, 178, 184, 199, 201
Textbooks, 7, 32, 33, 36, 43, 48–56, 147, 165
Turkey, 9, 10, 175–179, 184–187

U

Ubuntu, 10, 210, 217–220
United Kingdom, 121–123, 136, 175
  England, 13, 22, 37, 175–178
  see Scotland
  see Britain
United Nations, 2, 36, 49, 51, 83, 121–123, 139, 175
United States, 31, 38, 83, 175, 177
Urban Education, 175–187

V
Victims, 29–35, 38, 47

W
Wellbeing, 9, 139–154
Western
   civilisation, 50
   democracies, 109
   enlightenment, 6
   philosophy, 220
   values, 51
   world view, 10, 219

X
Xenophobia, 7, 54, 55

Printed in the United States
By Bookmasters